Along the tracks of Cobb and Co.

The New South Wales Headquarters

History speaking for itself ...

Research and compilation by Hazel Johnson

For Ray Green, Cobb and Co. enthusiast and friend.

Author's Note

'Along the tracks of Cobb and Co. - The New South Wales Headquarters' (In & Around Bathurst) traces Cobb and Co.'s journey into New South Wales, highlighting the many proprietors from 1854 to 1924. The book features captivating stories of bushrangers, floods, coach accidents, and more.

Take a seat beside James Rutherford in 1862 as he embarks on his journey into New South Wales. As manager, Rutherford established Cobb and Co.'s headquarters and a coach factory in Bathurst, building his mansion home at Hereford by the Macquarie River. "James was not only a great organiser, he was also a great Australian, whose work was of national importance."

You may ask, What makes this book series different? To share the positive history of how Cobb and Co. and the postal service contributed to modern Australia, I have pieced together fragments written between the mid-1800s and mid-1900s—allowing history to speak for itself. These original texts may transport you back in time, as if you're jolting along the many tracks of Cobb and Co. My hope is that the excerpts I've chosen pay homage to the original records and recollections of Cobb and Co., as over time, detail and accuracy have been lost in the retelling of their story.

Courtesy of John Elliott, writer/photographer

As a proud Australian and a lover of history, I believe that exploring the journey of Cobb and Co. reveals a significant part of our national heritage. A.W. Robertson (Alex), John Wagner, James Rutherford, Walter Russell Hall, and William Frank Whitney are just a few of the proprietors who—along with many other pioneers—helped shape the great country we know today. Their hard work and resilience are reflected throughout these pages and have earned my enduring admiration.

Authenticity has been preserved, with spelling, punctuation, and grammar maintained as per historical sources. These features, in themselves, further enhance the story of change over time. Additionally, the development in photography, including the availability and quality of past photos, is evident.

I acknowledge that the accounts in this book series only fleetingly touch upon the rich, cultural history of Australia's First Peoples and their interactions with others during this period of colonisation.

> "The romance of road-coaching in Australia ... It abounds with incident and accident by flood and fell, by field and forest.
>
> Over miles of drought-stricken plains, through leagues of raging bush-fires, amid incessant rains and through the raging waters of swollen rivers, Cobb's coaches plunged along, beneath blazing sun-heat and in blinding storm, in heat and in cold, in midnight darkness and the crash of elemental war.
>
> The three great lamps have glowed in the blackest night as beacons of hope and messengers of civilisation, Cobb's mail-coach typifying a red link between the active world of affairs and the expatriated dwellers of the far Out-back."
> (A Pioneer of the Coaching Days: The Late James Rutherford, 20 Sep 1911, p.2)

Acknowledgement of Country

We acknowledge the Traditional Custodians of the land on which the Cobb and Co. stage coaches travelled. We pay our respect to Elders past, present and emerging, and extend our deep respect to all Aboriginal and Torres Strait Islander Peoples.

Titles

Book 1
Along the tracks of Cobb and Co. —The Great Northern Road
(Tenterfield to Warwick)

Book 2
Along the tracks of Cobb and Co. —The Western Run
(Brisbane, Toowoomba, Roma & Charleville)

Book 3
Along the tracks of Cobb and Co. —The New South Wales Headquarters
(In & Around Bathurst)

Book 4
Along the tracks of Cobb and Co. —Back to the Beginning
(Victoria & the Goldfields)

Book 5
Along the tracks of Cobb and Co. —Cobb's Coach Drivers

Book 6
Along the tracks of Cobb and Co. —The Roaring Days !
(Amusing Anecdotes & Tales of Grit and Graft)

Book 7
Along the tracks of Cobb and Co. —Queensland
(Brisbane & Beyond) (Release date … late 2025)

Print | Audiobooks | eBooks
Copyright by Hazel T. Johnson

First Edition 2023, Second Edition June 2024, Reprinted February 2025, Reprinted July 2025

Content mainly courtesy of Trove (The National Library of Australia) and their many partners including State Library of New South Wales, State Library of Queensland, State Library of Western Australia, and State Library of Victoria. Photographs taken before 1955 and maps created before 1955 are out of copyright (Australian Copyright Council). Thanks to the other contributors of photos and/or information, to assist in telling the story of Cobb and Co. in Australia. Special thanks to Ray Green, Christopher Morgan and Mary Fletcher. Spelling, punctuation and grammar as per historical sources. Every attempt has been made to ensure the correct use and acknowledgement of all sources. The information in this book is by no means exhaustive. Corrections and/or contributions welcome for the next edition. Cover image: 1900 Looking towards Holy Trinity, Kelso - Courtesy Bathurst District Historical Society.

Available from www.cobbandcotracks.au or local distributors

Further contact: email dvhtjohnson@gmail.com; Mobile phone +61 417984455

ISBN 978-0-6459759-4-9

This book was printed by: IngramSpark

Typeset in Garamond

Contents

4   Author's Note

8   **Chapter One:**
    Cobb's first wheel turned

14 **Chapter Two:**
    Cobb and Co. moves into N.S.W.

26 **Chapter Three:**
    The many proprietors of Cobb and Co.

42 **Chapter Four:**
    N.S.W. proprietors

54 **Chapter Five:**
    The town of Bathurst—Cobb and Co.'s N.S.W. headquarters

66 **Chapter Six:**
    Cobb and Co.'s coach factories

78 **Chapter Seven:**
    N.S.W. coaching routes—News along the tracks

114 **Chapter Eight:**
    Abercrombie House, Bathurst N.S.W.

130 Appendices

147 Reference List

Chapter One

Cobb's first wheel turned

A Snake Yarn to start the wheels turning

"According to a Northern contemporary (and these tropical papers hardly ever tell tarradiddles) man rushed into a pub on the banks of the Burdekin one day last week, yelling for help. Soon it was ascertained that a fair-sized black snake had crawled up inside one leg of his trousers. Willing hand helped the victim, and the reptile was, when extricated, found dead. As the man had felt many punctures, he was dosed with brandy for following two days, and then danger being past, tended like a prince for the rest of the week, at the end of which time he took up his swag and proceeded on his lonely tramp. A few days after the driver of Cobb's coach dropped in and, being told the tale, knocked the public into extravagant profanity by explaining that the man had played the same game at fully a dozen pubs and shanties along the road. The plan the gentle boozer adopted was to find a snake, kill it, and when in sight of a pub, lodge it in his trousers."

(A Snake Yarn, 12 Sep 1891, p.10)
ca. 1880 Cobb & Co. Royal Mail Coach Booking Office, Deniliquin, NSW
– Courtesy State Library of New South Wales

"To the present generation of Australians the name of Cobb and Co. is only a memory. They have heard, of Cobb's being connected with the early back country passenger traffic before the advent of railways, and have no idea of the important part this great and enterprising firm took as pioneers in developing the Australian continent ... When gold was discovered in Victoria, in 1851, and up to the middle of 1853, the only means of conveyance to the then existing gold fields, Mount Alexander, Bendigo, and Ballarat, was by paying a carrier so much for head for the carrying of the passengers' swags and tools, the men walking, and, of course, camping out at night. The average daily distance was 25 or 30 miles, and for this each man was charged £3, finding himself in food on the road." (The Contributor, 25 Nov 1908, p.1405)

"... back forty years in my life, and in my mind's eye I saw again the first conveyance leaving Melbourne for Forest Creek. This now historical first coach was owned by Emanuel King, who, at that time, February 1852, was conducting a barber's business in Bourke-street, about three doors east of the post-office. The conveyance was a two-wheeled van, drawn by three horses ... The fare to Forest Creek [Mount Alexander] was £3, the journey, 75 miles, occupying two days, the passengers camping out one night en route. This style of conveyance continued until the beginning of 1853, when Foster and Vinge, who had been for some years running the overland mail from Melbourne to Sydney, came upon the scene. They introduced four-horse coaches, and fares were still £3. 'King's' line was taken off, probably purchased by Foster and Co., in November, 1852." (Reminiscences of Cobb and Co., 14 Jan 1898, p.2)

"About the middle of 1853 a change came over this mode of transit" (The Contributor, 25 Nov 1908, p.1405) In mid-1853 "Freeman Cobb came to Melbourne ... with George Mowton, to form a branch of Adam and Co, famed in the United States as express carriers." (Death of the Founder of Cobb and Co., 28 Sep 1878, p.3) By 6 May 1853 Adams and Co. were "prepared to give through receipts for gold dust, specio, packages, etc., to any part of the United States, Canada, or Europe. Also to draw for any amount on England or America in sums to suit." (Advertising, 2 Jun 1853, p.7) While "about the end of 1853 was to be seen any day in Collins-street, at and about Adams' Express Office, which stood then just about where the Bank of N.S.W. now stands, a small, thin, wiry little man, slightly lame ... This was Freeman Cobb." (Reminiscences of Cobb and Co, 14 Jan 1898, p.2)

"Many of us witnessed the first efforts of Freeman Cobb to establish communication between the metropolis and the interior, and know how pluckily he in his two horse conveyance conveyed half a dozen passengers from Melbourne to Sandhurst in three days, through difficulties that were deemed at the time almost insurmountable" (Kyneton, 16 Sep 1859, p.3) "... carrying from Liardet's (Port Melbourne) to the City of Melbourne for a start but 'no road' across the swamp between Emerald Hill, now South Melbourne, and the river was such a quagmire that their waggons sank to the hubs" (a [?] Drive, 31 July 1937, p.4) "Hauling their waggons through the mud ... they gave it up." (Old Coaching Days, 10 Jun 1922, p.7)

"They advised their principals [Adam and Co.] in the United States against the carrying business, but told them that there was a good opening for a real up-to-date line of coaches to the diggings ... the United States companies turned down the coaching proposition." (a [?] Drive, 31 July 1937, p.4)

Following this, "George Francis Train ... says: *I told Freeman Cobb, who was then with Adams and Co., that I wanted him to start a line of coaches between Melbourne and the gold-mines, a distance of about sixty miles. I advanced the money for the enterprise, and a line was established, the first in Australia ... These were the first coaches seen in that continent.*" (My Life of Many States and Foreign Lands, 1902, pp.133-134)

It has also been stated that it was Freeman Cobb's brother, E. Winslow Cobb (Elisha Winslow Cobb), who started the coaching business. "Winslow Cobb, a pleasant American, founded the coaching system of Victoria. George Mowton, another American (of Adams and Co.), introduced the first buggy ... To add to our obligations, George Train taught us tall talk, and we have been pretty apt pupils." (Under the Verandah, 27 Mar 1869, p.17) Another excerpt supports that it was the Cobb brothers who commenced Cobb and Co. coaching "The name 'Cobb and Co.' is about all there ever was to associate Winslow and Freeman Cobb with the great system of passenger transport in Australia." (Stories of the Cobb & Co Coaching Days, 19 Dec 1920, p.18) Nevertheless, evidence does shows E. Winslow Cobb, Freeman Cobb, George Mowton and Geo. F. Train were all active business men in Melbourne during that time. Note: For more information see 'Along the tracks of Cobb and Co. – Back to the Beginning' Victoria & the Goldfields.

By 1859 "Cobb and Co.'s Telegraph Line of Coaches.— The development of coaching enterprise in this colony is certainly as astonishing as any other of the wonderful things we have occasionally to chronicle ... but we venture to say that no one, not even Cobb himself, imagined that his enterprise would so rapidly approach the magnificent development lately, witnessed, when the humble half dozen passenger conveyance was represented by a gigantic car, holding fifty travellers and harnessed to fourteen greys, as fine specimens of horse flesh as one can hope to find in the southern hemisphere, 'tooled' by whips who are equalled by few, and excelled by none." (No Title, 14 Sep 1859, p.3) Note: For more information see 'Along the tracks of Cobb and Co. – Cobb's Coach Drivers'.

In 1861 "King Cobb's dominions are wide, and his rule on the whole is beneficent. There is scarcely a civilized portion of the colony to which his sceptre has not extended; in fact, he may be said to reign supreme in the highways of Victoria ... There has been no real opposition to Cobb on the Sandhurst road for fully nine months ... Now ... the starting point for the coaches is twenty miles on this side of Melbourne, and the roads are infinitely better than they were ... Coach travelling, on the American leather-spring principle, is wearisome work at any time, but it becomes doubly distressing when the boxed up passengers have ... other miseries." (Advertising, 2 Jul 1861, p.2)

1856 The diggings, Forest Creek – Courtesy National Library of Australia

ca. 1855-1856 Melbourne, Criterion Hotel, Collins Street (Samuel Thomas Gill, lithograph by Campbell & Fergusson) – Courtesy State Library of New South Wales

1853 Bill of Exchange, Second of Exchange, Adams & Co, Melbourne, Victoria, Nov 1853 – Courtesy Museums Victoria

March, 1861 Malop Street, Geelong: Departure of the mail for Ballaarat (George Slater) – Courtesy State Library Victoria

1860 East Melbourne, Bourke St. – Courtesy State Library Victoria

1867 The 'Bendigo' Coach at Dunedin, 20 passengers. Mr. Fish holding the brake. Afterwards foreman at Melbourne Omnibus Co. – Courtesy The University of Melbourne Archives

Chapter Two

Cobb and Co. moves into N.S.W.

Henry Lawson

In the Days when the World was Wide

The good ship bound for the Southern Seas
 When the beacon was Ballarat,
With a 'Ship ahoy' on the fresh'ning breeze,
 'Where bound?' and 'What ship's that?'
 The emigrant train to New Mexico;
 The rush to the Lachlan side,
 Ah! Faint is the echo of Westward Ho,
 From the Days when the World was Wide.

The Lights of Cobb and Co.

Throw down the reins, old driver — there's no one left to shout;
 The ruined inn's survivor must take the horses out.
 A poor old coach hereafter! We're lost to all such things —
No bursts of songs or laughter shall shake your leathern springs
 When creeping in unnoticed by railway sidings drear,
 Or left in yards for lumber, decaying with the year —
 Oh, who'll think how in those days when distant fields were broad
 You raced across the Lachlan side with twenty-five on board.

Henry Lawson, "born on Grenfell Goldfield, June 17th, 1867, in a tent near south west corner of the old diggers' cemetery." (Henry Lawson, 28 Feb 1921, p.2) He "is the deepest, the clearest voice, his figure the most nobly prominent ... It is sufficient to read Lawson to know that Lawson is a tramp, that he tramps for the love of it, facing hardship and danger in his desire to see, and know, and understand ... he has actually 'been there'; he has swagged it through the back country, and farther out 'where the dead men lie'; worked on fringe selections, shorn in the sheds, roughed it in the cities, where he went gaily broke, and in one desperate struggle with fortune he even fell back on the precarious profession of schoolmastering." (Henry Lawson, 14 Dec 1907, p.2) Verse Two above is "a stirring extract from one of Henry Lawson's songs, headed 'The Lights of Cobb and Co.' Cobb and Co., it will be remembered, was an historical name in this State. Cobb and Co. carried most of the passengers and mails in the back country for very many years, until the railways gradually superseded the old coach. I have always thought that 'The Lights of Cobb and Co.' was one of Lawson's best pieces."

(A Few Notes on Henry Lawson, 15 Sep 1927, p.25)
1896 'In the Days when the World was Wide' (Henry Lawson) 1915-1922;
Portrait of Henry Lawson – Courtesy State Library Victoria

Goldfields—North to the Lachlan

Back to 1850 when there were early signs of mineral potential: "This colony (New South Wales) is becoming a mining country as well as South Australia. Copper, lead, and gold, are in considerable abundance in the schists and quartzites of the Cordillera." (The Golden Dream, 16 Sep 1850, p.4) While in 1851 "Gold has been found in quantities at Mount Alexander, Clunes, and Buninyong, throughout an extent of country 30 miles in length. It has been found in smaller portions at the Anakie Hills and Bates-ford, in a line of country 40 miles south-east from Ballarat. It has been washed in small quantities from the alluvium of Anderson's Creek, south bank of the Yarra, ninety miles east from Ballarat. Anderson's Creek probably belongs to a separate auriferous range, which has yet to be explored. The Wardiyallock ranges, the upper branches of Mount Emu Creek, Fiery Creek, and the Hopkins are everywhere intersected and strewn with quartz, evidently a continuation of the same system of rocks as those around Buninyong. The whole of these watercourses, with the Moorabool and Leigh, if not also the Avoca and other rivers on the northern slope of the dividing ranges, will, there is every likelihood, prove auriferous. Taking these considerations in conjunction with our knowledge of the gold fields several hundreds of miles to the northward, in the territory of New South Wales, we think we are justified in supposing that the Australian Gold Fields will rival, if they will not speedily excel, the world famous fields of California." (News from the Diggings, 29 Sep 1851, p.2)

Later, in 1861 "Lachlan Gold-fields ... Since my last communication the new regulations ... partially amended by Captain Browne, have become law ... All sinkings above fifty feet are to be taken up on the frontage system ; a party of four men are allowed forty feet along the lead, and half a mile on each side until gold is struck, then the claims will be blocked up to fifty feet on each side. A surveyor has been appointed by the miners ... and for the last ten days he has been busily employed in registering claims, drawing parallels, &c. One very wholesome rule with regard to shepherding has been adopted which is, that all claimholders must be on their claims between the hours of nine and eleven a.m. daily, and unless as such, claims are liable to be jumped ... last week a small nugget, weighing some 7dwts, was found on the bar of the river, by Mr. Turpy and a few other Lambing Flat notabilities while fishing for cod, though it happened one of them was fortunate to find gold instead." (Lachlan Gold Fields, 6 Dec 1861, p.2)

The following year Gold Escorts Tenders were "required for the conveyance of the gold and escort between the Lachlan gold-fields and Bathurst via Orange, in connection with the escort which leaves Bathurst weekly for the Mint. The vehicles employed must be of a thoroughly serviceable description (a preference being given to the American coach), and capable of carrying at least 10,000 ounces of gold, with an escort of any number of men not exceeding seven. The tender must state at what rate per trip (or otherwise at what cost per head per trip), including five gold boxes, the work can be performed. This escort will be required (upon the arrival of the escort from Sydney) to leave Bathurst each Wednesday for the Lachlan, and leave the Lachlan in time to arrive at Bathurst with the gold, to meet the down escort to Sydney, which leaves Bathurst each Tuesday night." (Advertising, 21 Mar 1862, p.2)

Security concerns were clearly needed as shown by the robberies that occurred. "MAIL AND GOLD ESCORT ROBBERY. Reward Of £1000, And Pardon To An Accomplice ... the Gold Escort from the Lachlan was attacked on the road between Forbes and Orange by a band of armed men, said to be ten in number, and described as dressed in red shirts, red caps, and with their faces blacked, who fired on and wounded the Police forming the Guard, opened the Mail Bags and Letters, and carried off a large amount of Gold Dust and Money ... Charles Cowper." (Advertising, 21 Jun 1862, p.10) While "an order has been issued ... to the sergeants in charge of the various gold escorts, directing them not to communicate to any person the amount of treasure while on its route to its destination. These commands have obviously been given in order that the marauding parties now out may be kept in ignorance of the quantity of gold dust, and bank notes that is being transmitted from the different diggings to the metropolis." (Local and General Intelligence, 2 Jul 1862, p. 2)

Meanwhile, "a very large quantity of gold is accumulating in the banks at the Lachlan ... in consequence of the insufficiency of the escort guard. The Oriental Bank alone has upwards of 13,000 ozs. awaiting to be forwarded to Sydney. The government have lost no time in taking the necessary steps to provide an efficient escort, and they have given instructions to the Inspector-General of Police to provide suitable vehicles, to be built in the colony, for carrying out this object. It is intended to have an advance and rear guard mounted. In addition to this there will be three guards with the coachman, sitting in the vehicle. The vehicles will be so constructed that no passengers can be taken. Two of the guards will be seated with their backs to the driver, and the other by his side." (Local and General Intelligence, 5 Jul 1862, p.2)

Cobb and Co.—Off to the Lachlan

"In no branch of commercial enterprise do our American colonists shine more than in coaching and conveyancing ... Ever on the look-out for 'fresh fields,' and the roads thereto, no sooner does one hear of a new gold-field being established, whether it is in this or any of the neighbouring colonies, but almost simultaneously comes the intelligence that Cobb and Company's telegraph line is extended to the place." (Local and Provincial, 14 Jun 1862, p.2) "We understand that the three spirited proprietors of Cobb's American coaches have determined, now that the railway is complete from Geelong to Ballaarat, to transfer the principal portion of their stock-in-trade to the line between Sydney and the Lachlan." (Weekly Register, 3 May 1862, p.3)

"PRELIMINARY NOTICE. For the Lachlan Gold Fields Direct. Cobb and Co. will despatch a number of Coaches for the Lachlan Diggings direct ... Intending passengers can be booked at any of Cobb and Co.'s offices in the Colony of Victoria. The Coaches will leave Ballarat on or about the 28th of May. The day of starting will be published in another advertisement. Fare from Sandhurst. £5. E. J. Brayton, Agent." (Advertising, 24 May 1862, p.1)

Following this, detailed preparations were undertaken to launch the new route: "The latest extension of the line of coaches by the firm of Cobb and Co. has been the establishment of a branch to run between Sydney and the Lachlan. For the last month or so, some of the proprietors have been busily engaged in making the necessary arrangements between the places mentioned for providing stable accommodation, horse feed, and other requirements. The length of the journey to be performed ... would be about 240 miles, requiring about ten coaches, and about one hundred and fifty horses. Arrangements were made for the performance of the journey in two days and a night—the mail contract, we may mention, in passing, being to deliver it in five days and a half. The whole number of horses, coaches, harness, and other equipments necessary for the establishments of the new line, were taken from the surplus stock on the several lines in this colony, the Sandhurst, Castlemaine, Ballarat, &c ...

It having been the intention of the company to make Sandhurst the point of departure, for the last few days, coaches, drivers, horse-grooms, and helpers of all kinds have been arriving in Sandhurst preparatory to a grand start for the Lachlan ... at present it is not the intention of the proprietary to establish a line between this place and the Lachlan, in consequence of there being no intermediate townships of sufficient importance for a payable traffic to exist. All the necessary preparations for a start having been completed on Tuesday, about three o'clock in the afternoon, the coaches, ten in number, left the stables of the company in Mundy street, and making somewhat of a grand splash as they proceeded through Market Square, drew up in front of the Shamrock Hotel, in Pall Mall. Here the coaches were speedily occupied by the persons engaged to proceed to the Lachlan, who comprised the ten drivers, between twenty and thirty grooms and stablemen, and about fifty passengers. The proceedings connected with the departure of such an imposing turn out, excited, as may be imagined, a considerable degree of interest among the townspeople, and the neighborhood of the hotel was occupied by a goodly number of people.

The appearance of the various conveyances and teams was well worthy of being looked at by the admirers of horseflesh, who might have noticed especially two fine teams of bays, another composed of black horses, and a handsome team of all greys ... coaches of various sizes, capable of holding fifteen, nineteen, and twenty-six passengers, and were of the same kind and build as those employed on the road between Sandhurst and Castlemaine, the uneven nature of the roads between Sydney and the Lachlan preventing the use of the large description of coach employed by the company on other roads. Eight of the coaches had seven, and the other two five horses, the whole being accompanied by a waggon containing provender for the road. In addition to this number, the balance required for coaching the entire line between the Lachlan and Sydney, will be despatched from Sandhurst this morning. Previous to the departure from the Shamrock Hotel, the whole of the employees, of the company on and in the coaches were liberally treated with champagne, hospitably administered also to their friends, who in a parting cup wished a successful and speedy journey to the Lachlan, to which we may be allowed to add, and a profitable return for so enterprising a speculation. We may add that to the kindness of Mr. Wagner, one of the proprietors, and to others connected with the company, we are indebted for the details of the above information.—Bendigo Advertiser." (Modern Colonial Coaching, 6 Jun 1862, p.5) "Off to the Lachlan.—On Monday morning last twelve coaches, well horsed, several forage waggons, and a lot of loose horses, belonging to Messrs. Robertson and Britton, the coach proprietors—the successors and present representatives, of Cobb and Co., of Victoria coaching celebrity—passed through Deniliquin en route to the Lachlan." (Deniliquin Police Court, 13 Jun 1862, p.3)

Cobb and Co. arrived on the Lachlan when the "first instalment of this celebrated Victorian line arrived in Forbes on Monday afternoon, consisting of two out of ten coaches, each drawn by five horses of good mettle and in splendid condition. The coaches were filled with passengers, and some excitement was created as they drove through the town, pulling up at the Newmarket Hotel, Court-street. The enterping spirit of the celebrated coaching firm of Cobb and Co. is well known among Victorians, while the fact of making a bold appearance in New South Wales speaks for itself. If to merit success be to win it, the new firm has a respectable chance ... Saturday's Free Press thus announces the arrival of the coaches in Bathurst: *On Thursday the town of Bathurst was pleasurably excited by the arrival of the coaching plant of the celebrated firm of Cobb and Co., of Melbourne.*

It was like the triumphal entrance of a first-class equestrian troupe on a heavy scale. There were eight comfortably covered compact coaches, horsed by fifty-two high mettled and well-trained roadsters, driven by bearded and moustached whips, apparently of no mean stamp—Jehus of the first order. Six of the teams comprised respectively seven dashing animals, which were handled with less seeming anxiety than one of our own 'towneys' would manage his own tandem turn-out. Had a band of music preceded the 'line,' the town might have hailed for a half-holiday. In about an hour after there appeared, as supplementary to the 'rolling stock,' two large waggons, with seven splendid animals to each, making a total of sixty-eight horses. As it was impossible to find stable-room for so large a number of horses and coaches at any one of the inns in the town, the whole establishment encamped for the night on the flat between the Vale and Denison bridges. Yesterday two teams, consisting of the significant number of seven horses each, and two coaches, were started for stations on the road between Bathurst and the Lachlan. We understand that arrangements on a very liberal scale will be made by the firm, with as little delay as possible, to convey passengers to and from the metropolis and the respective diggings." While advertised on the same page "The Braidwood Penny Bank.—It is now a year since it was first established ... ninety-three depositors". (Local and Provincial, 2 Jul 1862, p.2)

By 17 July, Cobb and Co.'s line of coaches had commenced operations between Forbes and Bathurst—approximately halfway to Sydney. As one observer also noted at the time, "I have just learned that the line will be open from Sydney through to the Lachlan in another week or ten days." (The Lachlan Goldfields, 16 Jul 1862, p.2)

Along the tracks—Mail, gold & bushrangers

1861 – "MAIL ACCIDENTS. As the Sydney mail was coming through Wingello Park, one of the wheels came in contact with a stump, and the driver was unseated. The horses then ran away, breaking the pole, and otherwise much injuring the coach. One of the passengers (a lady) was somewhat hurt by another person falling on her when they were getting out of the coach. A sapling being substituted for the pole, the vehicle was brought on, reaching town some three hours after time.—The same evening the pole of the Yass coach was broke, and afterwards one of the wheels came off; but the horses being well under control no further damage was sustained.—On the same day, when the coach from Queanbeyan via Gundaroo reached Collector, the fresh horses, which it seems are kept in a paddock, could not be found. Mr. Gannon and another passenger had horses lent to them by Mr. Winter, the innkeeper, and brought in the mail bags on a third horse, the driver being unable to ride owing to having a boil on his leg. After delivering the mail at the post-office, Sir. Gannon was proceeding home, and just opposite Mr. Butler's the horse he was riding fell, breaking his knees very badly. Mr. Gannon was somewhat shaken, but fortunately sustained no serious injury.—Goulburn Herald." (Lachlan Gold Fields, 6 Dec 1861, p.2)

1862 – "COBB AND CO'S TELEGRAPH LINE OF ROYAL MAIL COACHES ... carrying her Majesty's Mails and Gold Escorts, leave Cobb and Co's Booking Office, Bathurst ... For Penrith and Sydney, Paramatta, Forbes via Orange, Forbes via Carcoar and Cowra, Lambing Flat via Cowra, Orange, Mudgee ... For further particulars apply at Cobb and Co.'s Office, William-street, Bathurst." (Advertising, 15 Oct 1862, p.1) See *Appendix 2: Overview of Cobb and Co.'s Coaching Lines (N.S.W.)*

M'GUINESS AND PADDY CONOLLY

1862 – "Two bushrangers known as M;Guiness and Paddy Conolly, were recently captured between Burrangong and the Lachlan, but subsequently effected their escape." (The Sydney Monthly Overland Mail, 21 May 1862, p.5)

Gardiner

1862 – WILD COLONIAL BOYS "From the Turon, from Louisa Creek, from Forbes on the Lachlan, and from Lambing Flat, were the roads along which thousands of pounds worth of gold had to be sent, and these roads climbed five-mile-long hills, wound through dense scrub, and in one way or another exposed their traffic to unforseen and hardly resistable attack. Young fellows from the outback farms, the 'wild colonial boys,' with a taste for adventure and no great love of work, and in whose training the moral element had been entirely omitted, made easy recruits for the old convict bushrangers. The 'industry' spread. To stick up a mail coach, or a bank, had a spice of adventure in it—and Australians were never wanting in pluck. The game, however, did not need anything like the pluck and daring one would imagine to be essential. This is not the place to tell the life story of Frank Gardiner, for example, king and exemplar of all gold stealing bushrangers, but a mention of his career will suffice to show how capture and death could be avoided. Times out of number Gardiner was either captured or surrounded by the police; but either his guards could be bribed, or his high official captor, in the moment of triumph, did something ineffably foolish. Gardiner haunted the roads between Bathurst and Lambing Flat, sticking up coaches, also, between Yass and Gundagai. In 1862, he secured £12,000 worth of coin and gold from the escorted coach between Forbes and Bathurst. When, finally, he was caught and sent to goal for life, his good luck stuck to him. Mysterious influences stirred the heart of Premier and Governor, and Gardiner went free to America to live out cheerful days." (In the Days of Cobb & Co., 15 Oct 1932, p.6)

Peisley

1862 – "GALLANT CAPTURE OF BUSHRANGERS ON THE LACHLAN. The settlers on the Lachlan and its neighborhood have for some time been levied upon by a gang of four bushrangers, well mounted and armed, but until a few days since, these desperadoes succeeded in eluding detection and capture. We are not in possession of a detailed account of the many depredations committed, but have reason to believe that none of them were attended with loss of life, although it appears that a stockman named Frederick Smith had a very narrow escape of being shot ... It appears that the bushrangers visited a publichouse and store kept by Alick Lowe, on the Lachlan, and bailed up all the inmates, taking from them about £8 and a gold watch belonging to Mrs Lowe ... Fred. Smith ... who had suspicion that they were on no good ... On observing him, the bushrangers rushed out of the house, and called on him to stop, but as he would not, one of the villains fired at him, thirteen grains of shot entering his back, and a bullet whizzed over his head ... They tracked the robbers ... the third ... soon run down and capture, but the others escaped ... one of them being without a hat, having lost it while escaping from his pursuers, said it blew off while they were galloping after a kangaroo." (Gallant Capture of Bushrangers on the Lachlan, 24 Jun 1861, p.3) While in 1862 "The gang of western bushrangers is not yet broken up. Peisley has been hung within the precincts of the Bathurst gaol, having richly merited his fate. Gardner is still at large, and has had the impudence to write a letter to the local newspaper. It seems strange that the police cannot succeed in laying hands on this desperado. Unless he receives assistance, or is aided in his concealment by some persons in the neighbourhood, he ought by this time to have been hunted out of his hiding places. It may be that there are some residents on his 'beat' who are afraid of him, and who purchase security by conniving at his deeds, or there may be some depraved enough to sympathise with him and to receive a share of his gains as the price of their covert fellowship. If there is any sufficient ground for suspecting this to be the case, the police should keep an eye upon all shanty keepers of doubtful reputation. Next to bushrangers, those who aid and abet bushrangers are most deserving of being brought to punishment." (Summary, 3 May 1862, p.4)

Vane

"AMONG THE BUSHRANGERS. BEN HALL'S GANG. 'John Vane, Bushranger.' Edited by Charles White, Sydney: New South Wales Bookstall Company. Mr White, who has done more for the literature of bushranging than any other writer takes as the theme of his latest contribution to the subject the life of John Vane, a prominent member of Ben Hall's gang who terrorised New South Wales in the early sixties. With Vane, who died a year or two ago, Mr White had long been acquainted, and this romantic story, as thrilling as any work of fiction, was taken down from Vane's own lips, after he had regained his freedom and begun to reform. From 'cattle duffing' Vane passed to bushranging, his first exploit in that direction being the robbery, partly in fun, of a Chinaman, who erroneously thought he had secured his little bag of gold when he had fixed it under his horse's tail. Other exciting events are related and we are told how having gone so far that retreat was difficult, he joined Ben Hall's gang on the Lachlan River. Brushes with the police were frequent, but though occasionally bullets took effect in non-vital parts, the bushrangers seemed to lead charmed lives. Ben Hall was always against avoidable bloodshed, but he was not able on every occasion to control the worst of his followers whose crimes included, at least, one cold blooded murder.

An authentic version is given of the famous 'fight at Keightley's,' celebrated in melodramas and 'penny dreadfuls'. There was no sensational ride by a lady on horse back for the money required for a husband's ransom. The facts were these:—Keightley, a gold commissioner, or at all events, a Government officer, lived at a place called Dunn's Plains, near Rockley. He was a noted shot and had more than once expressed a desire to fall in with the bushrangers when he had his gun with him. Asked what he could do against five armed men, his reply was, *Well, I could turn a couple of them over with this gun*. His chance came sooner than he had expected. His house was surrounded by Hall, Gilbert, O'Meally, Burke, and Vane, and after an exchange of shots in which Burke was mortally wounded, Keightley and Dr. Pechey, who was staying with him, gave himself up after eliciting a promise that their lives would be spared. The death of Burke, however, had infuriated the bushrangers who had serious thoughts of shooting Keightley. However, it was decided that it would suffice if he were relieved of the £500 to which he had become entitled, that sum having been placed by the Government on Burke's head. Mrs. Keightley offered to go to Bathurst to get the money, and Dr Pechey accompanied her ... The journey was made in a trap, and the wife stayed at Bathurst, Dr. Pechey returning with the £500. Vane's strongly expressed opinion is after years was that Burke was shot not by Keightley, but by Gilbert who thus avenged some insult, real or fancied. Soon afterwards Vane, tiring of the life, and foreseeing the fate which actually befell his companions, all three of whom were shot in encounters with the police, allowed himself to be persuaded by a Roman Catholic priest to give himself up. He was liable to be hanged but the priest, Father McCarthy, pledged his word that he would escape this fate, and as a matter of fact, Vane got off with a sentence of 15 years imprisonment. After serving six years at Darlinghurst his release came unexpectedly, and he spent his remaining years gold-digging, shearing &c., in the western part of New South Wales.

As a picture of the lawless lives led by the desperadoes of the sixties, the book has a certain historical value" (Among the Bushrangers, 10 Oct 1908, p.3)

Hall

BUSHRANGER'S STIRRUP-IRONS. "Mr. R J. Lackey, stipendiary steward of the North and North-Western Racing Association, has in his possession the bushranger Ben Hall's stirrup-irons. *They are as thin as a threepenny-bit*, says Mr. Lackey, *as a result of many years of wear, first by Hall, then for about 14 years by my father, and after-wards, for a like period, by myself*. But they are tangible evidence of the roaring days, when Hall had the Lachlan in a ferment. Mr. Lackey is a son of the former owner of Nelungaloo Station near Forbes, where the bushranger was shot.

HOW HALL WAS SHOT. Mr. Lackey said there were many stories of how Ben Hall was cornered and shot, and what led up to him being trapped. He said that Hall, finding things were getting too hot for him in the Forbes district, had actually planned to clear out. One night Hall hid in a clump of natural scrub on Nelungaloo, or a portion of the adjoining property which was subsequently added to that station while he sent his go-between and mate, known as Coobung Mick, into Forbes to withdraw money which he had in a bank. Whether Coobung Mick got the money from the bank was not stated; but he visited several hotels until he reached a merry stage and began to talk about Hall. Next thing Coobung Mick knew, he was talking in the presence of the police. POLICE TRAP. That night, mounted police left Forbes and Parkes and surrounded the patch of scrub in which Hall was hiding. When dawn broke a [First Nations] person was sent forward on his belly to see if he could find any sign of the bushranger. Crawling to the edge of the scrub with his gun, he raised himself on his knees and, seeing Hall, his gun went off, either as a signal to the police, or by accident or from fear of the danger he was in being so close to the bushranger. Hall fired back, and the opening shots were the signal for the police party to start firing, resulting in Hall's body being riddled with bullets." (Ben Hall, 2 Oct 1941, p.10)

The Escort Robbery

SPECIAL CRIMINAL COMMISSION. "Before his Honor the Chief Justice and a mixed jury ... Alexander Fordyce, John Bow, John Maguire, and Henry Munns, were indicted for that they, on the 16th June, 1862, at Eugowra, did assault and rob James Condell, Henry Moran, William Haviland, and John Fegan, and steal 2719 ounces of gold, £3700 in notes, and various minor articles ; and that immediately before the said robbery they did feloniously wound James Condell ... Mr. R. Forster, attorney for the prisoners, stated that be had only just been placed in possession of the means of retaining counsel for the defence, and applied to the court for the postponement, of half-an-hour, in order to enable him to secure the service of counsel ...

There were very few offences now that the law punished with death ... The law allowed a person assaulted on the highway, and threatened with firearms, to shoot the marauder dead ; and if the person so assaulted did not do so, and should he be wounded, then the law came in and did no more than it would have allowed the individual himself to do in self defence. In fact, when the robbery was committed and the wound inflicted, society was injured, and its whole force and strength was then transferred to the jury, into whose hands were committed the dealing out of the punishments that the law ordered, and the protection of the community at large ...

He [Forster] admitted that the chief testimony against them was that of the accomplice Charters, but urged that he could scarcely be regarded as an accomplice, having been forced into the matter by the ruffian Gardiner, and having, throughout, been kept in bodily fear and danger of his life by the threats of his companions, whose eyes were never off him ... Inspector **Charles Sanderson** ... I went out on the 16th in search of the robbers ... we found remains of a camp ... follow the tracks and came upon a pack horse ... I found on the horse 1239 ounces of gold ... a police cloak, two police rifles ... there are bullet holes in the cape ... I arrested the prisoner Fordyce at O'Maley's ... **Sergeant James Condell**, sworn ... I saw two bullock teams across the road ... a party of men came from behind the rocks, and the word 'fire' was given, and they fired on us; I saw the men; I thought there were ten men in all; we returned the fire, and the men retired behind the rocks; directly afterwards they rushed out again and fired; the coach was not going at this time, as the horses had turned and shied at the first discharge; after the second fire, the horses took fright, and started, and I was knocked from the box seat ... the coach ran on after I fell for about fifty yards, when it was capsized; I saw a lot of men rush down on the coach shouting, and saw constable Haviland assisting Moran away; Moran was wounded; one of the attacking party cried out, *there's the —— wretches; shoot them*; immediately after this two shots more were fired ... I remained in the scrub ... I also had a revolver of my own ; in the fall I lost it from my hand ... blood was flowing ... two holes about two inches apart in my left side ... **Mr. Butler** : The men who fired on us were disguised in red caps and red shirts ... and some of their faces were blackened ... **Sir Fredrick Pottinger,** sworn ... I started in pursuit of the robbers ... we found some of the letters and papers from the mailbags near where the coach was attacked ... about two miles further on we found two of the gold-boxes broken open ... we tracked on till sundown ... fences had been cut ... On the 7th July I apprehended the prisoner Manns at Merool ; he was in company with two other persons at the time—one of whom is supposed to be John Gilbert—the other gave the name of Darcy ... one of them gave me the slip and darted into the bush ... we found on Manns £131 in bank notes, and in a sack in front of his saddle we found an escort bag containing 213 or 215 ounces of gold ... Manns and Darcy were both rescued from our custody by a party of armed men ... the bank notes have not been recovered since ... I arrested Bow, and Sanderson arrested Fordyce at O'Malley's near Weddin Mountain ... I apprehended Maguire and Charters, and two others ... Another man named John Brown was apprehended the same night at a different locality ... **Patrick Lyons,** being sworn ... I believed the gold I saw in those bags to be Lachlan gold, and I believe so still ; the gold found on the Lachlan is of a particular character ... **John Fegan**, mail driver, being sworn, deposed : I was driving the mail on the 15th of June last ; there were three or four bullet marks in the body of the coach on that day ; I lost four horses that night, and got back two of them on the following day ; one of the horse I then missed I saw a week afterwards ; I lost two coats at that time ; the horses I lost were four geldings ; they were the property of Ford and Co., my employers ; Ford and Company are the proprietors of the coach ; one of the horses stolen from me was brought back by inspector Sanderson, a fortnight after; I do not know the parties who robbed the coach ; I did not observe any of them very particularly, and should not know them even if they were brought before me ... **Daniel Charters** ... On the 12th June I was driving some horses towards my sister's place, about sundown, and I met Frank Gardiner. John Bow, Alec Fordyce, and John Gilbert ... They were all on horseback. Gardiner rode straight up to me, and said, *Good evening* He bid me the time of day and I returned it ... Gardiner asked where I was going ...

He then said *I want you to come with me for a few days* ... I was unarmed and by myself ... I turned back and went with them ... I knew it was Gardiner ; I had seen him several times before ... I have known Bow six or seven years. He was a stockkeeper for John Nowlan ... I have known Fordyce as a stockkeeper for six or seven years ... I knew Gilbert by sight. He is about twenty or one and twenty years of age. He is a slight young man, about five feet seven in height ... we came to Eugowra Creek, just at dark ... There were Gardiner, Gilbert, myself, Henry, Charley, Billy, Fordyce and Bow ... Towards morning I saw the blackening used to blacken their faces ... We then had some breakfast—some sardines and bread, oysters ... every man pulled off his coat and waistcoat and pulled out his crimean shirt so as to hang down outside and over his trousers ... The crimean shirts were all different colours—some dark, some striped, and only one red ... We then went down all abreast, to a large rock about twenty yards from the road ... I remained with the horses ... The same seven men that went down came back together ... I head him say that there was £3655 in the lot ... I got my horse and left ... I know John O'Mealley, he was not in my company on that Thursday, Friday, Saturday or Sunday ; Hall and O'Mealley were not in my company that week ...

Why was it that [Charters] made no attempt to escape? The Judge then directed the depositions of Charters and Richards to be handed to the jury, at the request of the foremen. The jury then retired to deliberate ... The foreman ... announced a verdict of 'not guilty' as against Maguire, and 'guilty' against the other three prisoners of the first count of the indictment—wounding before the robbery ... His Honor said it now became his painful duty to pass sentence of death upon the prisoners ... Their guilt was confirmed by the testimony of numerous witnesses. There was ample evidence to justify the verdict ... even the prisoner themselves could not expect that any Government, charged with the protection of life and property, could think of extending to them what, in such a case, would be falsely denominated mercy ...

The policemen, who had been fired upon in this dastardly manner, were engaged simply in the performance of their duty bringing to town the gold and money belonging not alone to rich persons, but also to the poor and industrious of an extensive district—many of them having wives and children to maintain with the proceeds of their labour ... Take the case of the witness Charters as an illustration. Here is a young man, twenty-five years of age, with education, the owner of a herd of cattle, and with every facility of obtaining an honest livelihood ; here has this young man deliberately joined a band of ruffians to waylay, to rob, to murder—for it was only God's Providence that prevented their crime issuing in actual murder ...

Crimes like this made life insecure and property useless, and no one could doubt that they deserved the punishment which the law set against them ... he (the Judge) did not hesitate to say that crimes such as that of which the prisoners were found guilty, the only penalty that would prove effectual was the penalty of death ... He could feel for them as men, but he told them candidly that if sacrifice of their lives would be the means of, in any degree, checking the present lawlessness that prevailed, that the cause of society the cause of mercy and humanity—would be served by their deaths ...

The sentence of the Court on the prisoners severally was, that they be taken back to the place whence they came ... and that they be then and there hanged by the neck until they are dead. His Honor added, *God have mercy on your souls*" (Special Criminal Commission, 28 Feb 1863, p.12)

"Coaching ... Messrs. Ford and Co. and Messrs. Cobb and Co. have arranged to tun their lines of coaches from Lambing Flat to the Lachlan and to Bathurst in one day, passing, as at present, through Cowra." (Country News, 16 Aug 1862, p.3) while "Cobb & Co.'s contract for the conveyance of gold has been accepted ... The Forbes claims in the Caledonian reef are still yielding well ... Sticking-up still continues ... In the Bathurst district extensive goldfields have been discovered ... The mailman who succeeded the one who was murdered by the bushrangers has been dragged from the mail-cart by bushrangers. The horses bolted with the mail." (New South Wales, 30 Aug 1862, p.5)

"Mr. Peter Toohey was driving the Mail ... when about three miles on the Lambing Flat side of Wattamundera a man on horse-back, having his face painted with mud, called upon him to stand, at the same time presenting a revolver to enforce his commands, instead of obeying which Mr. Toohey, with great presence of mind, and more courage than is commonly met with, laid whip to his spirited horses and bounded past the robber despite his attempt to fire by snapping his revolver three times. The highwayman gave chase, but, to the credit of Messrs Cobb and Co. be it said, the coach horses were more than a match for the apparently good steed of the robber, and Mr. Toohey and four passengers reached the station of Mr. Allan at Wattamundera in safety ... It is really time that the mail lines of roads were patrolled by mounted constables, as it is dangerous to travel in a mail conveyance." (New South Wales Mems., 20 Sep 1862, p.3)

GILBERT, O'MEALLY & HALL

1863 — "Miscellaneous ... Gilbert and his mates have taken to the Weddin Mountains ... It has been discovered that the names of the men who fired at the police horses, at Wombat, and wounded one of the troopers in the knee were Gilbert, O'Meally, and Ben Hall ... Two bushrangers stuck up Smith's public-house, ten miles from Mudgee, on Tuesday morning at nine o'clock. They took nineteen pounds and one of Cobb's mail horses ... The Singleton Times ... reports the capture of the notorious Ben Hall and two other bushrangers at Murrurundi. The Carcoar correspondent ... reports that the district had never been in such a state of alarm as it is at present from the constant recurrence of depredations and outrages by bushrangers. He says, *Every person you meet in town is armed to the teeth, and prepared at a moment's warning to render any assistance that may be necessary*" meanwhile "Gold has been struck in thirteen feet alluvial sinking at Billabong ... The operatic season was brought to a close on Saturday night ... the town of Adelong has been visited with a frightful storm, attended with a flood. The wind levelled everything in its fury. Such a storm has not been witnessed for the last twenty years ... A violent storm visited Gundagai on Friday last. The roof of Mr. Joseph Carberry's Inn at Five-mile was blown away, whilst the stables and outbuildings were almost entirely destroyed ... There has been a great flood at Tamworth ... A man named Buckley fell down a well at Rushton's public-house, Braidwood, on Sunday night, and was drowned ... A child six months old, named Devon, was accidently smothered by being overlaid by its mother on Thursday ... The Pastoral Times records the death of a [First Nations] woman named Opossum through her crinoline catching fire ... A man broke into a house in Kelso on Friday morning, and got into the bed occupied by the master of the house and his wife. The man was soon discovered, and kicked out of the bed and the house. The husband shortly afterwards followed the man, and shot him dead." (Miscellaneous, 21 Sep 1863, p.3) See *Appendix 3: £4,000 Reward for the apprehension of John Gilbert, John O'Mealy, Benjamin Hall, and John Vane*

The Bushrangers' Cave

by Ethel Mills, The Grange, Stanthorpe

Such wattle, ah! Such wattle; it is golden as the sunlight
Which bathes the frowning rock-cliffs, where the white clematis showers
Its wealth of starry blossoms o'er the mosey granite ledges;
But the wattle guards the secret with its tangled screen of flowers.

A secret! Would you know it, you must part the guarding branches;
Never step beyond the thicket, for scant foothold lies below,
Where a steep and jagged crevice guards the entrance to the stronghold
Where the outlaw braved the troopers half a century ago.

'Tis a cave where runs deep water past isolated boulders,
Not a place to choose to live in save when hope and luck has fled,
To be hushed to sleep by eddies as they whisper in the darkness
Tales of long-forgotten sunlight to the clustered bats o'erhead.

An eerie place, uncanny— let us up again to daylight;
Let us leave these darksome waters where eyeless creatures dwell;
But amid the wealth of blossoms and graceful twining creepers
We must shut our eyes to picture all this Heaven turned to Hell.

The flat below was sounding with the firing of the troopers,
The rocks above re-echoed as the deadly rifles rang;
The powder-blackened faces were alight with lust of battle,
While below, unchanged, unheeding, the earth bound river sang.

"Short and merry life an outlaw's," so the ancient ballads tell us;
Short was his but scarcely merry when the flat below was red
With the blood of trusted comrades, while the hunters watched above him
For the quarry driven earthward with the price upon his head.

A man outlawed and hunted, watching there in utter darkness;
A charge or two still left him, and an eye as true as steel,
And troopers only human you could scare expect they'd follow,
Where in unfamiliar darkness lurked the serpent for the heel.

Did he know some secret outlet, or, wounded, to some by-way
Creep away and die by inches, watched by greedy vampire eyes,
We shall never know; the wattle guards the secrets of his passing,
And above the golden wattle all God's golden sunshine lies.

(1897 Original Poetry – The Australasian, 2 Jan 1897, p.42)
1911 Wattle, Government Printing Office – Courtesy State Archives & Records Authority of N.S.W.

1894 Story of Australian bushranging (Patrick William Marony 1858-1939) –
Courtesy National Library of Australia

ca. 1894 Bourke [i.e. Burke] ; Ben Hall ; Frank Gardiner, King of the Road ;
Gilbert ; Dunne [i.e. Dunn] – Courtesy National Library of Australia

1863 Ben Hall (Freeman Brothers)
– Courtesy of Mitchell Library,
State Library of New South Wales

1880 Ned Kelly, the bushranger
(Alfred May and Alfred Martin Ebsworth,
Melbourne) – Courtesy State Library Victoria

The Mudgee to Wallerawang Mail Coach stuck up at Aaron's Pass,
six miles from Cunningham's Creek, May 29, 1874 – Sunday Times, 19 Dec 1920, p.18

ca. 1860 Pickering, Charles Percy (1825-1908) Frank Gardiner and [John Gilbert?]
bushranger – Courtesy State Library of New South Wales

1863 The Death of O'Malley (Back and white lantern slide of a painting)
– Courtesy National Museum Australia

Chapter Three

Proprietors of Cobb and Co.

Journey through the many proprietors of Cobb and Co.

As noted in a 1922 account, "It would be wearisome, and indeed impossible, to follow the various firms which carried the banner of Cobb and Company ... the growth of the railway system, which took place in the 'sixties and 'seventies, meant, of course, the gradual disintegration of the coaching business. To-day the name of Cobb and Company, as far as the directory tells us, survives in but one country township." (Story of Cobb and Co., 20 May 1922, p.5)

In contrast, the 'Along the tracks of Cobb and Co.' book series embraces that very challenge. It sets out to accurately identify the many proprietors of the firm from 1854 to 1924. While the 1922 reflection acknowledged the difficulty—if not the impossibility—of tracing the numerous companies and individuals operating under the Cobb and Co. name in the 1850s and beyond, this series approaches the task with purpose and precision. Through meticulous research, it seeks to honour not only the well-known entrepreneurs and agents but also the many unsung proprietors whose efforts built and sustained the network. In doing so, it pays tribute to the hundreds of individuals whose collective efforts forged new routes and shaped the social and economic fabric of colonial Australia.

ca. 1905 A group of people in a Cobb & Company coach, Torquay, Victoria
– Courtesy Museums Victoria

"King Cobb is a comparatively modern potentate—there are many who remember when he first made his descent on these shores, and there are many who can recall the time when his name was unknown in the land—but by untiring energy he has established a pretty wide dominion, when in the order of things he shall be swept away by the advancing genius of steam, and his sceptre shall have passed into the hands of his rival, he will not be entirely unregretted. We shall say of him that he served us in our need, that he treated us well and liberally, and when we see his chariots, dismantled and uncared for, rotting in the yard of some ancient horse'ry, we shall remember many pleasant journeys and many jovial hours that we have passed under his [?]. If at times the road was a little rough or the travellers a little crowded, it only made them more sociable, and the necessity for making the best of the position conquered their reserve ... He has his faults; he is slow, he is not unfrequently uncomfortable, and he is too ambitious of emulating a carpet-bag in the point of never considering himself too full to containing some extra luggage, animate or inanimate, but then he has his good sides, and we shall relinquish him with regret." (King Cobb, 15 Aug 1871, p.2)

"The ubiquitous Cobb, the Hydra-headed Cobb, the Argus-eyed Cobb. But why Cobb? as Betsy prig said of Mrs. 'Arris, *there aint no Cobb*. Cobb's dead, defunct, gone out, has passed in checks, so far as Australia is concerned. Is he, and has he ? Cobb, being dead, yet liveth. *Cobb est mort, vive Cobb*. Go where you will, you shall find him. Here is a paradox, polyonomous yet mononomous. He may be any-body, Robertson and Wagner, Crawford, Chaplin, Quick, or who not, and yet he is Cobb after all." (Cobb's Box, 6 Feb 1875, p.4) *Appendix 1: Supporting evidence for many Cobb and Co. proprietors*

Cobb and Co. commenced in Australia

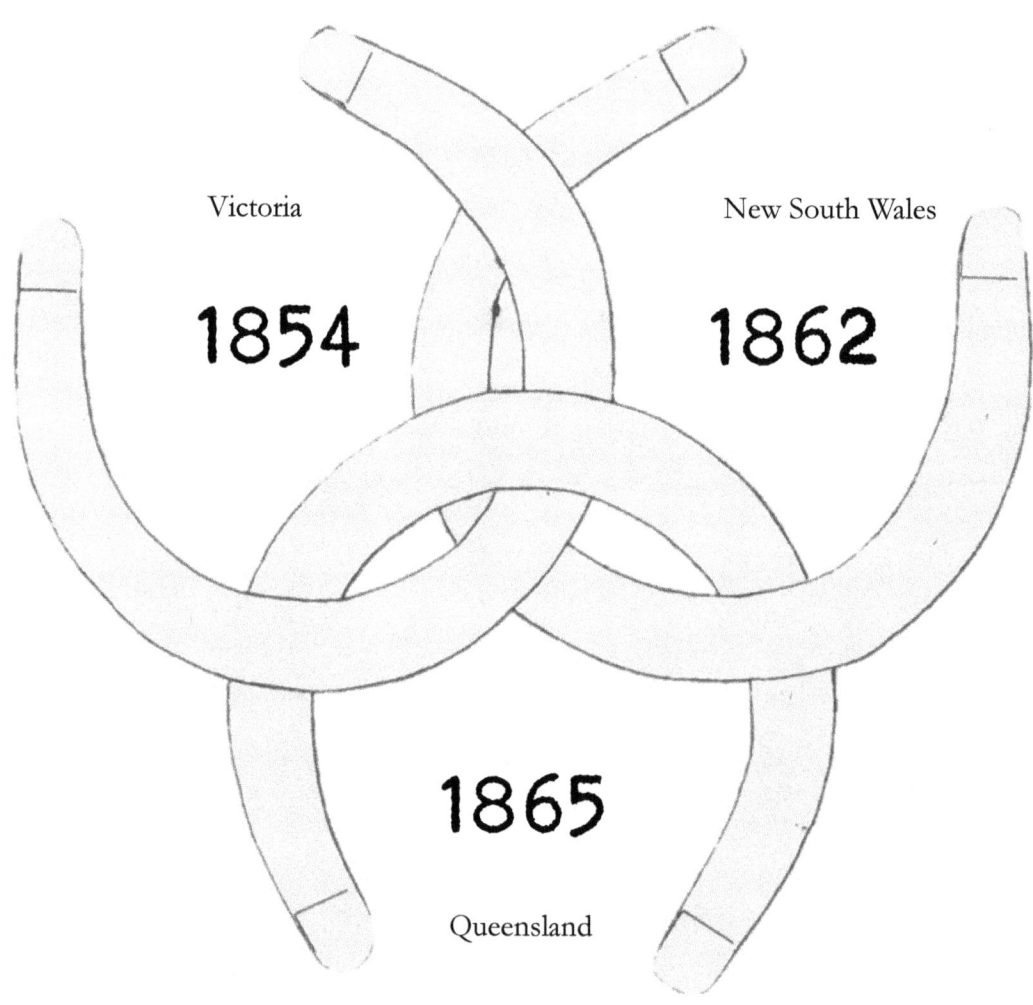

1862 The Floral Album, three intertwined horseshoes, ink (H. O. Lamb) – Courtesy Mitchell Library, State Library of New South Wales

Proprietors of Cobb and Co. coaching lines, Victoria

Proprietors of Cobb and Co. —1854

*Freeman Cobb, John B. Lamber/Lambert, James Swanton, John Murray Peck

Proprietors of Cobb and Co. —1855

*Freeman Cobb, James Swanton, John Murray Peck, Arthur Blake

Proprietors of Cobb and Co. —1856

*'Messrs. Cobb and Co.' [possibly Thomas Davies from this point in time]

Proprietors of Cobb and Co. —1857

*Thomas Davies Pre-18 April 1857-23 Sep 1857 ... sold to *Alexander Walker

*Chas. Colclough

*Watson and Hewitt (George Watson and Cyrus Hewitt) ... sold lines to *Swanton, Blake, and Co. (James Swanton, Arthur Lincoln Blake)

*F. B. Clapp and Co. (Francis Boardman Clapp)

Proprietors of Cobb and Co. —1858

*Watson and Hewitt ... sold lines to F. B. Clapp and Co.

*Swanton, Blake and Co. ... became Victoria Stage Company

*W. H. Brayton

Proprietors of Cobb and Co. —1859

*Victoria Stage Company, partners Arthur Lincoln Blake (Head manager of business, Melbourne), Charles Culwell Gardiner, Jacob Rogers, Pegleg Whitford Jackson, George Loop Woodworth, John Francis Britton, Levi Rich, Oliver Blake Clapp, Christopher Ives, John Murray Peck, James Joseph Blake, McCormick, as at 19 Sep 1859 ... change of partners 30 Nov 1859

*F. B. Clapp and Co.

*W. H. Brayton ... left district

Proprietors of Cobb and Co. —1860

*Victoria Stage Company, partners Arthur Lincoln Blake, Peleg Whitford Jackson, John Francis Britton, Oliver Blake Clapp, Christopher Ives, John Murray Peck, Charles Culwell Gardiner, as at 25 Jun 1860 ... company soon dissolved

*F. B. Clapp and Co.

*Watson and Hewitt

*William Warren

Proprietors of Cobb and Co. —1861

*F. B. Clapp and Co. ... now known as *Australian Stage Company, 16 Jan 1861-25 Jan 1861, partners William Randle, Cyrus Hewitt, William Williams, Matthew M'Caw, John R. Ricards, jun., John Halfey, A. L. Blake, F. B. Clapp, G. B. Perkins, William Woods, Thomas Ogilvie, J. D. Robinson, Hugh M'Phillimy, C. C. Skarratt, T. A. Lascelles, J. T. Fallen, David Jones, Walter Craig, Alexander Kelly, Charles Croaker, B. H. Fernald, William Malcolm, Joel Tompkins, Oliver Cooper, J. L. Huntley, Francis Tozer, as at 7 May 1860

*Australian Stage Company, new partners 25 Jan 1861

*M'Phee & Co.

*Michel and Hughes by 13 Jun 1861-10 Jul 1861

*Henry Hoyt advertised 5 Jun 1861

*Robertson, Britton and Co. ... 1 Feb 1861 A. W. Robertson retired from Bendigo Stage Company that continued with partners William B. Bradley, Walter R. Hall, William F. Whitney, Edward Moore, Frank May ... which then sold plant to *Watson & Hewitt ... Watson and Hewitt ceased by 2 Apr 1861 ... selling to *Robertson, Britton and Co. by 3 Jun 1861

Proprietors of Cobb and Co.—1862

*Australian Stage Company

*Robertson, Britton and Co. partners A. W. Robertson and John Britton, as at 13 Jun 1862 ... some, but not all, of Robertson and Britton's lines were then advertised as *Robertson, Wagner and Co. whose partners were A. W. Robertson, John Wagner, James Rutherford, W. B. Bradley, Wm. F. Whitney

*Henry Hoyt

*M'Phee & Co.

Note: Evidence not found to date, as to when James Rutherford, W. B. Bradley, and Wm. F. Whitney joined A. W. Robertson and John Wagner, trading under the style of Cobb and Co.

Proprietors of Cobb and Co.—1863

*Australian Stage Company

*Robertson, Britton and Co. & *Robertson, Wagner and Co.

*Henry Hoyt still being advertised 3 Dec 1863

*Meigs & Anderson advertised 5 Dec 1863

Proprietors of Cobb and Co.—1864

*Australian Stage Company

*Robertson, Britton and Co. & *Robertson, Wagner and Co.

*Meigs & Anderson

*J. J. Stiles

*R. Davey

*John Cawker

*A. Lane

*G. Whorlom

*M'Phee and Co./John M'Phee

*J. C. Horr

*Thomas Stoneman

*Cameron and Jones advertised from 17 Jun 1864-21 Sep 1864

Proprietors of Cobb and Co.—1865

*Australian Stage Company

*Robertson, Wagner and Co.

*Meigs & Anderson

*J. C. Horr line ... to *M'Phee and Co./John M'Phee

*Ballarat Stage Company

*Thomas Stoneman

Proprietors of Cobb and Co.—1866

*Australian Stage Company

*Robertson, Wagner and Co.

*Meigs & Anderson/Meggs and Anderson

*M'Phee and Co.

*Ballarat Stage Company

*Thomas Stoneman

*E. Moore and Co.

*Meigs & Anderson, Thomas Stoneman, Joshua Vines ... became *Western Stage Company 27 Dec 1866

Proprietors of Cobb and Co.—1867

*Australian Stage Company still advertised 9 Jan 1867

*Robertson, Wagner and Co.

*M'Phee and Co.

*Western Stage Company

Proprietors of Cobb and Co.—1868

*Robertson, Wagner and Co. partners Alexander W. Robertson, John Wagner, George John Watson, William James, as at 14 Jan 1868
*M'Phee and Co.
*Anderson and M'Phee
*Western Stage Company
*Matthew Veal and Co.
*Scott & Nugent

Proprietors of Cobb and Co.—1869

*Robertson, Wagner and Co.
*M'Phee and Co.
*Anderson & M'Phee
*Western Stage Company
*Matthew Veal and Co.

Proprietors of Cobb and Co.—1870

*Robertson, Wagner and Co.
*M'Phee and Co.
*Anderson & M'Phee
*Western Stage Company
*Matthew Veal and Co.

Proprietors of Cobb and Co.—1871

*Robertson, Wagner and Co. 15 Aug 1871 "Dissolution of 'Cobb and Co.' partnership in the colonies of Victoria, New South Wales, and Queensland, has been this day dissolved by mutual consent A. W. Robertson, J. Rutherford. W. B. Bradley, Wm. F. Whitney, John Wagner"

Note: Robertson and Wagner took Victoria; the Echuca, Deniliquin, Hay, Booligal, and Wilcannia road, and west of it (Cobb and Co., Melbourne)
*M'Phee and Co.
*Anderson & M'Phee
*Western Stage Company
*Matthew Veal and Co.

Proprietors of Cobb and Co.—1872

*Robertson, Wagner and Co., A. W. Robertson and J. Wagner listed on mail tenders not as Cobb & Co.
*M'Phee and Co.
*Anderson & M'Phee
*Western Stage Company
*Matthew Veal and Co.
*J. Cawker

Proprietors of Cobb and Co.—1873

*Robertson, Wagner and Co.
*M'Phee and Co.
*Anderson & M'Phee
*Western Stage Company
*Matthew Veal and Co.
*J. Cawker

Proprietors of Cobb and Co.—1874

*Robertson, Wagner and Co.
*M'Phee and Co.
*Anderson & M'Phee
*Western Stage Company
*Matthew Veal and Co.

Proprietors of Cobb and Co.—1875

*Robertson, Wagner and Co.
*M'Phee and Co.
*Anderson & M'Phee
*Western Stage Company
*Matthew Veal and Co.

Proprietors of Cobb and Co.—1876

*Robertson, Wagner and Co.
*M'Phee and Co.
*Anderson & M'Phee
*Western Stage Company partners Thomas Stoneman, Charles Anderson, Joshua Vine, as at 13 Dec 1876
*Matthew Veal and Co

Proprietors of Cobb and Co.—1877

*Robertson, Wagner and Co.
*M'Phee and Co.
*Anderson & M'Phee
*Western Stage Company
*Matthew Veal and Co.

Proprietors of Cobb and Co.—1878

*Robertson, Wagner and Co.
*M'Phee and Co.
*Anderson & M'Phee
*Western Stage Company
*Matthew Veal and Co.
Note: Death of Freeman Cobb

Proprietors of Cobb and Co.—1879

*Robertson, Wagner and Co.
*M'Phee and Co.
*Anderson & M'Phee
*Western Stage Company
*Seth Sharp

Proprietors of Cobb and Co.—1880

*Robertson, Wagner and Co.
*M'Phee and Co.
*Anderson & M'Phee
*Western Stage Company
*Seth Sharp/S. Sharp

Proprietors of Cobb and Co.—1881

*Robertson, Wagner and Co.
Note: A. W. Robertson & John Wagner lesses of Pericoota, Tattaila
*M'Phee and Co.
*Anderson & M'Phee
*Western Stage Company
*Seth Sharp/S. Sharp

Proprietors of Cobb and Co.—1882

*Robertson, Wagner and Co.
*M'Phee and Co.
*Western Stage Company
*Seth Sharp/S. Sharp
*Vines and M'Phee

Proprietors of Cobb and Co.—1883

*Robertson, Wagner and Co.
*M'Phee and Co.
*Anderson & M'Phee
*Western Stage Company
*Seth Sharp/S. Sharp
*Vines and M'Phee
*T. Cawker

Proprietors of Cobb and Co.—1884

*Robertson, Wagner and Co.
*M'Phee and Co.
*Western Stage Company
*Vines and M'Phee

Proprietors of Cobb and Co.—1885

*Robertson, Wagner and Co.
*M'Phee and Co.
*Western Stage Company
*Vines and M'Phee

Proprietors of Cobb and Co.—1886

*Robertson, Wagner and Co.
*M'Phee and Co.
*Western Stage Company
*Vines and M'Phee

Proprietors of Cobb and Co.—1887

*Robertson, Wagner and Co.
*M'Phee and Co.
*Western Stage Company
*Vines and M'Phee

Proprietors of Cobb and Co.—1888

*Robertson, Wagner and Co.
*M'Phee and Co.
*Western Stage Company
*Vines and M'Phee

Proprietors of Cobb and Co.—1889

*Robertson, Wagner and Co.
*M'Phee and Co.
*Western Stage Company
*Vines and M'Phee

Proprietors of Cobb and Co.—1890

*Robertson, Wagner and Co.
*Western Stage Company
*Vines and M'Phee

Proprietors of Cobb and Co.—1891

*Robertson, Wagner and Co.
*Western Stage Company
*Vines and M'Phee

Proprietors of Cobb and Co.—1892

*Robertson, Wagner and Co.
*Western Stage Company
*Vines and M'Phee

Proprietors of Cobb and Co.—1893

*Robertson, Wagner and Co.
*Western Stage Company
*Vines and M'Phee

Proprietors of Cobb and Co.—1894

*Robertson, Wagner and Co.
*Western Stage Company
*Vines and M'Phee

Proprietors of Cobb and Co.—1895

*Robertson, Wagner and Co.
*Western Stage Company
*Vines and M'Phee

Proprietors of Cobb and Co.—1896

*Robertson, Wagner and Co.
*Western Stage Company
*Vines and M'Phee
*A. Grant

Note: Death of A. W. Robertson 16/18 Jul 1896

Proprietors of Cobb and Co.—1897

*Robertson & Wagner
*Western Stage Company
*Vines and M'Phee

Proprietors of Cobb and Co.—1898

*Robertson & Wagner
*Western Stage Company
*Vines and M'Phee

Proprietors of Cobb and Co.—1899

*Robertson & Wagner sold line to *George Alexander McGowan (Mac)
* Western Stage Company
* Vines and M'Phee

Proprietors of Cobb and Co.—1900-1904

* Robertson, Wagner and Co. dissolved with A. W Robertson's death (16/18 Jul 1896) but some lines still advertised as Robertson, Wagner and Co.
*Western Stage Company
*Vines and M'Phee

Note: Death of John Wagner 27 Jan 1901; Death of John Murray Peck 19 Nov 1903

Proprietors of Cobb and Co.—1905-1929

*A. N. Vines (1905-1919)
*H. Womersley (1919-1921)

18 Dec 1920 Cobb and Co.'s Charleville Factory closed

Cobb and Co. retired from coaching business in the west (Queensland)

By 14 Aug 1924 Yeulba and Surat ... Last Queensland horse-drawn coach owned by Cobb and Co. supplanted by a modern motor service

1929 Voluntary Liquidation of *Cobb and Co. Ltd, Queensland, Alfred Uhl, Liquidator

Note: 6 Sep 1920 Death of Francis Boardman Clapp

* * *

1 Nov 1963 "Victoria was the last state in which this occurred ... The Colac Herald has now been informed that Mr. William Thomas Fletcher, who still have relatives in this district, ran his Cobb & Co. coach from Deans Marsh to Lorne 'until at least 1925'. This certificate is to conduct the service which was issued by the deputy registrar general of Victoria was produced at the 'Colac Herald' office this week"

1 Dec 1823 "Lorne via Ocean Road. Large comfortable cars leave daily from garage at 8.30 a.m., arriving at Lorne midday. Coaches daily from Dean's Marsh to Lorne. Daily Service to Torquay ... Fletcher's Services Pty Ltd" Not listed as Cobb and Co. (Advertising, 1 Dec 1923, p.1)

18 Nov 1925 "Lorne Cars leave Garage daily ... for Great Ocean Road ... Fletcher's Services Pty Ltd. 29 Gheringhap St., Geelong, Telephone 2481 [?]." (Advertising, 18 Nov 1925, p.2)

Proprietors of Cobb and Co. coaching lines, New South Wales

Proprietors of Cobb and Co. —1862

28 May 1862 Messrs. *Robertson and Britton, with James Rutherford manager N.S.W.

13 Jun 1862 *Robertson, Britton and Co., partners A. W. Robertson and John Britton ... some, but not all, of Robertson and Britton's lines were then advertised as *Robertson, Wagner and Co. whose partners were A. W. Robertson, John Wagner, James Rutherford, W. B. Bradley, Wm. F. Whitney

Proprietors of Cobb and Co. —1868

*Robertson, Wagner and Co., partners Alexander W. Robertson, John Wagner, George John Watson, William James, as at 14 Jan 1868 ... (group possibly running 'Cobb and Co., Melbourne' before official Cobb and Co. partnership dissolution)

Proprietors of Cobb and Co. —1871

*Robertson, Wagner and Co. 15 Aug 1871 ... "Dissolution of 'Cobb and Co.' partnership in the colonies of Victoria, New South Wales, and Queensland, has been this day dissolved by mutual consent A. W. Robertson, J. Rutherford. W. B. Bradley, Wm. F. Whitney, John Wagner"

30 Dec 1871 New partnership James Rutherford, Walter R. Hall, William B. Bradley, William F. Whitney, Colin Robertson (Cobb and Co., Sydney)

Note: Robertson and Wagner took Victoria; the Echuca, Deniliquin, Hay, Booligal, and Wilcannia road, and west of it (Cobb and Co., Melbourne)

Proprietors of Cobb and Co. —1874

13 Jan 1874 William Brown Bradley retired from partnership known as Cobb & Co.

Partners James Rutherford, Walter R. Hall, Wm. F. Whitney, Colin Robertson, as at 13 Jan 1874

Proprietors of Cobb and Co. —1876

After 6 May 1876 partners James Rutherford, Walter Russell Hall, William Franklin Whitney

Proprietors of Cobb and Co. —1881

Note: James Rutherford, Walter R. Hall, William B. Bradley, William F. Whitney lessees of Woollagoola Beriarh, and Gooagoola

Proprietors of Cobb and Co. —1885

Partners James Rutherford, William Franklin Whitney ... dissolution of Cobb and Co. partnership 15 Oct 1885

Proprietors of Cobb and Co. —1887

Note: Cobb & Co. Mail Contracts address listed as Sydney

Proprietors of Cobb and Co. —1888

Note: Cobb & Co. Mail Contracts address listed as Bathurst

Proprietors of Cobb and Co. —1894

Note: Cobb and Co. listed on N.S.W. mail contracts; Death of William Franklin Whitney 31 Oct 1894

Proprietors of Cobb and Co. —1895

Note: James Rutherford and/or Cobb and Co. listed on N.S.W. mail contracts

Proprietors of Cobb and Co. —1898

Note: Cobb & Co. no longer listed on mail contracts in New South Wales

Proprietors of Cobb and Co. —1899

*Robertson, Wagner and Co., sold Hay and Deniliquin lines to *George Alexander McGowan (Mac)

Note: Death of James Rutherford 14 Sep 1911

Proprietors of Cobb and Co. coaching lines, Queensland

Proprietors of Cobb and Co.—1862

28 May 1862 Messrs. *Robertson and Britton, with James Rutherford manager N.S.W.

Proprietors of Cobb and Co.—1865

1 Jan 1865 Mr. Grant, Queensland managing director

Proprietors of Cobb and Co.—1871

*Robertson, Wagner and Co., partners prior to 15 Aug 1871 A. W. Robertson, J. Rutherford, W. B. Bradley, Wm. F. Whitney, John Wagner

30 Dec 1871 New partnership James Rutherford, Walter R. Hall, William B. Bradley, William F. Whitney, Colin Robertson

Proprietors of Cobb and Co.—1874

13 Jan 1874 William Brown Bradley retired from partnership known as Cobb & Co.; As at 13 Jan 1874 partners J. Rutherford, W. R. Hall, Wm. F. Whitney, Colin Robertson

Proprietors of Cobb and Co.—1876

After 6 May 1876 partners James Rutherford, Walter Russell Hall, William Franklin Whitney

Proprietors of Cobb and Co.—1881

*Qld Cobb and Co. Limited, Aug 1881 company was incorporated, shareholders were W. R. Hall, J. Rutherford, F. Shaw, I. T. Barthelomew, T. Gallagher, C. M. Kirk, F. C. Shaw, H. W. Shaw, H. B. Taylor, R. M'Master, J. Coyle, W. J. Richardson, L. Uhl, J. Coyle (Charters Towers), W. Jenkins, John Bock

Proprietors of Cobb and Co.—1907

"A special meeting of Cobb and Co., Limited, was held yesterday afternoon for the purpose of receiving the liquidator's report on the winding up of the old company ... Mr. J. Story presided ... it had been decided to form a new company under the name of Cobb and Co., Limited, the old company being styled Cobb and Co. The liabilities of the company's per balance book were £66,879 8s. 1d., and the assets £47,023 5s. 9d., showing a debit balance of £19,856 2s. 4d. The new company was formed with a capital of 30,000 shares for every £200 shares held in the old company, shareholders were allotted 100 £1 shares in the new company paid up to 15s. The report was adopted." (Messrs Cobb and Co, 18 Mar 1907, p.4)

Proprietors of Cobb and Co.—1920

Directors of Cobb and Co., Ltd., Queensland: A. Uhl (chairman), W. N. Morcom, Dr. E. D. Ahern, W. Ross Munro, and H. Uhl with Mr. G. W. F. Studdert, F.A.I.S. as secretary.

Proprietors of Cobb and Co.—1928

"Cobb and Company Limited. The days of vast coaching enterprises ... had gone ... A chain of stores in the Surat and St. George districts was opened, and certain coaching was done, but per motor car. Then the coaching was dropped and just the stores continued. Lately a fire destroyed the St. George stores and stock, and though business was continued in temporary premises the company has had enough if it ... they have put up a proposal to go into liquidation." (End of Cobb and Co., 15 Nov 1928, p.2)

Proprietors of Cobb and Co.—1931

"The report of the liquidator of Cobb and Co., Ltd ... Since the last report there have been further decreases in the price of wool. This, together with the present trade depression, has made it difficult to collect outstanding debts. The property at Surat was sold during the year for £200. Efforts have also been made to dispose of the Dirranbandi property at a satisfactory price without effect." (Cobb and Co., 23 Oct 1931, p.10)

Cobb and Co. Name—1948

"Right To Name ... Gordon Wallace Fitzgerald Studdert, merchant ... When the company voluntarily liquidated in 1929, he was general manager, and by agreement acquired the company's Surat business, together with the right to use name 'Cobb and Co,' for £5,100." (Historic Firm Recalled, 30 Nov 1948, p.6)

Other possible Cobb and Co. proprietors ... further evidence sought:

- Alex. W. Robertson, George John Watson, William James, and John Wagner (Written in 1868)
- James Rutherford, one share; John Wagner, one share; A. W. Robertson, one share; B. and C. Robertson and Pollock, one share; Walter Hall and W. F. Whitney, one share (Written in 1924)
- Alick and John Robertson, John Wagner, Walter Hall and James Rutherford (Written in 1925)
- J. Rutherford, Walter Hall, W. Franklin Whitney, W. Bradley, R. Brunig (Note: A. C. Brunig, Manager, Ballarat 1861)
- Frank Whitney, Walter Hall, James Rutherford and a wealthy Melbourne racing man named Power (Written in 1925)
- Australian Stage Company, of which Russell and Warren are partners (Written in 1861)
- A. W. Robertson and John Wagner became partners with Mr. Watson, and subsequently Walter Hall and E. James. (Written in 1918)
- James Rutherford, half share; Mr. H. Barnes and Mr. John Robertson each one-quarter (Written in 1917)
- James Rutherford, half share; Mr. H. Barnes, one quarter share and Mr. John Robertson three quarters share (Written in 1955)

Early Cobb and Co. proprietors

Cobb and Co.—Freeman Cobb, John Murray Peck, James Swanton, John B. Lamber, Arthur Lincoln Blake

"Freeman Cobb is an American ... arrived in Melbourne, having come out as agent for Adams, and Co., the well-known express company of New York ... after him came a few of the first of those vehicles that have attained a world-wide celebrity ... Following him came James Swanson, John Lamber, and John M. Peck ... finding that there was a demand for conveyance to the newly broken-out-diggings, the four I have named formed themselves into a company and started a line from Castlemaine and Bendigo ... These and for years after, were the palmy days of Cobb's coaches! ... One by one they have left, these hardy, pioneers of the road, these men who recked not of danger, who smiled in the face of difficulties, who calmly looked at impossibilities and overcame them. Furious driving, I grant you, a reckless disregard, sometimes of their own and the passengers' necks, probably. But what else could have been done ? let me ask. There was no time to be shilly-shallying on the edge of a swamp—no use hesitating at taking a header down a steep gully with a broken boulder or slimy bottom. It was a shake of the reins, a crack of the stinging whipcord, a heigh ! ho! houp la ! a mad plunge, a creaking of springs, a straining of harness, a flying of mud and gravel and a get out on the other side at full gallop, for you know her Majesty's mails must not be delayed ... One by one, I say, have these pioneers, of the road quitted. Of the four only one remains, namely, John M. Peck, and he has given over coaching long ago." (Cobb and Co., 24 Jul 1875, p.5)

"The original Freeman Cobb, after selling out his interest in Victoria, went to California, where, unfortunately, he invested in some wild cat banks and mines, in which he lost his money, but, with the indomitable pluck which characterised him, he, with the wreck of his fortune, crossed over to South Africa, at the time diamonds were first discovered at Kimberly. He at once started a coaching business ... from Port Elizabeth to the mines, but his health failed him, and he died there in 1873. Mr. John Peck died recently in Melbourne, where for many years he was the head of a large and profitable stock and station agency business. Jas. Swanson and Anthony Blake went home to America some years ago." (The Contributor, 25 Nov 1908, p.1405)

"Pioneer of the Coaching Days. The announcement of the death of Mr. John Murray Peck, which took place in his 73rd year, at his residence, Pascoevale ... will be received with sincere regret by his numerous friends, who held him in high esteem for his business capacity and excellent qualities of heart and mind ... Mr. Peck was born at Lebanon, New Hampshire, United States, and coming to Melbourne in 1853 with Mr. Hiram Cobb, he entered into partnership with that gentleman in conjunction with Messrs. J. Swanton and J. Lambert, and founded the famous firm of Cobb and Company, whose name subsequently became a household word throughout the state. In 1857 Mr. Peck visited the United States, and returned, bringing with him the first shipment of the 'Jack coaches' which were run by Cobb and Company, mainly on the Mount Alexander-road. Shortly after Mr. Peck's return from the States, Mr. Cobb retired from the partnership, and the Victorian Stage Company was formed, consisting of 13 partners, who were all Americans or Canadians, and in June, 1860, that company sold their coaching business to Messrs. Watson and Hewitt, who were subsequently succeeded by Messrs. Robertson and Wagner." (Death of Mr J. M. Peck, 21 Nov 1903, p.1)

Cobb and Co.—A. W. Robertson (Alexander), John Wagner

"It may here be stated that the two members of the firm, who originated the campaign in New South Wales in 1861—A. W. Robertson and John Wagner—were British Americans, being natives of Canada, and, were splendid types of the men who, in all new countries, are resolute and resourceful colonisers. As employers, they were just and liberal in all dealings with their vast army of employees, as evidence of which there was never during their 40 years of coaching business the slightest friction between them and their employees. It can truthfully be said, too, that never had a firm a more capable, loyal, and faithful body of servants. Several of them filled important positions in the public life of the Australian States; amongst whom may be mentioned Mr. John Taverner, the present Agent-General for Victoria in London, who was a stage coach driver on the Bendigo to Swan Hill Road in Victoria. Mr. A. R. Outtrim, the present M.L.A. for Maryborough, and ex-Minister for Mines in that State, and F. A. Byrne, driver, agent, and manager, and ex-M.L.A. for Hay, in New South Wales. In this connection it may be mentioned that the father of Mr. Alfred Deakin, an old coaching man, and member of the old-time firm of Bill and Deakin, was accountant to Robertson, Wagner, and Co. for several years." (The Contributor, 25 Nov 1908, p.1405)

Other early coach proprietors

"I have not forgotten the early coaching proprietors in Australia, who also filled worthy positions as pioneers in developing the States, and in this connection I have in my mind's eye Charles Henry Jones on the south line, Crane and Roberts, Mylecharane and Elliott, on the western. Nowland Bros. and Gill Bros, on the northern roads; Foster and Vinge, at one time the overland contractors, Sydney to Melbourne. In Victoria there were James Bevan and Co., on the Beechworth line; Bill and Deakin, and Howard, with the 'Argus' line, subsidised by that great newspaper to ensure delivery of the paper on the goldfields, each copy selling in 1854 at 2s 6d. In Tasmania, Mr. Samuel Page was the colossus of coaching, and was subjected at times to a spirited opposition from Mrs. Cox, who had a love for coaching. In South Australia the pioneer was Mr. W. Chambers, who was carrying the principal mail contracts in that State as early as 1849, and who sold out in the early 50's to J. Rounsevell, ex-sergeant of police in Adelaide, who carried on the business for several years, when it came into the hands of Hill and Fuller.

In Western Australia, there was no large service in coaching, until the finding of Coolgardie, followed by other great discoveries, where a highly efficient mail and coach service was established by Sydney Kidman (the Cattle King) and James Nicholas, the latter an old-time driver for Cobb and Co. in Riverina. The service then established assumed very large proportions, and was a well-equipped and well-managed business." (The Contributor, 25 Nov 1908, p.1405)

1860 Two men seated in a buggy, Cyrus Hewitt on left, beard, wearing top hat; J. M. Peck on right, moustache, also wearing top hat – Courtesy State Library of Victoria

J. E. Bishop, Coach Builder. Joseph Bishop arrived in Melbourne during the goldrushes, ultimately establishing a coach building business at Beechworth, which was later transferred to Euroa. The family moved to Melbourne in the late 1880s, where one son became the proprietor of the trade journal 'The Australasian Coachbuilder and Saddler.' – Courtesy The University of Melbourne Archives

Alexander William Robertson –
Courtesy Geln Eira Historical Society

1872 **Alex Walker** [identity not confirmed as Cobb and Co. Alex Walker] (Thomas Foster Chuck) – Courtesy State of Library Victoria

James Rutherford – National Advocate (Bathurst), 19 Nov 1913, p.3

1872 **James Rutherford** (T. F. Chuck) – Courtesy State Library of Victoria

1880 **Peleg Whitford Jackson** –
Courtesy State Library of South Australia

1890 **John Wagner** (1827-1901), (U. Catani)
– Courtesy State Library of Victoria

Pre-1911 Portrait of **Walter Hall**
(T. R. Dibdin) – Courtesy Mitchell Library,
State Library of New South Wales

1900-1915 **Frank Whitney** amongst workshop,
Mandurama, New South Wales (E. A. Lumme) –
Courtesy National Library of Australia

Chapter Four

N.S.W. Proprietors

Cobb and Co. journey into New South Wales

"The story of Cobb and Co. is really the story of James Rutherford, and the company saw its greatest days long after the man whose name was its trademark had ceased to have any connection with it.

Much more properly, it should have been 'Rutherford and Co.'—but the original name will be remembered when that of the man who was really its guiding spirit is forgotten." Rutherford as a "prominent pioneer of the old-time Roaring Days of the stage-coach, which antedated the advent of the railways ... was the life and heart and soul of the eastern and north Australian Cobb and Co. ... he never allowed an obstacle to daunt or to stay him in anything he wished to accomplish."

(A Relic of the Past, 14 Jan 1931, p. 9; A Pioneer of the Coaching Days:
The Late James Rutherford, 20 Sep 1911, p.40)

1908 A meeting of three Cobb and Co. mail coaches and a motor vehicle at Winton, coaches from Middleton, Longreach and Kynuna – Courtesy National Archives Australia

The main roads of New South Wales

"The railways of to-day follow generally the main roads built by the Government with convict labour, the tracks made by the explorers and beaten by the bullock-teams of the first pioneers, the routes followed by the drivers of Cobb and Co.'s coaches, and the travelling stock routes carved out by the drovers and overlanders.

In 1861 the colony of New South Wales had only 74 miles of railway open to traffic—Sydney was connected by rail with Parramatta, and a portion of the line to Goulburn (completed in 1869) was under construction. The colony possessed also four main roads, with branch traffic feeders, namely, the Northern, the Western, the Southern, and the South Coast. The first, 405 miles in length, extended from Morpeth to Maryland, New England; the second (338miles) from Sydney to Warren, via Bathurst, Orange, and many other important townships thence prolonged to the Darling, at Bourke, by a line 175 miles in length; the third (385 miles) from Sydney to Albury—prior to the construction of the railway, the great highway between Sydney and Melbourne; and the fourth (250 miles) left Campbelltown, and ascended the coast range, along the top of which it ran to Coal Cliff, thence traversing the Illawarra District, paralled to the coast, and passing through the rich lands watered by the Shoalhaven, the Clyde, and the Moruya, as far as Bega, whence, as a minor road, it extended to the southern limits of New South Wales.

With the exception of bullock-dray and drovers' tracks, this was the colony's intercommicatory stock-in-trade when James Rutherford came from Victoria to New South Wales as manager for Cobb and Co. in New South Wales and Queensland, and interviewed the firm's Sydney representative, Walter R. Hall (the last survivor of the enterprise) at his office in Pitt-street, on what is now the site of Garling's-chambers. Rutherford went straightway to Bathurst (of which 'City of the Plains' he was elected Mayor in 1868), and there fixed his headquarters, established a coach factory (where Cobb and Co.'s vehicles were built, repaired, and renovated, and where a great deal of general work for the public was performed), and built himself a mansion home at Hereford, by the bank of the Macquarie River, near Kelso, and Bathurst remained his home till the time of his death—a period of fifty years." (A Pioneer of the Coaching Days: The Late James Rutherford, 20 Sep 1911, p.26)

The proprietors of Cobb and Co.

Cobb and Co.—James Rutherford (Jas.)

"AN AMERICAN AUSTRALIAN. JAMES RUTHERFORD. (By Archdeacon Oakes, in Sydney Telegraph.) The most enterprising man in our Australian history—that, of course, is only an opinion, but *by their fruits ye shall know them*, and the results of this man's restless energies and capable business administrations challenge comparisons with confidence. Sterling traits stood out in bold relief in his character, quickness in decision, largeness in idea, energy in execution—he was the type of man to whom all Australians, but more especially those living outback, are under the deepest obligations ... All his undertakings were carried out on scales of vast magnitude ... The name of James Rutherford was a synonym for all that was honorable, just, and equitable" (The Founder of Cobb & Co., 12 Dec 1924, p.4)

"GRAND-DAUGHTER OF JAMES RUTHERFORD ... Mrs A. W. Riordan, of Mount Dandenong, who writes:—*As a grand-daughter of James Rutherford, of Cobb & Co., I was greatly interested in the article published in your issue of 21st July. A fire which burned down my grandmother's house in Bathurst destroyed the family records, with the result that very little is now known of James Rutherford's early days in Victoria.*

If the facts mentioned in your article are correct, it is clear that you have access to some source of information of which the Rutherfords are ignorant, but which would be of value to them ... The history of the Rutherford family is no less interesting than that of Cobb & Co. Originally from Roxburghshire in Scotland the family went to Ulster about 1660, where they were prosperous farmers until the 'troubles' of 1798, in which year the then James was ambushed and murdered by Irish rebels, his house then being burned down and the occupants butchered, with the exception of his wife, her infant son—also a James—and nurse in New York State, where the second James later had a farm 40 miles from Buffalo.

James, of Cobb and Co., was born on this farm in 1827; before arriving in Australia to try his luck on the gold fields he had been a poor school-teacher. Soon after arriving in Victoria he married Ada Nicholson, the descendant of a former officer of the Royal Navy who had joined the American rebels and later commanded the migrated U.S.S. 'Constitution' better known as 'Old Ironsides.' Commodore Nicholson left, much property in America and his widow was so alarmed by the possibility of her daughters being married for their money that she abandoned the estates and came to Australia, a strange choice when a gold rush was in progress. The outcome, however, was a happy one; Ada was married for her own sake by a man destined to build up a large fortune, solely by his own energy and ability. This fortunate partnership ended with the death of James at Bathurst in 1911, at the age of 84, still energetic enough to break in his own horses.

James was not only a great organiser, he was also a great Australian, whose work was of national importance. Original in everything he did, he refused to let his children go to the same schools, sending them to Scotland, Germany, Switzerland, and America. My father, the fourth James, who rowed for Geelong Grammar School in the '80's, was the only one who was not sent abroad to complete his education.

If the information in the 'Free Press' article is correct, it is a remarkable co-incidence that great-grandchildren of the first Australian James should now be living in a district which furnished the means that made possible the vast expansion of Cobb & Co. specially as no member of the Rutherford family had lived in Victoria since 1862, until my husband, who was then a regular soldier, was stationed in Melbourne on his return from the Staff College, Camberley, in 1937.—A. W. Riordan. (Mt. Dandenong).

The information was taken from an article in the 'Digest of World Reading' by Mr J. Bennett, of 'Free Press,' on American colonisation in Australia. As far as Mr Bennett can recollect, he gathered the information in the Oxley Memorial (Historical) Library in Brisbane, possibly from the late William Lee's authoritative work on Cobb and Co ... Following this, the article moved to the subject of DOGS "Sir.—I am one who can tell Upwey Lady and others where the dogs go, that are out for an evening's run. They go to some garden nearby, choose the choicest plant, sit down and empty their bowels, then make a path across seedling beds crushing the seedlings into the ground, then to the front door which they foul. And should there be a home in the district where some unfortunate people own a female dog (as dear a pet to them as Upwey Lady's is to her) they immediately start a persecution day and night for two or three weeks, even though the female, poor creature, a strict prisoner, is never seen by them, if doctors could only realize what nerve storms are caused by packs of uncontrolled dogs, they would appeal to the Government to make it an offence for anyone to keep a dog that is not under its owner's control all the time, kept strictly on his or her own property. One of the Victims. (Fern Tree Gully)" (Readers' Letters, 6 Aug 1948, p.6)

Back to James Rutherford "Mr Rutherford came to Australia in 1852 with a little money at his back and joined Messrs A. W. Robertson, W. F. Whitney, W. R. Hall, and W. Bradley, taking over a small firm called Cobb and Co ... supplmenting their enterprise with investments in pastoral properties." (Cobb and Co., 1 Oct 1936, p.67)

For example, 1867 "It is hereby notified for general information, that the interest of the previous occupants in the licenses of the undermentioned Runs of Crown Lands has been transferred, during the quarter ending the 31st March, with the sanction of the Government, to the parties hereafter particularised. W. Alcock Tully, Chief Commissioner of Crown Lands. Warrego District. Transferrer George Sydney Smith. Transferrees James Rutherford and Alexander Wm. Robertson. Name of Run. Yanda, Trankey East." (Advertising, 9 Apr 1867, p.1)

"In 1861 it was decided to separate the firm's business, Mr Rutherford and other partners taking up the New South Wales and Queensland's interests and Mr Robertson and Mr Wagner remaining in Victoria ... With the most indefatigable industry, and extraordinary success, he devoted himself to the organisation of the business of mail carrying in New South Wales and Queensland, and it is said of Cobb and Co.—that is, of Mr Rutherford, who was the main spirit in the firm—that it opened roads where never else our railways would have penetrated. In 1875 Mr. Rutherford purchased the property known as Hereford, which originally was the grant of Lieut. William Cox, for constructing the first road over the Blue Mountains. Here he built himself a residence, now known as 'Hereford Court'." (The Founder of Cobb & Co., 12 Dec 1924, p.4)

At Hereford in 1907, "several shearers were charged at the Bathurst Police Court last week with breach of agreement with James Rutherford, of Hereford. After shearing a few, the men had on Tuesday held a meeting and decided that the sheep were too wet to shear. Mr. Rutherford persuaded some of the men to resume work ... The evidence for the prosecution stated that the sheep were in a coverered shed from Saturday to Tuesday, and so could not have got wet. The bench imposed a fine of 40s in one case with £3 12s 6d costs. The other cases were postponed." (Shearers Fined, 5 Nov 1907, p.4)

While "at the police court yesterday before Messrs. C. E. Smith, P.M., and J. M. Ryan, J.P., George Casey, aged 39 years, and his son Rodney Casey, aged 18, were charged with breaking into two sheds on Hereford Estate, on the night of the 11th inst., and stealing therein a number of sheepskins, a bag of corn and a quantity of bacon ... Thomas Denis, laborer on Hereford Estate, deposed that he locked up the bacon house on Thursday evening. It contained ham, bacon, etc. ; on the following morning he found the door open, the lock broken and a quantity of hams, shoulders, and pigs' heads missing ; the door of the shed containing sheep skins was also broken open, and he missed a bundle of 30 skins and about 14 or 15 loose ones" ([?] Police Court, 16 Aug 1898, p.2)

In 1865 "NEW MODE OF TIREING WHEELS. Mr. Rutherford, of the firm of Cobb and Co., has, at considerable expense, adopted a new method of fixing tires on, wheels by machinery ; he has had a large circular tank made of boiler plate fixed in the wheelwright's yard, in Howick-street ; the tank is filled with water and a circular plate made of cast-iron, perfectly level, is fixed above it and attached to a powerful lever ; the untired wheel is laid upon the iron plate, to which it is firmly secured by a screw, and the heated tire is then put over the wheel, and being hammered to its proper position, the level is moved, and the iron plate and the wheel are immediately submerged in the water ; after a short immersion they are again raised from the water, and the tire is hammered into its proper position, the wheel is again submerged, and the heated iron thoroughly cooled. The whole process of fixing the tire is accomplished in about two minutes, and the rapid and uniform cooling of the iron prevents the charring of the felloes of the wheel, which takes place under the old process, and renders the work more complete and durable.

The saving of time and labour by this contrivance is very considerable, and we have no doubt that Mr. Rutherford will be amply repaid for the expense incurred. We have not seen or heard of anything of the kind in any other wheelwright's establishment in the colony, but should think that others will speedily follow the example of Mr. Rutherford. Bathurst Free Press." (No Title, 7 Mar 1865, p.4) Also reported in 1865 "On Wednesday, the 22nd instant, about seven o'clock in the evening, as Mrs James Hammond, of Grabben Gullen, was looking after some pigs that were in the sty close to the house, she felt some thing bite her toe, and looking down she discovered a large snake. She made all possible speed to the house, and got a young man that happened to be there at the time to chop off one of the small toes, together with a portion of the outside of the left foot. Mrs Hammond displayed the greatest courage on the occasion, as she held her foot tightly grasped round the ankle on a block for the operation. The young man in the meantime, provided with a tomahawk and axe, laid the tomahawk along the outside of her foot from the small toe, and then struck it down with the axe. He had to repeat the blow four times before he took the piece clean off." (General News, 7 Dec 1865, p.4)

By 1868 "Mr. James Rutherford, of the firm of Cobb and Co., has been elected Mayor by the unanimous vote of the aldermen." (Bathurst, 22 Feb 1868, p.2) While in 1891 he was described as a "Generous Citizen.—We notice that Mr. James Rutherford, of Hereford, who is a large property holder in Lithgow, has presented the local Council with the choice of two eligible and valuable sites for the establishment of gasworks which have been decided on." (Local and General, 20 Jul 1891, p.2) An article recounting the foundation of the once-renowned Australian firm Cobb and Co., published in 1936, reflected on the early 1900s and included further details about James Rutherford. It noted that throughout his life, Rutherford was an ardent protectionist." He believed that the future of this country depended upon the development of its industries and that the only way in which that might be achieved was a systematic policy of protection.

In 1873, with Mr John Sutherland, Mr Daniel Williams, and others, he founded the Lithgow iron works. The venture was started with a subscribed capital of £100,000. For some years the management was in the hands of Mr Sutherland, and when the original capital had been, lost and another £100,000 had been put into it, Mr Rutherford himself assumed the management, stayed the loss, and turned the business over to Mr Sandford as a profit-earning concern. The works were afterwards leased to Mr Sandford and ultimately sold to him ...

While absorbed in the widely extending ramifications of his business, Mr Rutherford yet found time for active participation in the local affairs of Bathurst. He was the originator of the street tree-planting scheme, which has so beautified the transmontaine city, was an alderman for many years, helped the local agricultural society, and was a munificent patron of the noble Bathurst Hospital, towards which he devoted much of his wealth and business wisdom. The School of Arts also received his generous aid. He was for 10 years upon its committee and for 30 years had presidential control of the institution ... He was a devout churchman, and was a warden and trustee of the Bathurst Anglican Church ...

In addition to his other interests, Mr Rutherford has been one of the most prominent pastoralists in New South Wales and Queensland. For over forty years he, in conjunction with his partners in Cobb and Co. and eventually himself, owned Buckinguy Station, which is still his property. He also owned Murrumbidgerie Station, near Dubbo, which a few years ago, in order to foster closer settlement, he divided and sold.

A large part of it is now under wheat. Mr Rutherford also owned Wyagdon, near Peel, which is now being sold, and his estate at Hereford, near Bathurst, is one of the most beautiful in the district.

In Queensland his properties consist of Burrenbella, near Cunnamulla; Connemara, Warcon, on the Condamine; Aubathata, near Charleville; Davenport Downs, on the Diamantina; and Ingledoon, adjoining it, the last two being large cattle stations. All these properties have been worked on the most scientific bases, and Mr Rutherford—recognising that they should be equipped, in addition to all his other stations, with the latest appliances which make for success—recognised the necessity for artesian boring and the most up-to-date scouring plants, with the consequence that the that the C. and B. wool has more than once topped the London market ...

News was received yesterday [1936] of the death of Mr James Rutherford, at Mackay, Queensland, from bronchitis, after a very short illness. Mr Rutherford had reached the age of 84 years, but preserved to that unusual period of maturity physical and business activities of such a marked character that no fear of his sudden death was entertained of those with whom he was intimately connected ... The deceased left a large family, only one son out his eleven children having predeceased him. Two of his sons are graziers, one is a surgeon (who was with him at the time of his death), and another an electrical engineer (at present in Mexico). His daughters are Mrs H. P. Street, of Sydney; Mrs James McMaster, of Rockgedgiel; Mrs J. F. Fitzhardinge, of Sydney; and Mrs Walter Scott, of Glazzon. A fifth daughter is a graduate of Sydney University and is practising medicine in Sydney. The body of the deceased pioneer will be embalmed and brought from North Queensland for interment in the family vault at Bathurst." (Cobb and Co., 1 Oct 1936, p.67)

The son who predeceased James Rutherford of Cobb and Co. was "Mr. James Rutherford. The death occurred at 'Molong' private hospital, Darlinghurst, on Thursday, of Mr. James Rutherford, who had been in a critical state of health for some time following upon an operation for gall-stones. Mr. Rutherford was the eldest son of the late James Rutherford, of Hereford, Bathurst, where he was born 68 years ago. The late Mr. Rutherford was well-known in the Wellington district, where he resided for a number of years at the well-known 'Wolombi' Station. He was greatly interested in the turf, and his 'Wolombi' stud was well-known. He had bred and raced many good gallopers. During his residence in this district he was a keen supporter of both the Wellington Jockey Club and the Picnic Race Club, where his colors were always prominent. After his dispersal sale at this station he went to reside at 'The Hermitage,' on the Molong Road, between Molong and Orange. Later he sold this property to Mr. McLeish, and took up his residence in Sydney. He was a constant visitor to Wellington, and was among the visitors at the last Picnic Race Club meeting. The late Mr. Rutherford is survived by four daughters and one son, Mrs. Adrian Riordan (whose husband is connected with the Defence Department), Mrs. Thomas Machattie, of Moonambil, Coonamble, Mrs. Newecomin and Miss Thelma Rutherford, and Mr. Norman Rutherford, of Bathampton, Bathurst, the latter being at the bedside of his father at the end. The remains were cremated on Friday afternoon." (Mr. James Rutherford, 24 Sep 1934, p.2)

Interestingly, in 1948 *"BATHAMPTON MAN'S FOSSIL WAS 125 MILLION YEARS OLD ... The other day I had a par from Mr. Norman Rutherford, of Bathampton, about a fossil remain in which he was interested. It came from Roma (Queensland), and shaped like an animals tooth, it was thought that it may have been the tooth of a prehistoric monster akin to the crocodile. Inquiries, were made of the museum authorities at Brisbane, and later at the Australian Museum in Sydney.*

Mr. Rutherford now has a report on the fossil. It is a belemnite, and is about 125 million years old. The museum points out that the rocks of the Roma district are mainly of Lower Cretaceous age, and were laid down under marine conditions about 125 million years ago.

Belemnites are somewhat tooth-shaped in appearance, and are actually the shells of an extinct group of cephlialopods allied to the squids and cuttlefishes. The shells are usually three to five inches in length. Mr. Rutherford's fossil certainly has been lying around for an awfully long-time." (Bathampton Man's Fossil was 125 Million Years Old, 8 Dec 1948, p.8)

In summary, James Rutherford "A magistrate of the territory, the one-time mayor of his town, a foremost man in the affairs relating to its hospital, its school of arts, its agricultural society, and other local institutions, the founder of the free industry in the Lithgow Valley, a foremost judge and breeder of equine stock, and a large investor in station properties in New South Wales and in Queensland, James Rutherford will chiefly be remembered as a pioneer of that romantic and old-time industry symbolised by the world-wide name of Cobb and Co.

He was a man of hearty and engaging personality. Tall and spare, of the true American hickory type, he might well have passed as an Australian of Scottish descent. He was gifted with the grace of humour, and like Yorick, in the character given him by Hamlet, was 'wont to set the table in a roar.' Like his illustrious countryman, Abraham Lincoln, he dearly loved a witty story, and was himself a born raconteur, and a great favourite with the 'boys' wherever his travels over the length and breadth of New South Wales and Queensland carried him. The public institutions of his adopted town attest his charity, and those whom he has helped bear witness to him large sympathy, his kindly heart, his private benevolence and beneficence" (A Pioneer of the Coaching Days: The Late James Rutherford, 20 Sep 1911, p.26)

COBB AND CO.—WALTER RUSSELL HALL

"There was scarcely any enterprise in which members of the firm of Cobb and Co. did not embark. One member—Walter R. Hall—was an original proprietor in Mount Morgan, and died a millionaire. Their station properties were scattered far and wide throughout N. S. Wales and Queensland. Of these may be mentioned Peracoota, near Moama, afterwards sold to F. S. Falkiner and Sons, for £225,000; Midkin, Claverton, Burrendilla, Daveport Downs, Murrumbidgeree, and many others." (The Founder of Cobb & Co., 12 Dec 1924, p.4)

Back in 1864 "ACCIDENT TO THE MAIL. On Thursday afternoon as the mail coach for Bathurst from Sydney was proceeding with three passengers along the Junction Hill, one of the horses shied at a large stone, and before the coachman, Jacob Russart, a steady useful man, who has been driving on the roads for years, could get the horse under control, he went over the side of the road and dragging the whole team with him, in a moment the coach, passengers, and horses were all precipitated together down a steep declivity, the coach it is said rolling over and over, at least a dozen times. Two of the passengers, a lady and a gentleman, whose names we have not yet learnt, and the driver were reported to be very much hurt but had no bones broken. One of the horses broke a leg, and another is not expected to recover. The third passenger, a young man, escaped unhurt. Mr. Walter Hall, Messrs. Cobb and Co.'s Sydney agent, who had been supoenaed in a case in the Circuit Court, and was returning to Sydney, telegraphed immediately on his arrival at Hartley to Mr. Rutherford, who made arrangements to visit the sufferers as early as possible, and accordingly, in company with Dr. Machattie, went away yesterday morning at day-break. Russart, one of whose hip was dislocated, was brought on by the driver, together with the mails, in the day coach.—*Bathurst Times*, Oct. 22." (Government Gazette, 26 Oct 1864, p.6)

While in 1911 "MR WALTER RUSSELL HALL. The following is from our issue of October 14, 1911, dealing with the association of Mr Walter Russell Hall—first with Cobb and Co., then with Mount Morgan in both of which he retained an interest up till practically the end of his days, twenty-five years ago: *News was received in town yesterday that Mr Walter Russell Hall, one of the largest shareholders in the Mount Morgan Gold-mining Company, had passed away peacefully at half-past one o'clock, at his residence, Pott's Point, Sydney. Mr Hall had been suffering from acute bronchitis and a weak heart. The deceased gentleman was born at Kingston, in Hereford, England, on the 19th of February, 1831, and was, therefore, over eighty years of age. He received his education at Kingston and Taunton, in Somerset. He was the son of a flourmiller. After spending some time at Newcastle-on-Tyne, he came out to Sydney, arriving in the early fifties. From Sydney he gravitated to the gold diggings of Victoria, and was present at the Eureka Stockade riot. Although he did not take an active part, he was acquainted with some of the prominent spirits in the riot. From there he went to the Bendigo diggings, and later to the Ovens district. He did not meet with any special good fortune at fossicking, and gave it up in favour of other work. Afterwards he became agent for the firm of Cobb and Co. at Wood's Point, Victoria. Later he became a partner in Cobb and Co., and also acted as the firm's agent in Sydney. While he was connected with Cobb and Co. it was necessary that he should make long trips for the purpose of opening up some of its 'lines,' one of which was from Brisbane to Gympie, when the goldfield at the latter place was opened. About this time or later he went all through Queensland in connexion with Cobb and Co's lines of coaches as far north as Cloncurry. Much of his work in New South Wales consisted of going over the different coaching lines for the purpose of inspection. At this period gangs of bushrangers were at large. Although he met with some notable adventures with the gentlemen of the road, he was never stuck up, as it was known that he never carried cash, but paid his drivers by cheque, it being said that he carried only a cheque book. Subsequently Mr Hall and his friends tried railway contracting and built which is now portion of the main railway between Brisbane and Sydney, the section being somewhere in the vicinity of Glen Innes. As this did not prove financially successful it was decided by Mr Hall and his friends not to enter into the business of railway construction. About this time Mr Hall became interested in tin mines in the same district, principally at Vegetable Creek. While with Cobb and Co. he joined in the purchase of several pastoral properties in New South Wales. The first of these he took up for breeding horses for the coaching lines, which by this time had become very extensive.*

Although very successful with Cobb and Co's coaching line and in his ventures in the pastoral industry, Mr Hall always took an interest in mining, notwithstanding that in his early career it had brought him no favours. About thirty years after he landed in Australia he became interested in Mount Morgan. He came in when it was first taken up, and, as already stated, was one of the largest shareholders. His connexion with Mount Morgan was owing principally to his brother, the late Mr T. S. Hall, who was then manager of the Queensland National Bank at Rockhampton, and to his acquaintance with the late Mr William Pattison, Messrs W. K. D'Arcy, T. S. Hall, W. Pattison, and Mr Hall himself ranked about equal in the number of shares when the company was formed. Since then Mr Hall has been a visitor to Mount Morgan every year except once when he was in England and the last two years, when his health failed him. Mount Morgan was the source of a very large portion of his fortune and few watched its development with more interest than he did. But he also exhibited a keen concern in the welfare of the town and its people.

The children of the place specially interested him. This was illustrated by a remark that he made on an occasion when he gave a treat in the grounds of the Mount Morgan Rugby Football Union, at which practically all the children of the town—numbering several thousands—were present. He described them as the biggest dividend from Mount Morgan. Mr Hall made a large number of handsome donations to Mount Morgan. He was always very liberal in matters of education and sport. It would take a good deal of space to enumerate his many acts in these directions.

Among the most recent of his donations was one of £250 to the Mount Morgan Technical College. His personal liking for the members of the company's staff was marked by many a dinner and many a merry evening. His kindness was shown in many ways. He was particularly gracious to anyone from Mount Morgan who visited Sydney. The injured or sick man going south to be treated by a specialist was always carefully looked after.

For thirty or forty years Mr Hall was a member of the Australian Jockey Club, most of the time being a member of the committee. He always had a string of horses and was well known as one of the patrons of the turf whose business it was to make good sport and to keep it clean. He was a director of several financial institutions in Sydney and was well known as a very sound and able financier, and above all things, as one who would not tolerate any tricks with stocks and shares or have anything to do with anyone who did so. It is said—and on the best of authority—that he never bought Mount Morgan shares although the price on several occasions has been very low, nor did he sell any when they reached tempting prices, at one time as high as £17 10s. He was a director of the Mount Morgan Company for very many years and right up till the time of his death. Mr Hall married many years ago, his wife being the daughter of Mr Kirk, of Kirk's Bazaar, and Avoca, South Yarra, and cousin to Mrs T. S. Hall. There was no issue of the marriage." (With Cobb and Co., 22 Oct 1936, p.61)

COBB AND CO.–WILLIAM FRANK WHITNEY (FRANK)

Cobb and Co. became involved in a number of legal cases. "SMITHYMAN V. WHITNEY AND OTHERS.— The hearing of this action, brought by Thomas Smithyman against Frederick Whitney, James Rutherford, and Walter Hall, trading as Cobb and Co., claiming £5000 damages for injuries alleged to have been sustained by plaintiff by reason of his being thrown out of a coach of defendants while travelling from Wellington to Orange ... the object of the defence being to establish the fact that no negligence was attachable to the driver of the coach, that the night on which the accident occurred was foggy, that the coach at the time was on the proper road, and that the injuries sustained by the plaintiff were only of a trivial character ... The jury returned a verdict in favour of the plaintiff for £1000" (Law Intelligence, 28 Jul 1881, p.4)

Another example in 1888: "SUPREME COURT. HALL V. COMMISSIONER FOR RAILWAYS ... This was an action brought by Walter Hall, James Rutherford and Washington Frank Whitney, trading as Cobb and Co., railway contractors, against the Commissioner for Railways ... The action arose upon a contract entered into by the plaintiffs for the construction of a line of railway between Glen Innes and Tenterfield. Plaintiffs claim ... in connection with sleepers passed and on which payments were made and which were afterwards rejected, and for damages arising out of the condemnation and rejection ... There was a delay of 10 months in the construction of the line due to the condemnation of the sleepers. The contract would have been finished in November, 1885, but it was not concluded until August, 1886." (Law, 25 May 1888, p.3)

In 1894, Mr. W. F. Whitney, who passed away recently at Coombing Park, Carcoar, was among the founding partners of the renowned coaching firm Cobb and Co. His fellow co-founders included A. W. Robertson, John Wagner, W. R. Hall, W. B. Bradley, and James Rutherford. "Twenty years ago (says the 'National Advocate') the operations of the firm were nothing short of enormous. As coach and buggy builders, they did a business the many ramifications of which extended almost from end to end of the eastern coast. As coaching contractors they harnessed 5000 horses a day alone, employed, directly and indirectly, some thousands of hands, and paid in wages the startling sum of over £200,000 a year, the while their contracts for the mails were of such an extensive character that they ran into £100,000 a year at least.

As squatters, too, the business which they did was on a corresponding scale; the properties worked by them extended over three colonies; whilst, as mining men, they enterprised in gold, silver, copper, iron, and coal; and, as one of a syndicate, established the Lithgow Ironworks, which at one time paid in wages over £3000 a month." (Cobb and Co., 17 Nov 1894, p.1016)

"Mr. Whitney, though not the most prominent member of the firm were always in active sympathy with the movements and enterprises of his partners. Mr. Whitney was a Canadian by birth. He was a man of simple habits and gentle temperament. He had wisely and fortunately no strong political views, taking no active part in municipal matters or public politics. His tastes lay more in the direction of live stock of most useful kinds. He loved a horse, and was considered a consumate judge of a good one when he saw him. Like most Canadians or Americans, he preferred a good harness horse to the saddle hack, and liked to sit behind a pair of flyers. He was very much attached to his family, and loved his home beyond all other places. He was a very hospitable man, and always glad of call from his friends. Frank Whitney, as his intimate friends called him, will be missed not only at Carcoar, at Orange, and at Bathurst, but throughout the entire Western districts. He was a genial, kindly, unassuming man, who came into collision with no one, but kept well with all. As one of the partners of the famous firm of Cobb and Company he was highly esteemed and respected everywhere, and as an individual he was liked and loved by all who knew him. His family consisted of two sons and five daughters, one being the wife of Dr. Keity of this town. He was ill for some time before his regretted death, and we believe that the disease he died from is not quite ascertained. He, it is said, suffered little or no pain during his illness. Knowing him well and intimately we convoy our sincere sympathy to his family in their heavy hour of sorrow." (The Late Mr. F. Whitney, 6 Nov 1894, p.2)

To honour the legacy of Frank Whitney following his death at Coombing Park in 1894, employees of Cobb and Co. initiated what became known as the 'Whitney Monument Fund'—a subscription effort aimed at raising funds to erect a memorial in his name, as reported by a Forbes newspaper. "Mr. Whitney was so well known and esteemed by all the employees of the firm, as well as by numerous friends and others in both New South Wales and Victoria, that they deem it their duty to raise a lasting monument in honor of his sterling worth as a man and an employer. The subscription lists are being kept strictly within the limits of the firm's employees, and no one donation is to exceed £1, and though the marble structure will cost between £400 and £500 the money will be easily and speedily raised in subscriptions not exceeding the amount we have stated. It is probable that the monument will be erected somewhere in Orange, though the exact spot has not yet been decided upon." (Memorial to Mr. Whitney, 25 Dec 1894, p.5)

Further legal action followed. "PARTNERSHIP CASE. WHITNEY AND OTHERS v. RUTHERFORD ... In the Equity Court, Sydney ... This was a suit arising out of a deed of partnership whereby, it was alleged, on January 1, 1886, the defendant and William Franklin Whitney (since deceased) agreed to become partners as coach proprietors, railway contractors, mail contractors, general graziers, &c, for five years. The business was to be carried on under the name of 'Cobb and Co.' The partnership did not determine at the expiration of the five years, but was continued to the death of Mr. Whitney. The head office was at Bathurst ... Subsequent to the death of Mr. Whitney the business was continued under the management and supervision of the defendant with a view to a general winding up and realisation as and when favourable opportunities for the same might occur.

An audit had been made of the accounts as from January 1, 1890, to June 30, 1896, and this disclosed entries of transactions of which the plaintiffs disapproved. The plaintiffs claimed that there was a large balance due owing to Mr. Whitney's estate by the partnership or the defendant ... The defendant denied that the books or accounts were kept wholly under his control or supervision. His position as general manager necessitated, he said, frequent journeys, which took him away from Bathurst for considerable periods. The books were kept by an accountant, whose duty it was to see that they were properly kept. Mr. Whitney had always an opportunity of taking part in the management of the business to such an extent as he thought fit. While the defendant was actually in Bathurst, and also while he was absent therefrom, Mr. Whitney frequently visited the Bathurst office and investigating the accounts and went through the books of the firm which were kept there, and while Mr. Rutherford was absent from Bathurst it was the duty of Mr. Whitney to, and he did, attend the office, deal with the correspondence, and generally manage the business of the firm ... The suit stands part heard." (Partnership Case, 1 Mar 1900, p.3)

1941 saw the "death Of Mrs. Whitney. Pioneer Landholder. Memories of Cobb and Co. A pioneer landholder and widow of a partner in the once famous firm of Cobb and Co., Mrs. Isabella Whitney, died at Coombing Park, Carcoar, at the age of 96 years, on Tuesday. Mrs. Whitney was born at Muswellbrook, and married the late Mr. William Franklyn Whitney, at Mount Arthur, Wellington, in 1863. She was a sister of the late Mr. J. S. Leeds of Orange. She lived for more than 50 years at Coombing park, which was established as a sheep station 100 years ago. A noted pastoralist up till the time of her death she was managing director of the Whitney Pastoral Co. The name of the Whitney family has been well known in the Orange district for a long time, and the fountain near the entrance to Robinson Park is a memorial presented to the borough authorities by the employees of Cobb and Co. in remembrance of Mr. W. F. Whitney, who died at Carcoar in 1894. After leaving Mount Arthur with her husband, Mrs. Whitney went to Buckinguy, one of the Cobb and Co. properties, and while she was there three of her ten children were born.

When Coombing Park was purchased by Cobb and Co. about 1880 from Mr. Thomas Icely, Mrs. Whitney went to live there, and continued her residence up till the time of her death. On the death of her husband she took charge of the properties with the assistance of her son-in-law, Dr. Keity, until the Whitney Pastoral Co. was formed. She was a remarkably efficient business executive, and worked consistently and successfully for the improvement of the breed of cattle and sheep particularly beef shorthorns and mutton sheep ... One of her hobbies was tapestry work, which was greatly admired by her friends. In addition to the development of pastoral properties, Mrs. Whitney was one of the historic figures of the gold rush days, as a member of the firm of Cobb and Co., when the firm had its head office at Bathurst. In 1870, the Co. was harnessing 6,000 horses a day in the three eastern States, their coaches were travelling 28,000 miles a week, the annual pay sheet was more than £100,000, and £95,000 was received each year in mail subsidies. Of course, there are few left who can remember, but vivid stories are told of the days when plunging horses wheeled from the Cobb and Co. depot in Anson Street.

In 1871, the business was separated, Mr. Whitney remaining in the N.S.W. and Queensland firm, with Messrs. Rutherford, Hall and Bradley. After the death of Mr. Whitney, Mr. Rutherford was the sole surviving member of the original firm. The last Cobb and Co. coach was taken off the Yeulba-Surat (Queensland) run in 1924, and is now in exhibition in the Queensland Museum.

The late Mrs. Whitney was remarkably hale and active to within a short time of her death. She was buried beside her late husband at Orange, the Rev. A. G. Halliday officiating. Four daughters survive, Meesdames Cargill (Coombing Park), Keity (Coombing Park), King (Sydney), and Hood (Albury). There are 13 grandchildren and 21 great-grandchildren." (Death Of Mrs. Whitney, 29 Aug 1941, p.1)

Cobb and Co.–William Brown Bradley

Written in 1868, "FEARFUL SUFFERING IN THE BUSH.—A Man Compelled to Drink his Horse's Blood.— The report I send you to-day will serve to show what a man may endure in these sterile regions. I have had many cases of hardship to record ; but this of Mr. W. B. Bradley's, of the firm of Cobb and Co., is certainly one of the most fearful I have ever known. Men have wrestled with the terrible agony and died, but since I have been on the river, no one has gone through as much and lived to relate the event I shall nothing extenuate or set down, but as nearly as possible tell the tale as I have gleaned it from the sufferer himself. He says :—*I started from Yanda, on the Darling, about the 9th of April last, with a buggy and two horses, for Gidyagabambo, back country belonging to us south of the Darling, a distance of eighty miles without water. I had horses I depended on, but after going thirty miles through the bush one of them knocked up and I had to camp. When I started I had only two bottles of water, which were now consumed. This camp I considered about thirty miles south of Toorale ; I say south, but having no compass cannot be certain. I started next morning, one horse still very well, and went about seven miles when I believed myself too much to the east ; changed my course due south or what I supposed south, and travelled forty or fifty miles, and found myself among mountains. These mountains or high ridges running in all sorts of forms and directions, caused me to admit that I was in unknown country ; and no water. The day had been very warm, and a painful sensation in the throat and tongue was felt; the horse was completely done ; here I camped. By daybreak I was after the horses, and found they had left me in the night ; found their tracks and with much toil (for I had eaten nothing since I started, in fact hunger I never felt); followed them for ten miles in a N. W. direction. About ten o'clock I came up to my best horse, the other nowhere to be seen ; and being in a fainting state from thirst, opened with my knife the neck vein, and drank more than a quart of blood. This horrible draught gave me much relief, but it was voided almost as soon as taken. I here rested, being quite exhausted, my poor horse never leaving me ; in fact, whenever I lay down, which I did towards the end of the journey every mile or so, he would stop, come back, and neigh. When I again started I led him N. W., the course he was going when I recovered him ; this point, I felt sure was the nearest to the river. About 3 o'clock I found a kurragong tree, and as well as I was able—for my knees trembled and my arms felt powerless—stripped away some of its bark, which I chewed, and found the sweet moisture of much benefit in clearing my throat and tongue ; and I felt convinced should anyone be in the like strait and have strength to procure plenty of this bark, it would preserve life for a day or two. At 4 p.m. I again drank blood with exactly the some result ; my poor horse, Sydney, a TAB, was now literally staggering. All day it had been very hot, but at night it became quite cool, and I resolved to long-hobble my horse and follow him ; the reason of my hobbling him was that, weak as he was, he could out-walk me, and even then I had to follow the sound of the chains. After going about six miles thus, he started into a reeling canter and stopped in a dry creek called Mulranya ; here I knew where I was, and followed him to Marrandina and lay down ; when I again started the horse was gone. Ten miles had now to be got over, which took me about seven hours, when I reached one of my own tanks at Nulltrania, fifteen miles from the Darling, where I had sheep. The horse, Sydney, likewise found the tank, drank, rolled, and died ; the other horse got in the next day, and plunging headlong into the water, was drowned.*" (Town And Country, 23 May 1868, p.11)

In early 1874, a formal notice marked a significant change in the leadership of Cobb and Co. On 9 January, William Brown Bradley officially retired from the partnership, leaving the firm "and that the said partnership will henceforth be carried on by James Rutherford, Walter Russell Hall, William Franklin Whitney, and Colin Robertson. Witness our hands this 9th day of January, 1874. J. Rutherford. W. R. Hall. Wm. F. Whitney. Colin Robertson. W. B. Bradley. Witness—George Pinnock. " (Notice is hereby given, that Mr. William Brown Bradley has retired this day from the partnership known as Cobb & Co., 13 Jan 1874, p.76)

It was said that Mr. W. B. Bradley, of Cobb and Co., sold out to his partners with the amount variously stated. "About 35,000 is mentioned by those who ought, to know, as the figure." Meanwhile, "the Melbourne Cricket Club is so prosperous that it has adopted a rule limiting the number of subscribing members to 1500 ... Jack Kettle, well known among the old cricketing heroes of Sydney is dead. He kept up his wickets for seventy odd years, but old Death, with a 'grubber,' found a weak spot in his defences at last." (News and Notes, 14 Sep 1881, p.3)

Cobb and Co.–Colin Robertson

1932 – "Mr. John Horton ... who claims to be the oldest surviving driver of Cobb and Co.'s coaches; gives some of his recolections in this ... Gundagai ... he met dealer who ... set out to taking his horse and cart across the flooded creek ... Horse and cart were swept downstream ... The following day a horseman ... was washed off its feet by the curent. When the flood waters had receded some days later the missing horseman and his mount, dealer's horse and cart ... were found together against the root of a tree 300 yards down the creek ... Two weeks later brought illness, which resulted in him [John Horton] retiring from the service ...

Yass to Young ... Mr. Horton recalling an instance where a loaded team took a week to travel a mile. As the condition of the roads prevented him from running to schedule, Mr. Horton soon tired of his position and returned to Goulburn ... he was offered a job by Mr. Colin Robertson, manager of Cobb and Co.'s Goulburn branch ... taking over the Goulburn-Yass run in succession to Fred Gilliam, a brother of George Giliam of Ashton's circus fame ... Mr. Horton commenced driving with Johnny Dailey, at that time one of the State's veteran coach drivers. That was in 1870, the winter proving to be one of the wettest sesons experienced for years. Lake George was almost overflowing and the coaches did not have a dry trip for almost five months. One trip from Goulburn to within three miles of Yass occupied 17 hours, the fact that O'Brien's Bridge was completely under water preventing the coach from reaching Yass that night. The passengers ... were compelled to spend the night at a hotel on the Goulburn side of the bridge. The bridge presented a sorry spectacle the following morning, the flood waters having washed away about 6ft. of the approach on the Yass side, and the decking was buried, beneath tons of debris. The arrival of a two seater buggy enabled the lady passenger, with the mails and luggage to be transferred across the river. One of the constables walked into Yass and returned with the down mail for Sydney and Mr. Hurley, then M.P. for Campbelltown. The iron bridge at Yass had been washed off its piers and lay at the bottom of the river ... With one passenger aboard, the coach commenced its return trip to Goulburn, but on arrival at Gunning it was found that the creek had flooded and the water reached along the main street to as far as the Telegraph Hotel. Asked if he would be willing to take the trip through the water, Mr. Hurley replied that he was agreeable if Mr. Horton considered the undertaking would not incur any great risk. The sergeant of police issued a warning against attempting a crossing, but was told that the mail had to be Goulburn by 10.15 a.m ... The coach succeeded in getting through and a cheer went up from the spectators ... Mr. Hurley complimenting Mr. Robertson, the coach proprietor, on Mr. Horton's performance ... [Another] driver [who also survives] ... Mr. William Barry ... entered the employ of Cobb and Co." (Cobb and Co. Coachman, 21 Nov 1932, p.4) See *Appendix 1: Supporting evidence for many Cobb and Co. proprietors*

ca. 1953 Hereford Bathurst Residence of John Nicholson [a view],
(William Butler Simpson) – Dixson Library, State Library of New South Wales

1892 Coombing Park Station homestead, Carcoar region, New South Wales,
woolshed and stable to left, residence [unfinished] to the right, Mt. Macquarie in the background
(Evan Antoni Johann Lumme 1865-1935) – Courtesy National Library of Australia

ca. 1880s Hereford, Bathurst – Courtesy Bathurst Historical Society

1900-1915 Mr Whitney holding horse, Coombing Park, New South Wales
(Evan Antoni Johann Lumme 1865-1935) – Courtesy National Library of Australia

1874 Walter Russell Hall (drawn by Helena Forde, Sydney) – Courtesy State Library of New South Wales

ca. 1910 Lithgow panorama, Lithgow with the ironworks and Great Cobar copper refinery in the background (Lithgow Blast-Furnace Group) – Courtesy Flickr

ca. 1880 Workmen, Lithgow Ironworks – Courtesy Flickr

Chapter Five

The town of Bathurst-Cobb and Co.'s
N.S.W headquarters

Bathurst Map

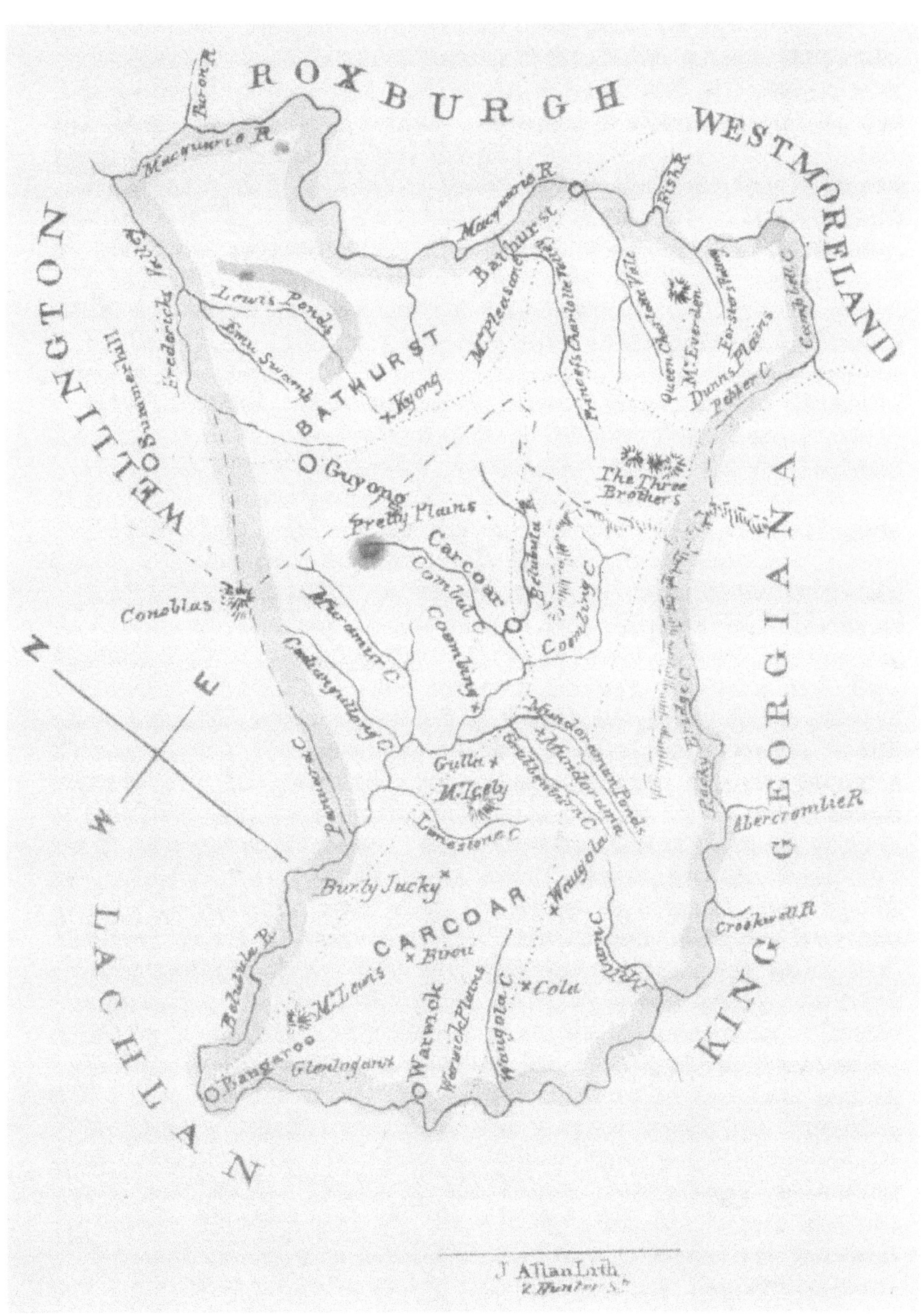

1848 Bathurst Map [William Henry Wells ; J. Allan, Lith.] – Courtesy National Library of Australia

On the road to Bathurst—Before Cobb and Co.

By October 1851, the Abercrombie diggings had become an established goldfield (Tarahish) and considered successful for "all those who persevere in the search for gold. We are much in want of a police force, and an armed escort ; not that any depredations have yet taken place, but as our population becomes denser it is reasonable to expect that some bad characters, such as gamblers, drunkards and thieves, will find their way to this now secluded spot, and disturb the peace and good order which prevails there. A very large quantity of gold is ready to be removed as soon as a convoy is provided, but no one will risk sending it along the road without an armed guard. There have been for the last few weeks some very suspicious looking characters lurking about the roads leading to Bathurst and Goulburn, and it is expected that they will not remain idle much longer. I will now put you in possession of some late particulars as to the diggings. Cramp's party of three obtained on Friday last 5¾ ounces of gold, and on the following day got 4 ounces before dinner. Mr T. Connor's part of four washed 2 ounces in half-a-day. Stephenson's party, consisting of the same number, have been getting from 4 to 6 ounces per day for the last three weeks. The average earnings are from 1¾ to 2 ounces per week a man. There are about 270 people at the diggings, and fresh faces are to be seen every day. The emigration from Bathurst and the Turon is very considerable." (The Abercrombie, 18 Oct 1851, p.1)

A few years later, in 1855, a traveller documented his journey through the same region, offering a vivid account of the landscape and road conditions. "Leaving Hartley, whence the coach starts at five o'clock in the morning, a drive of about an hour brings the Mudgee-road in view, and at eight o'clock Solitary Creek is reached. The country, thus far, consists of precipitous mountains, on the summits of some of which the rocks are seen standing out in bold relief, giving the elevations which they crown the appearance of immense ruins, and low fertile valleys, watered by creeks formed by the streams which descend from the hills. The farms around here are more numerous than at any other part of the road, and appear to be fertile and carefully cultivated. After passing Hartley, the road for some distance improves. Where the roadway lies below the level of the adjoining grounds, as it does in most places, trenches have been cut parallel with it on the elevated ground, to carry off the water during heavy rains. This plan has operated excellently where the trench has been dug at a reasonable distance from the road ; but some parts, owing to the slight nature of the intervening embankment, this latter has been washed away, thus aggravating the evil which it was intended to prevent. A very beautiful description of granite, intersected at intervals by slate, is now the prevailing formation, but quartz is abundant for several miles.

In many places this latter is seen imbedded in the slate, and some practised diggers, who were among the passengers, expressed their conviction that gold exists in these hills. Shortly after leaving Solitary Creek, Cox's River presents itself—a tortuous stream, traversing a marshy valley between the hills. The river is crossed by a small-wooden bridge, which, in times of rain, must be rather a dangerous passage, as it is evident that the stream must, at such periods, become swollen to a very great extent. Passing Cox's River, the road, which for some time has resumed its old character of roughness, begins to ascend in the direction of Mount Lambie, and the long hours of driving which are expended in the ascent speak forcibly of the altitude of the chain of mountains which here intervenes. For some time the traces of recent bush fires have become visible, and here is seen the remains of a bridge burned down by the raging element, the roadway having fallen in, barely leaving room for a dray to pass over at considerable risk. The summit of the Lambie having been at length attained, after innumerable windings, the magnificent prospect which was seen on the previous day from Mount Victoria itself from an opposite view, the narrow pass which leads into Hartley through the Victoria being itself dimly discernible. From the utmost heights of Mount Lambie, which was cleared of all the large trees except one, which stands to this day, by the party which formed the view, it is said that Sydney may be seen by the aid of a telescope. Here, it is said, was a station from which those in charge of the original road parties communicated with Sydney, through an intervening station, by means of the telegraph.

In the hilly valley, which lies beneath, several clearances are visible, and some fine farms are seen, and mounting a spot called the Sodwalls—a name derived from the architecture of the houses thereabouts, which, are built of the green turf. The ground here is said to be peculiarly prolific in potatoes, and some green patches, which contested strongly with the surrounding forest, afforded proof of the fact. Several wheat fields also gave good promise of an abundant yield. The driver pointed out a place among the lower ranges which he called Bindo, reported to be very rich in natural curiosities. Among others, it is said that there are some extensive caves formed in the granite in the recesses of the hills.

Descending Mount Lambie, the country becomes more level than it has been since leaving Hartley, the farms become numerous, and the fields comparatively verdant. Hereabouts we passed a party of workmen reconstructing a bridge which had been burned down by the recent bush fires. Several of the settlers along the road have suffered considerably by these conflagrations, and the hostess of the inn at which we had breakfast, apologised, for the absence of eggs, by saying that her fowls had all been consumed in a barn which fell prey to the flames. Passing Durack's Inn, a couple of hours driving brings the coach to Robert's Inn, where horses are changed for the last time previous to arriving at Bathurst. This latter appeared to be one of those remarkably neat and well-kept places of public entertainment which are frequent along the road. A short drive now brings the Bathurst plains in view, at the far side of which are seen the red brick buildings of the town ; the tower of a chapel, or the chimney of a mill or manufactory here and there raising its head aloft. These plains are some thirty miles long by twelve in width, and appear to be bordered by a large extent of thinly wooded country. Large herds of cattle, intended for slaughter, and in the very best condition, feed throughout its extent. Some small farms, including a few vineyards, which have been formed in the plains, are covered with luxuriant crops of every description. A drive of seven or eight miles across the plains ... This river, which was rendered so low by the recent drought as to allow of the conveyance driving through without any inconvenience, is a wide straggling water-course, about 100 yards wide from bank to bank. During continuous or heavy, rains, its channel becomes quite full, overflowing in some places the adjacent grounds. A large creek, passed over by a bridge, intervenes between the crossing place and the town.

In the town of Bathurst there are four churches and chapels ... In a large square in the centre of the town are situated the courthouse and gaol. Great complaint is made in reference to the situation of this latter establishment. It is said, and with justice, that in its present site it is an eye-sore, at once giving a gloomy aspect to the town and interfering with its trade. The chief object of interest around the town at present is the new bridge over the Macquarie, recently commenced, and intended to connect Kelso and Bathurst ...

Since the early part of last week, when some refreshing showers fell throughout the district, no rain has visited this quarter. At present however, thick masses of clouds lower overhead, and a change appears to be approaching. Reaping is going on, and although the growth of the wheat is somewhat stunted, the yield is reported to be generally better than was anticipated.— *Empire*." (Notes of a Journey Through the Western District, 2 Feb 1855, p.3)

Cobb and Co. arrive in Bathurst

In July 1862, Bathurst experienced a remarkable snowstorm —"On Sunday night last there was the heaviest fall of Snow in Bathurst, that has been known, it is said, for the last twenty years. It commenced about dark, and continued with more or less intermission until a late hour of the night. There was no wind, and the appearance on Monday morning was similar to a Snowey December day in England ; the fences were fringed along the rails to the depth of about three inches, and the branches of trees down to the smallest twig, were thickly clothed with snow. The Coachman of the Orange Mail reports that the fall was very heavy along the road. The fogs which had been so prevalent for some time, seem to have fled from before this winterly display." (Local and Domestic, 2 Jul 1862, p.2) Nearly four decades later, in 1900, Bathurst was once again blanketed in snow. "Latest particulars state that Bathurst is snow-bound. By common consent all business has been suspended. The train from Sydney was blocked by the snow, and at Rockley the resources of the railway officials were taxed to the utmost to secure safety to the trains. Heavy land slips are reported from Clifton-road, where all the traffic has been blocked. The stock in some districts have been unable to procure food for the last 12 days, owing to the ground being covered with snow. Unless a change occurs within the next 48 hours, serious loss must result." (Late Telegrams, 8 Jul 1900, p.1)

During that same winter, "the town of Bathurst was pleasurably excited by the arrival of the coaching 'plant' of the celebrated firm of Cobb and Co, of Melbourne ... We understand that arrangements on a very liberal scale will be made by the firm, with as little delay as possible, to convey passengers to and from the Metropolis and the respective diggings.—Bathurst Free Press," (Sydney News, 3 Jul 1862, p.3) having been advertised the week before as "Cobb and Co's. Telegraph Line of Coaches, to The Lachlan. On and after Thursday the 4th July a six horse coach will leave Cobb & Co's Booking Office, Bathurst, every Thursday, Saturday & Tuesday. For the Lachlan via Orange, Arriving at Lachlan same Evenings and returning from there Every Monday, Wednesday and Fridays. For particulars apply at Cobb and Co's Office, Bathurst. James Rutherford. Manager N.S.W." (Advertising, 28 Jun 1862, p.3)

One of Cobb and Co.'s booking-offices was the "Club House Hotel. The undersigned begs to inform his numerrous friends and the public generally that he has converted his large club room into fifteen separate bedrooms, which are all well furnished ; and having taken the premises recently occupied by Mr. Flanagan, he has removed his billiard table thereto. The old billiard-room will be set apart as dining and commercial room. As the proprietor imports from England direct all Ales, Wines and Spirits used in his Establishment, the public may depend upon being supplied with liquors of the very best description. Strangers visiting Bathurst during the Assizes are invited to call at the Club-house Hotel, where they will have every attention. Table d' Hote daily at 1 o'clock. The above Hotel is also a stopping place and Booking-office for Cobb and Co.'s Telegraph line of Mails and Coaches. W. Chapman." (Advertising, 3 Sep 1862, p.3) Another booking-office was The Royal Hotel.

"Wanted, a good wheelwright, to go to Bathurst. Apply at Cobb and Co.'s Office, Royal Hotel, George-street." (Advertising, 11 May 1863, p.8)

"Mr. Rutherford ... first came to Bathurst for the purpose of making the town the headquarters of the west for the great firm of Cobb and Co. and lead the great procession of Cobb's coaches, himself driving ten greys of a class seldom seen. Shortly afterwards he established the coach factory on a large scale in Howick street, next to Mockett's mill, where the whole of the coaches for the interior of the colony were made. Very many men were employed there, and when the whistle blew for 'Knock off', the number of men making their way homeward would surprise the young men of to-day if it were possible to see them.

The stables were lower down on portion of the 'Black Bull' premises, and a number of men were also employed there as grooms, etc, while some of the well known 'whips' were to be seen there abouts. What a treat it was to see a Cobb's coach starting off. Where will you see such horses, and where will you see such drivers? The coach loaded with light-hearted passengers, a groom holding the spirited leaders' heads, the hand-shaking; then 'right,'—the groom releases the leaders heads, and they're off, the leaders prancing and jumping in the air, some of the young ladies screaming. But the 'whip,' popular Joe Jenkins, or maybe Harry James, the Keegans, Martin Murphy, John Fagan (who afterwards became a wealthy squatter), or one of the other drivers would sit with perfect control of the equine beauties. John Fagan, it was who drove the escort laden with police and gold in [18] '62 when the Ben Hall gang stuck it up at the Eugowra Rocks, an ideal spot for the work. Half the width of Howick-street, near the old factory, would always be taken up with coaches.

The coach factory was carried on under David Brown, a Scotchman brought here by Cobb and Co., probably from Victoria, where the great firm commenced business. On all the main roads in New South Wales and Queensland at some time or other have I seen Cobb's coaches. The firm also acquired some grand station properties in New South Wales and also in Queensland. Little did I dream when I saw Cassidy selling Cobb and Co.'s bullocks at the old saleyards that I would later on work on one of the properties and see the cattle fatten and put on the road for Bathurst and Sydney." (After 40 years, 6 Nov 1917, p.1)

The town and the people

Bathurst was "so named by Governor Macquarie, in 1815, in honour of Lord Bathurst, then Secretary of State for the Colonies, is the principal town in western district of New South Wales ... The present means of access are rail and coach, but it will soon be in direct communication by rail ... Raglan is the present terminus of the line ... Bathurst may be considered the third town of New South Wales, and its importance is steadily increasing ... The principal thoroughfares are George and William streets ... places of worship ... Courthouse and Gaol ... numerous schools ... School of Arts ... banks ... hospital ... hotels (Tattersalls, the Royal and Club, being the leading) ... a good cricket ground and a fine reserve for horse racing ... Population of the city is 1,000 ... The census returns for 1871 give 16,826 as the population of city and district ... It is impossible to calculate the number of persons employed in the gold-fields ... of Wattle Flat and Sofala, Hill End and Tambaroora, Tuena, the Abercrombie, Coolah and Rockley, as well as at the copper mines of Cow Flat and Campbell's River ... The newspapers are the *Bathurst Free Press* and the *Western Independent* ...

The manufactures in Bathurst are several tanneries, a coach factory, and two flour mills ... Soap, candles, glue, boots and shoes, and earthenware are also manufactured extensively in the town. Beer is brewed at Glanmire ... From June, 1872, the city has been lighted with gas." (The Australian Handbook and Almanac and Shippers' and Importers' Directory, 1872, p.86)

In 1917 an old Bathurstian further described the town. "Below the bank was a most important one-storey building where the jeweller's shop is now. It was the railway station of Bathurst—Cobb's office ... Mr. Rutherford put in a lot of his time there. The head clerk's name was Pryce—a tall man of gentlemanly appearance. Next to Cobb's office was Mr. Pedrotta, the gunsmith. It was there that the Ben Hall gang went in '63 for the purpose of getting firearms, etc., when they paid the surprise visit to Bathurst. On the corner was Flanagan's butcher's shop, where a big business was done. Flanagan built and resided in the cottage known as 'Rosehill,' and planted a fine orchard there. The bridge was for years known as 'Flanagan's Bridge.' About a quarter of a mile further on was the slaughter house. Jack Ryan, who afterwards carried on business at first with Mick White as 'White and Ryan' and afterwards on his own, was a shopman at Flanagan's. He first started, in a one storey building next to the Royal, on the Grand Hotel side. In earlier times it was occupied by Charley Hughes, a well known butcher. On that corner was a saddler's shop, where business was carried on by Lamrock and Cornwell. Now that block is finished and we will cross over to the Square. The market buildings were commenced in '71. James Douglas was the contractor. So now the good old square, that had for so long been a recreation ground where the volunteers (which force had only been about two years in existence) were to be deprived of portion of their 'run,' where they so proudly drilled, led by their own band, under that prince of band masters, Mr. McCarthy, with their red-braided grey uniforms. What a fine body of men they were. Later on the uniform was changed to the red coat and black trousers with red stripe. The old Square prior to the markets being erected was also used by circuses and other shows; but the liveliest night of the year, was Queen's Birth night, when people came in from all round the district to take part in the great display of fireworks.

Well, to get back to William-street, and go back behind the mid [18]seventies: Below Saville's Hotel, where Lee's buildings now stand—that is, Hunter's and the chemist's—were several one-storey shops. One next to Saville's was McMinn's jeweller's shop, it was at McMinn's that the Ben Hall gang called, after they had visited Pedrotta, the gunsmith. Here they expected to make a good haul of jewellery, but the women's screams proved the salvation of McMinn's treasure, for the bushrangers rushed out of the shop and vaulted into the saddles held by one who remained on watch. Two of the gang were lower down William-street, but, a revolver being fired in the air, they turned back, and, joining their mates, all galloped up William-street to the Market Square, where they turned to take a cut across, intending to meet George-street at Keppel-street, the gaol square not then being fenced, but all open ground. But as they turned to cross the Market Square some of them came into contact with a large heap of metal, which had been placed there for the purpose of metalling William-street for the first time. They nearly came a cropper. Mind you, the square was not illuminated as at present. The town was then lit up with kerosene lamps. The town had only been incorporated twelve months at the time of the visit of Mr. Hall and his friends. Across Howick-street from Flanagan's corner is a low white building which was occupied by Louie Paetal, and a great business was done there. Louie Paetal's 'pipe hospital' was known as well as any place in town. With most of the young fellows in town nothing in the pipe or tobacco line was any good unless it came from Louie's.

Of course, being away so long, I cannot say what became of him but he must have made a competency before he left or died. On the corner where the jeweller's shop, Lorimer (hairdresser), and Yeo and Mansell are situated there were some old white shops kept by Mrs Clarke. Here Steve Dennis, a Kelso young man, carried on hairdressing, tobacconist, etc, with considerable success. All the young men of the day patronised Steve; they thought that he was more stylish than the other two old hands. Dave Hill, carried on bootmaking where Mr. Evans, the now busy bootman is.

In those days ready-made boot were little worn, and Dave made for all the young men of the town. On the spot where Gartrell's (baker) and Edgley's (clothing) shops stand was the old Scotch Kirk. Looking up from Bentinck-street to William-street, portion of the old kirk can still be seen. The present buildings, when completed in the early seventies by the late Mr. Gilmour, were occupied by the City Bank in one part, and the other by Robinson and Boys, as clothiers. A great sport carried on a saddler's business where the hotel now stands—John Gumbleton. As a pigeon shot he was considered one of the best, and no match was shot off without Gumbleton taking part. Then came Billy Meares. What an identity he was, and what fun did he give the neighbors. Billy was always, 'in holts' with someone; still he did a great business there, and the yarns and tales about him were many. Amongst his employees were Messrs. John Meagher, Jim Kelaher (afterwards 'Kelaher and Eviston'), and L. Peate. Below Meares (now Edgley's) was a great old identity—Mr. Josiah Parker, chemist. At the time Dr. Kerr brought in the nugget of gold shown to him by the [First Nations person] who was shepherding sheep for him, it was exhibited about Mr. Parker's shop, and weighed at Stanger's stores opposite, where it was found to go to 106lbs [?] in weight. I fancy the 'First Nugget Hotel' was then given its name. Below Parker's was a jeweller named Ramsay. A son, Fred., was a member of the old volunteer band conducted by McCarthy, some of the other players being Alf. Dowse, Tom McKell, Jack Jones, Bill O'Brien, Willett (kettledrum), and the big drum by Tom Nixon, a well-known brick layer.

Further on came a couple of hotels, the First Nugget being kept by John Eyers. He had the name of stocking the best, and naturally did a roaring trade. Eyers was a large money-lender, and must have died a wealthy man during my long absence from the old town. I passed by Bonnor's produce store, which was higher up William-street, about where Yeo and Mansell now are. George Bonnor afterwards became a world-renowned cricketer; he was employed here with his brothers, Jim and William, in the 70's. Well, next to the First Nugget is the Haymarket Reserve. In the centre was a small brick building used as an office by the Borough Council and connected with which was a weighbridge. It was a busy spot, for farmers brought their loads of hay and straw to be weighed by the clerk, a man named Horton. To-day a load of hay in trusses is never seen, but at that time you could scarcely look down a street without seeing a load of truss hay bound up with stringy bark, or a load of bundled straw. Opposite the Haymarket was a large produce store carried on by Jacob Knight, who had at that time been an old resident of the district, having carried on farming on the Mount Pleasant and Kelloshiel estates. Then there was the old lock-up, a white building. Lower down was R. and W. Oakes' saleyards in which the business done was enormous. Fat cattle and sheep were sold on Monday and Thursday morning, and in the afternoon horses were freely disposed of. Jim Cassidy mostly did the selling, many exciting events took place there. About there was the scene of Bathurst's earliest settlement. The gaol, the court house, and women's factory, were there.

The Police Magistrate and Dr. Busby (Government Medical Officer) both resided in the court house, the apartments of the one being on the ground floor and the other upstairs.

In later times, behind where the terrace of two-storeyed buildings stands was a large old-fashioned cottage surrounded by trees. It was the residence of Captain Battye, who was then superintendent of Police for the Western Districts. But at the time of my departure from Bathurst it was occupied by Mr. Lydiard, Super. Of Police. Captain Battye had some exciting adventures with convicts and bushrangers. Two sons, Bertie and Artie, were great athletes. Artie was an accomplished horseman and ran racehorses. He won the old Bathurst Cup with Gratis at a time when the Cup was worth winning. I understand now that the Cup has dwindled down to a tin-pot. Johnny Mutton had a large soap and candle factory at the bottom of William-street. It was burnt down in the early seventies, but soon after was rebuilt. I saw the fire, and I am not likely to forget how the tallow and grease flared up, illuminating that part of the district. On the opposite side of William-street were the military barracks in the old days, and afterwards the police barracks. It was a two-storeyed white building, where a large body of police and [First Nations] trackers were stationed, for besides being good old days, they were also bad old days, and those barracks were really the headquarters of the police who hunted the bushrangers, horsestealers, cattlestealers, etc., who made things so warm for squatters, settlers, travellers, and others, in the pre-railway and pre-telegraph days. The paddock was all paled in, and emus were to be seen walking around the fence for years." (After 40 Years, 13 Nov 1917, p.1)

1867 – ACCIDENT BATHURST "A shocking accident, caused by the misbehaviour of a drunken scoundrel, occurred on the river last night. It was 6 o'clock and dark, when the boat built by Cobb and Co. was engaged in conveying the mails and parcels brought by the coach across the river. There were a number of people waiting to be ferried over from the Kelso side, and, against the wish of the person in charge of the boat, seven or eight of these jumped in and amongst them a drunken ruffian who, seeing a female in the boat, stood on the gunwale, and commenced rocking it from side to side, despite all entreaties. The boat was very deep in the water, the sides being not more than a few inches above its level. When the centre of the stream was reached, an extra lurch given by the fellow turned the boat completely ever, and the passengers were precipitated into the river. All were saved but two—Mr. Caples and Mrs. Croft—who were drowned, and though the river has been dragged all day their bodies have not been recovered." (Bathurst, 6 Jul 1867, p.4)

1872 – ACCIDENT BATHURST "Cobb and Co.'s mail coach capsized ten miles out of Bathurst on the road to Sofala, at 11 o'clock this morning. There were twenty-three passengers in the coach. Mr. Biddell, confectioner, of George-street, was very much shaken ; Mr. Edward Edwards had a severe cut on the left leg near the thigh, and Mr. Murray suffered a severe injury to his right kneecap ... At the time of the accident the king-bolt fortunately broke and liberated the horses." (Bathurst, 21 May 1872, p.2)

1880 – BATHURST GHOST "The Bathurst Free Press states that in the western portion of the town ... a piece of ground has been in the occupation of a man ... the lawful owner up to the present has been unable to eject him ... in order to frighten any person from purchasing the premises, the man has lately been moving about the paddock near the street, covered with a large white sheet, thus attempting to lead people to believe that the place was haunted, and that the restless spirits were exercising themselves after nightfall.

This scheme of his succeeded to his own satisfaction for a time, until a few nights ago a young man was passing the spot referred to, when suddenly he saw what he took to be a ghost. He was alarmed, and in his flight stood motionless in the street, when seeing the 'spirit' moving towards him he became, still more alarmed. He had with him a faithful dog, and, calling the animal by name, told him to 'take to him.' The dog obeyed his master's command and made straight for the spirit ... the dog seized the sheet with which he was covered, tearing it from top to bottom and exposing to view the body of man. The dog then made for his legs and gave the ghost some severe bites." (Retaliating on a Ghost, 27 Jul 1880)

1881 – ACCIDENT BATHURST. "A narrow escape from a fatal accident happened yesterday afternoon to Mrs. Rutherford, wife of Mr. James Rutherford, of Cobb and Co. Mrs. Rutherford was returning from Bathurst in her buggy to her residence at Hereford, and when crossing the river the current, being very strong, washed the buggy down the stream. Mrs Rutherford, who showed remarkable presence of mind under the circumstances, succeeded in getting out of the buggy, and managed to hold on to some willows. After remaining in this perilous position for a considerable time two young men named Edwards and Honor, at considerable risk, dragged Mrs. Rutherford, who was in a very exhausted state, on to the bank. The buggy was subsequently recovered. The horse was drowned." (Narrow Escape at Bathurst, 21 Oct 1881, p.2)

1911 – BANK STICK-UP "Ex-Bushranger in Bathurst. Yesterday afternoon, we had a call from John Bradshaw, the ex-bushranger. Bradshaw spoke interestingly of his sticking-up of the Quirindi Bank in 1880, for which he received a sentence of 12 years imprisonment, and told of how, on being released, he was sent back for another eight years on a charge which had been 'manufactured' against him. His total sentences thus amounted to 20 years, but he did not serve more than 17 years and 9 months. He has been a free man since November, 1898. To-night Bradshaw will deliver a lecture in William-street." (Ex-Bushranger in Bathurst, 4 Feb 1911, p.4)

1919 – "BATHURSTIAN WINS POEM COMPETITION. On board the Kildonion Castle, a troopship which arrived in Sydney recently held a poem competition, the subject being 'Anzac Day'. A pocket wallet was the prize, and was won by a Bathurstian, Corporal Geo. Dawson, with the following: —

ANZAC DAY.

It was on the beach at Anzac.
Australians fought and fell.
The stirring deeds of valour,
The world now knows so well.

For they with burning courage,
Gained those splendid heights,
Forward, for Australia,
They won that awful fight.

But now the war is over,
They're home boys from the fray.
A living 'fine' memorial,
Remember Anzac Day.

(Anzac Day, 27 May 1919, p.2)

1862 Bathurst Cobb & Co. Office – Courtesy National Archives of Australia

ca. 1888 Bathurst, N.S.W. – Courtesy of Mitchell Library, State Library of New South Wales

ca. 1871 Bathurst (American & Australasian Photographic Company) – Courtesy State Library of New South Wales

'Kilrush', John Meagher's Residence, Bathurst – Courtesy of Bathurst District Historical Society

1870-1875 Panorama of Ballarat taken from the Town Hall clocktower (American & Australasian Photography Company) – Courtesy Mitchell Library, State Library of New South Wales

1870-1875 The Royal Hotel, William Street, Bathurst (American & Australasian Photography Company) – Courtesy Mitchell Library, State Library of New South Wales

1874 Bathurst Post Office & Goal – Courtesy Bathurst District Historical Society

ca. 1878 Bathurst Courthouse – Courtesy Bathurst District Historical Society

A Sullivan family picnic on the Macquarie River on their property 'Avoca', Bathurst
(Augustus Sullivan) – Courtesy Mitchell Library, State Library of New South Wales

1904 St. Stanislaus College, Bathurst, Football team (Augustus Sullivan)
– Courtesy Mitchell Library, State Library of New South Wales

1890 Bathurst Show Sketches – Illustrated Sydney News, 1 May 1890, p.17

April 1900, First Motorcar in Bathurst at Show – Courtesy of Bathurst District Historical Society

Chapter Six

Cobb and Co.'s coach factories

The Coach

"Cobb was not the first by many who attempted to cater for the crying need of goldfields' passenger and luggage transit. But Cobb knew how it should be done; he had gained his experience in the great transcontinental coaching enterprise of the United States ... It is Mark Twain who describes the overlanding coach as a

'great swinging and swaying stage, of the most sumptuous description, an imposing craddle on wheels ... drawn by six handsome horses.'

Cobb's coach, as the writer recollects it, was like a huge packing case stood on end, with small packing cases before and aft, all painted red—the whole 'contraption' swung on a net-work of leather braced over two sets of wheels. The rivals whom Cobb and Co. displaced had everything made of steel—bolted and nutted and screwed. The ruts called roads played sad havoc with these rigid machines, which were always breaking down and stranding their passengers in the most appalling of places and situations. Cobb, the Yankee traffic revolutionist, altered all this.

Prior to his advent, diggers paid exorbitant fares in the expectation of being whisked to Bendigo—a trip which they had invariably to complete on shank's-pony for the greater part of the distance. The strong point of the American conveyance was its great pliability—the leather thongs and braces being the features in its construction which specially fitted the coach for surmounting the obstacles of the rough roads and open tracks of the bush."

(A Pioneer of the Coaching Days: The late James Rutherford, 20 Sep 1911, p.40)
1854-1880 Thoroughbrace Coach used by the Nowland family, with accessories, trunk, spanner and jack;
It is possible that this coach was manufactured by Cobb & Co., however no physical evidence remains linking the object with this company (Abbott-Downing Company, Designer) – Courtesy National Museum of Australia

Cobb and Co. coach factory—Bathurst (1862-1893)

In May 1866, a report in the Bathurst Times revealed the surprising scale of Cobb and Co.'s coach factory on Howick Street—an operation so extensive that even local residents were largely unaware of its size and output. "We certainly had no idea ourselves of the existence of such a large factory until by accident we happened to saunter into the establishment a few days back. Being struck with the number of vehicles of all sizes and descriptions, in various stages towards completion, we were led to make a few inquiries, and as a subject which may not be uninteresting to our readers, we proceed to lay the information gained before them. The large contracts for mail services held by Messrs. Cobb and Co., requiring the employment of so many coaches, naturally led the company to the establishment of workshops in which they could more economically effect such repairs as were needed to their vehicles, and accordingly on the three principal routes, north, south, and west, shops have been opened.

One of the proprietary (our fellow townsman, Mr. Rutherford) had, before the company decided to commence operations in New South Wales, paid a visit to Bathurst, and seeing the importance of its position, as the key to the interior of the colony, selected it as the most suitable district in which to place the head quarters of the company. This, however, did not originate the idea of founding such a factory as now exists, for it was the intention to depend, in all parts of the colony, upon local firms for whatever building or repairs might be required; but it was soon found necessary to alter this resolution, and, in order to rely upon its own resources, the company, opened workshops of its own, similar to those established in Victoria, and as a first step brought here four experienced work men from the Castlemaine factory.

For a considerable time the company confined itself to its own work, but gradually an outside trade commenced, which has increased to such an extent, that twenty-five journeymen and four or five apprentices are now kept constantly busy, and at times are unable to meet the demand upon their labor. From all parts of the colony (even from Sydney) and from Queensland, work pours in to the Bathurst factory, and, as a consequence, it not unfrequently happens that orders have to be declined.

1866 THE SMITH'S SHOP

Entering the factory from Howick-street, we come upon the blacksmiths' and carriage makers' shop, in which four forges are kept in full work, setting ready the ironwork required by the other hands, and here the skeleton frames of every description of vehicle are constructed, from the lightest buggy shell to the largest and most substantial passenger coach. Generally speaking, imported carriage springs are used ; but occasionally, it is found necessary, in order to meet the fancy of a customer, to construct others of peculiar size and shape. Nothing appears to come amiss, however, to the workmen employed, or to their ingenious superintendent, Mr. David Brown, who has but to draw and explain his design to find it earned out with the utmost skill and rapidity. Colonial woods, as a rule without exception, are entirely eschewed by the company, and nothing but imported ash, hickory, elm, and oak are permitted to be used for building purposes.

In the construction of carriage frames, as for instance those of the large passenger coaches, it is necessary to obtain curved timber, and this is supplied by a steam box attached to a boiler in another part of the premises. Straight pieces of wood of the required dimensions are placed in the box, which is a long narrow square chamber, about twelve feet in length by eighteen inches in width, and being subjected to a jet of steam in the ratio of an hour to the inch thick, are taken out and placed in clamps that grip them into the necessary shapes, to force them out of which, when cool, would require treatment equally as violent. By the aid of this apparatus, the felloes of buggy wheels can be, and often are twisted in one piece, out of straight hickory rods, rendering only one join necessary to complete the circle. The company find it cheaper, however, to import American wheels, as well as nearly all their material—to select which they have agents both in America and England. It is only when the peculiar fancy of a customer renders it necessary to construct wheels of unusual height or strength that any are made by the aid of the steam-box, and therefore but one wheelwright is employed in the establishment, and he is mostly occupied in fitting together imported manufactures.

1866 THE PAINTER'S ROOM

At the rear of the smith's shop is the painter's room, in which three workmen are constantly engaged in the exercise of their skillful art—the difficulty of accomplishing which may be appreciated by any one who will attempt, without any guide, to draw a few of those delicate fine lines and curves which are usually to be found on the panels and wheels of all vehicles. In the same shop are two trimmers, whose business it is to execute the leather and upholstery work to carriages and buggies, the performance of which completes the labor of the establishment and render the vehicles ready to be delivered to the customers.

1866 THE SINKING PLATFORM

Passing out of the latter shop into the yard we come upon the 'sinking platform,' a simple contrivance invented by Mr. Brown for fixing tires to wheels, so as to supersede the old and rude method usually adopted for such purposes. A narrow brick furnace, of such dimensions as to admit of a tire of any height being placed in it, is near at hand. A fire is kindled of the refuse of the shop, and in a few minutes the iron is brought to the proper heat. The wheel which is to be tired is placed flat upon the platform, the tire is brought from the furnace, rapidly fixed in its position, and in an instant, by the aid of a lever, the platform, which is imbedded in a tank of water and hold up high and dry, sinks out of sight, and the job is finished. The surface of the platform is slightly concave, and besides other holes drilled through its surface to allow the ingress and egress of water, there is one large enough in the centre to admit the nave of the wheel, and thus the felloes lie flat on the platform, rendering the fixing of the tire a matter of perfect simplicity. The old method of cooling the tire, by pouring water on it, is open to the objection that the felloes are likely to be burnt and charred in places by the slowness of the operation. When once the tire is properly fixed it is obvious that the sooner it is thoroughly cooled the better, and Mr. Brown has certainly most successfully combated the difficulty by his invention, besides saving considerable time and labor.

1866 The engine

In another yard, connected with the hay sheds, a portable eight horse power engine is situated, which works extensive chaff-cutting machinery overhead, and supplies motion to a lathe and circular saw, as well as steam to the box which we have already described as being used for the purpose of curving wood. A tank, fourteen feet deep by twelve in diameter, is excavated and covered in close to the engine, being the reservoir of the rain-water collected from the roof of the building, and from this the engine supplies itself—sufficient water having been collected during the past dry season to supply all wants. In the loft above, all chaff used at the stables between Hartley and Forbes is cut and packed. In the manufacture of harness, the company have not found it necessary to engage, as it can be purchased in large quantities at very low prices from outside makers. They content themselves, therefore, with merely attending to repairs, and one saddler is found sufficient to do all that is required on the western route.

1866 The orders

The fame of the establishment appears to be spreading widely, for orders are received from all directions. A few weeks back two coaches were turned out for Messrs. Robertson and Nowlan, separate mail contractors at Rockhampton, Queensland, and buggies of various kinds are constructed for residents in all parts of this colony. The coaches required by the company for their mail contracts in Brisbane are built here, as well as those for the northern and southern lines in New South Wales, in which directions only small shops for light repairs have been established. The aim of the company is directed not so much to finish and ornament as to the substantiality of their work, and in this it appears to be generally admitted they are unexcelled, and, from their great resources, perhaps unequalled by any other firm in the colony. Even Sydney workshops do not enjoy so good a reputation, a fact which may be fully estimated from the circumstance that the wheels now fixed to the van used for conveying prisoners through the streets of the metropolis were manufactured in Bathurst, by Messrs. Cobb and Co., who, by-the-way, are now engaged upon other work for the Government.

The want of room for the erection of larger workshops is somewhat crippling the operations of the company, who could, with benefit to the public and profit to themselves, greatly extend their trade ; but we believe there are means of overcoming this difficulty which it is in contemplation to adopt, and it is not improbable that a factory of double the present dimensions will ere long be established. It is not more than four years since the first commencement was made, and not the least satisfactory, circumstance connected with the success achieved, is the knowledge that no injury what ever has been done to other local establishments of more modest pretensions. The Messrs. Cobb have cut out an entirely new trade, and established a factory which, without their energy and skill, might never have been called into existence ; and in doing this they have, whilst increasing the importance of the district, opened quietly and perseveringly, an avenue to labor, and set an example which might well be copied by those who rave so loudly upon the necessity of protection to native industry." (The Sketcher, 19 May 1866, p.12)

1879 – FACTORY ACCIDENT "Last night an employee at Cobb and Co.'s factory, at Bathurst, had a narrow escape from being killed. He was at work helping to fix a brake on a new dray for the Exhibition, when a heavy piece of iron fell, and nearly struck him on the head. It fell on his arm, but without doing any serious injury." (Telegraphic Brevities, 29 Oct 1879, p.2)

'We lead, those can may follow.'

In 1890, Cobb and Co. proudly declared, "We lead, those can may follow"—a fitting motto for a firm that had become a cornerstone of Bathurst's industrial landscape. "Situated in Lower William-street, and occupying fully an acre and a half of ground, is one of the oldest and most substantial industries of Bathurst. The business was established in 1862, not with a view to turning out work for the public but for the repair and manufacture of the coaches that were in requisition, the means then available in the City of the Plains not being at all adequate to the requirements of the great Australian coaching firm. Bathurst was one of the principal depots in the colony, and routes radiated on all sides—from Bathurst to Sydney, Mudgee, Dubbo, Forbes, Lambing Flat (now Young), and all intermediate places. The name of the firm that is now a household word all over the great continent of the Southern Seas … At the present time most of the coaching is being done in our northern sister colony, and some idea of its magnitude can be formed by the statement, of Mr James Rutherford that between 600 and 700 horses are now in active use throughout New South Wales. The Queensland business is a very extensive one, the value of the rolling stock being set down at £55,000. In 1871 it was merged into a limited liability company, about one third of the shares being allotted to the drivers and managers on the co-operative system, of which Mr. Rutherford speaks to our representative in terms of approval.

To Bathurstians there is something in the name which revives memories of the good old days, when, before the iron horse had reached so far into the interior, coaches were to be seen and heard at all hours of the day and night, departing for, or arriving from, their various destinations. Doubtless many a resident, on perusal of this article, will recall to mind the animated scene presented at Cobb and Co.'s central booking office in William-street on the departure of a thirty or forty passenger coach for Orange, Hill End, or some other centre of population, inaccessible save by the Royal Mail line of coaches. On such occasions there was an assemblage of humanity such as is now witnessed at our central railway depots at holiday times—an immense crowd, crushing and squeezing, laughing and teazing, swearing and sneezing, men, women, and children rushing hither and thither, all bent on securing the coveted seat on the coach—the box ; the confusion reaching its climax as the gruff voice, of the coachman was heard yelling out *Now*, then, *all aboard there !* Then followed a final scramble by a dozen or more excited individuals who had not been fortunate enough so far to obtain a footing in the ponderous conveyance. Well nigh frantic at the thoughts of being left behind, by superhuman efforts they generally managed, with the assistance of some benevolent souls on board, to get tucked in somehow. Crack went the whip, round spun the wheels, and another coach had started on its journey. Those were the palmy days of life and bustle in Bathurst.

They are passed now, but their memories will never be effaced from the minds of many still in our midst. Nor will such knights of the road as Hal Hamilton, Denny Doyle, Jim Hunter, Jim Love, Charlie Bissel, Joe Jenkins and old Johnny Fagan, whose encounters with the bushrangers would fill many a page of a thrilling book. But we digress.

Our instructions are to describe the establishment of Cobb and Co. for a place under the heading of 'Busy Bathurst.' In 1862 the firm commenced operations in Howick-street, and for a period of 16 or 17 years there carried on a highly successful business. An instance of the perfection to which they brought the building of coaches, it may be mentioned en passant that they hold the highest certificate of award obtained at the Sydney International Exhibition of 1879, for the best travelling coach, and only a few weeks ago we had the pleasure of inspecting a couple of coaches turned out for Port Douglas (Q.), that for workmanship and finish could not, we think, be surpassed in the colony. Though devoting so much of their time to the manufacture of coaches, the firm have more recently found time to do ample in the way of buggy building, to show that their prestige could be as equally well maintained in the construction of buggies and carriages as in coaches ; and the sequel has not been without proof, for at the present time Cobb and Co. enjoy the honor of being the premier coach and buggy and carriage builders of the West.

Now that the railway has extended so far into the interior, and coaching has been outdone by the iron horse, most of the business is confined to the construction of business and pleasure vehicles of the following kinds: landaus, barouches, Victorias, drags, vis-a-vis, sociables, double and single-seated buggies of every conceivable description, as well as dog carts, spring carts, drays, waggons, lorries, vans, coaches, etc. It might be here mentioned that the firm make a speciality of work built on the American and English principle in buggies and carriages, and they stand unrivalled as builders of those famous tray buggies, built after the Abbott style, and now known as the Cobb and Co. Eclipse Tray buggies, both double and single seated. This buggy has been wonderfully improved upon by the present manager, Mr. H. M. S. Brown, by the construction of a well designed and elegantly got up portable back seat, harmonious in every detail, and making it one of the most stylish and serviceable buggies procurable in the market. This being but one of the numerous original ideas of Mr. Brown, it is evident he intends that the motto of the firm shall be strictly adhered to—'We lead, those can may follow.' We are told by Mr. Brown that this buggy, of which he is so justly proud, was awarded first prize at the Bathurst show this year for the best double-seated buggy without hood, while one of their single-seated trays took the first prize for hooded buggies. To give our readers any adequate idea of the magnitude of Messrs. Cobb and Co.'s works it will be necessary to go into detail and deal with them as each department is come to.

1890 THE LAYOUT

The ground upon which the factory is erected has a frontage of 535 feet to William-street with a depth of 135 feet, the whole of the space being occupied by the works and manager's residence. The main entrance opens into a large court yard, about 55 x 100, on each side of which stands a wing of the main building, which extends the full depth of the ground, and intersects a large building at the rear, about 200 x 40.

Each wing is about 40 x 130, and the main building is subdivided into the construction departments and show room, while on either side it is surrounded by out buildings in the shape of engine room, harness room, timber sheds, &c. The works are admirably laid out, with every facility for turning out a great quantity of work in a thoroughly systematic manner.

1890 THE ENGINE ROOMS

As we pass through one of the main entrances we are astonished at the immense stacks of wood and coal that meet the eye, and begin to wonder is we have not made a huge mistake and got into some wood and coal depot ; but Mr. Brown soon dispels the doubting look, and lead us to watch the engineer stowing large quantities of wood and coal into the stoke hole of the boiler, beneath which is at work one of Robey's best 16-horse power engines, which drives all the machinery, as well as a fan for the use of the forges, thus obviating the necessity of bellows and a boy. Everything in the engine rooms denotes cleanliness, thorough care, and attention.

1890 THE MILL OR MACHINERY SHOP

In our exit from the engine room we pass a massive grindstone, driven by steam, and enter the mill or machinery shop. This department embraces an area of about 100 x 50 ; all round in most convenient places are situated a variety of useful and expensive machines, such as a band-saw, circular-saw, planing and champering machines, boring and spoke tanging machines, spoke-making machine, iron and wood lathes, emery machine, and many others, all in working order. In a corner of the machine shop is erected the office, upon the exterior of which we notice an immense number of first and second-class prizes obtained at the various local and metropolitan exhibitions. Here we also notice large black-boards with full-size drawings of different vehicles. In this department the foundation of every vehicle is laid down ; the rough planks are brought here, marked to pattern, sawn, planed, and dressed, then passed on to the body shop, where they assume whatever shape it is intended they should. The manager, Mr. Brown, being a thoroughly practical bodymaker, it is needless to say this department is efficiently presided over, and employing only the best skilled workmen available in Bathurst, the public need have no hesitation in entrusting Cobb and Co. with any class of work.

1890 THE SMITHING DEPARTMENT

From the mill we pass into the smithing department, which occupies about 50ft. x 80ft., and is fitted up with nine forges. Here, we are told, work the best coach-smiths in Bathurst, among them Mr. Peter Brown, son of the late manager, who has been in the firm's employ for over 20 years. The machinery in the smithing department comprises a steam hammer, drilling machine, shears, screwing machine, tire setting machine, and many others, all doing their particular work. Several traps are being ironed up as we pass along, and a great quantity of forgings are under way.

1890 THE BODY SHOP & WHEEL DEPARTMENT

Next in turn we come to the body shop where a number of bodies (not human) are to be seen in various stages of construction ; here the eye rests on an immense coach, there a vis-a-vis, next a hampshire, then a drag, and a number of carts.

In passing on through this labyrinth of bodies we note an express waggon just nearing completion, and one of the firm's popular £10 carts, as well as a host of other vehicles too numerous to individualise. In the wheel department are seen a number of Cobb and Co.'s superior made wheels, also American, savren and shellbourne ones.

1890 THE TIRING YARD

Passing on outside we come upon a heating furnace, a tire bending and tiring machine ; this tiring apparatus deserves more than passing mention, as we learn it is one of the best in the colony and only to be found within such establishments as the one under review, and Cobb and Co. of Bourke, where works are erected on the same principle and of almost equal magnitude. At one end of the tiring yard is erected a large timber and iron rack well stocked with English and colonial iron and steel, among which is a large quantity of the best Lithgow shoeing iron, largely used by our local farriers. The timber rack is well supplied with American and best colonial timbers.

1890 THE OFFICE & THE STORE

Returning thence we again traverse the smiths' department and enter the office, a regular *multum in parvo*. Here are all kinds of expensive fittings, from the beautiful ivory and silver mounted landau fittings down to the breeching staples of a cart, all arranged in apple-pie order. From the office we pass over to the store room, a veritable young warehouse, judging by the stock kept. Here are spokes of all sizes, felloes, hubs, axles, springs, clips, bolts, etc., etc., ad lib. ; also a quantity of American coach harness. Mr. Brown informed us that it is absolutely necessary to keep such a varied stock to ensure seasoned material being used in the construction of every article.

1890 THE PAINT SHOP & TRIMMING SHOP

Out of the store across to the paint shop we find ourselves in a large commodious department, well lighted and ventilated and replete with all the requirements of the trade. In one corner we see an excellent device, introduced by Mr. Brown, for the safe keeping of poles and shafts while being painted, instead of allowing them to lie about the shop ; close by is a large press fitted up with innumerable drawers, each containing different colors used in the preparation of paints. In vain we look round for any signs of shoddy material ; the names of Nobles and Hoare, Harlands, Blundel and Spence, and Champion's white lead stand as proof incontestable that Cobb and Co. believe in the best material obtainable. We now glance at the work under operation by the artistic members of the craft ; in this department we observe Mr. Ewing Hamilton, as head painter, who has been in the employ of the firm for the past 20 years, and who is just now working on a Victoria, one of the firm's manufacture ; a little farther away lies a new Hampshire buggy, well on the road towards completion, also a piano box and several others in more or less finished stages. Here also are to be seen a quantity of tray buggies, all filled in and hardening prior to being rubbed down, an indispensable process in the execution of first class work. From the paint shop we step into the trimming shop, another large department 30ft. x 20ft. At one end is erected a long bench for the work men, the space underneath lining fitted up with cupboards containing a big stock of all sorts of leather as well as linings, fringes, tassels, etc., to match each colored trimming.

In the opposite corner stands a large Singer sewing machine, which we are told is to be replaced shortly by one of Wertheim's latest improved. Amongst the vehicles being upholstered we specially notice a new style of sociable, built to the order of Mr. Macauley, of Tarana.

1890 THE SHOWROOM

The show room on the opposite side of the entrance courtyard has a frontage of 30ft. to William-street, and is about 100ft. deep. There is a splendid collection in stock. One stylish-looking turnout claims our attention, and we enquiringly turn to Mr. Brown. He informs us that the vehicle is an original idea of his own. It is a sulky or stylish two wheeler called the Browning roadster. We have seen a number of sulkies in various parts, but none to surpass the Browning roadster for neatness of design, and the ingenious mode of ingress or egress. The vehicle can be entered from the side or back, the back entrance being the principal feature of the contrivance. You simply catch hold of a handle, swing round the seat, step up, pull the seat too after you, thus avoiding all danger of a spirited horse, or the discomfort of climbing over a muddy wheel.

Our tour of inspection now being completed a word is necessary in closing. Ever since the establishment of the business, the management was in the hands (up to the time of his death) of Mr. David Brown, a thorough mechanic, a good citizen, and one who was universally respected. A number of first-class tradesmen now in Bathurst and elsewhere served their apprenticeship under him ; among them the present manager, who is not as might be supposed, a relation of his. Since serving his apprenticeship Mr. H. M. S. Brown has spent several years at some of the largest Sydney and provincial shops in quest of experience. This he is able to introduce into the business of the old firm under whom he learned his handicraft, and judging by the work that is now being turned out, and indications of an efficient, supervising management, Messrs. Cobb and Co. should have no fear that their welfare will be jealously guarded by their old pupil, and the name that the firm has made for itself be fully maintained by Mr. Brown." (Busy Bathurst, 27 Aug 1890, p.2)

1892 STILL GREAT ON WHEELS

Just two years later, Messrs. Cobb & Co., were "still great on wheels at the end of William-street, where they are just as well liked and appreciated as they are known from one end of the continent to the other. For Cobb is a household name, and no history is complete without it. In all parts of Australia, they run the public—legitimately, of course, and in coaches—and in Bathurst have the most extensive and complete carriage and buggy building factory this side of the Capital. They employ a large staff of men, a capable manager, and are always prepared to complete any order entrusted them." (Messrs. Cobb & Co., 24 Dec 1892, p.3)

1893 THE END OF AN INDUSTRIAL PILLAR AT BATHURST

The following year, at a "meeting of the Bathurst School of Arts, notice was given that Messrs. Cobb and Co. intended, on a certain date, to discontinue their occupancy of certain offices in that building, it became a matter for wonder, the reason, the why and the wherefore ; and because the firm had so long been looked upon as one of the institutions of the district (says the National Advocate, Bathurst).

Now, however, it is known to nearly everybody that the famous old coach and buggy building factory at the river end of Wiliam-street is to be removed to another colony; and this news has come with feelings of regret upon protectionist and free-trader alike, and owing to the fact that the loss which the change will entail is so very self-evident.

Time was when this business, so far as buggy building is concerned, was one of the industrial pillars of the West, but that was before the introduction of the cheap import; but even now the shrinkage that will be caused in our circulation in Bathurst through the determination of the firm to go into a properly protected country—in their line of business, at least—will be £5000 a year or more. Because of the operation of a £20 duty in Queensland the proprietors find themselves quite unable to further manufacture in a free-trade country ; and so they will transplant the works that have endured in Bathurst for 28 years in a colony where native industry in this line is protected—Queensland. We are constantly being told that an ounce of practice is worth a ton of theory, and here we have it—our free-trade citizens can digest the unpalatable fact that Bathurst is losing an industry that, has been established here nearly 30 years, and with it a considerable portion of its wages circulation, which, by the change about to be made, will, even if it does not increase by the encouragement offered in the younger province, benefit Queensland to just the extent that it deprives us." (Cobb and Company, 22 Mar 1893, p.6)

By 1917, the past location of Cobb and Co.'s factory had become unclear. "I have to thank your lady correspondent, 'Older Bathurstian' for her complimentary remarks, but must differ with her ... Any old hand knows that Cobb's factory was in Howick street on the William street side of the 'Black Bull ' and adjoining Hackett mill. Thirty nine years ago it may have been at the foot of William street. I do not know. On the Anniversary Day of 1875, the Oddfellows held a picnic at Sodwalls. Raglan was the railway terminus, and large crowds to get in early went to Cobb's in Howick street to get seats in the coaches before they reached the advertised starting place. I left Bathurst in the following spring and the factory was still there. Some old member of the Oddfellows might be good enough to say whether what I have written is correct. Jack Taylor looked after John Taits racehorses for a while when Tait kept the 'Black Bull,' but he will best be remembered as a coach driver. Joe Lewis kept the 'Bull' about the time of the good lady's wedding. Lewis afterwards kept the Royal Hotel for many years." (Cobb and Co's Factory, 9 Nov 1917, p.2)

While written in 1926: "Close association with the workings of Cobb and Co. is something of historical importance and pride, for did not this company provide the first organised means of transit in the Australian States before the advent of the 'iron horse.' Despite the modern methods of conveyance and comfort there was nothing more thrilling or enjoyable than to be on the box of a Cobb coach, drawn by numerous sturdy horses, and watch the masterly manner in which the driver handled the ribbons. The glories of the drivers of Cobb's coaches have been told in verse and story, and periodically lately southern papers have been telling of the lives of the last men to drive a coach ... But what has been related of the men who built the coaches?

Very little. They were not in the position to command public admiration, but they put such solid work into the construction of those vehicles, that gave life to the slogan *If it's a Cobb it will get you there*. A family record that is almost at illustrious as the enterprise of Cobb's is that of the Hooper family.

The aggregate years that the family were employed by Cobb's in building coaches total 115 ! And in Rockhampton at present there are descendants of this family, and also members who worked in building those coaches. The association with Cobb's is as follows—Charles Hooper, (father-deceased)—18 years, and the sons Charles Marshall, 27, George 25, and Frank 15. All the sons are still living with the exception of Charles, who passed away in Rockhampton on Thursday week, aged 62. The story of the family's record is highly interesting. It was away back in '54 that the father entered the service of Cobb's as a builder, and it was in Bathurst, where the coaches were first made in New South Wales. Like many other sons, those of Charles Hooper showed an inclination to follow their father's trade. It was about '84 that George and Charles, junr., were apprenticed in Bathurst. In 1893 Charles came to Queensland and took a prominent part in Cobb's factory at Charleville, which was a very important link in the Cobb chain. Charles was appointed foreman at the Charleville works, and worked in that capacity for 14 years." (115 Years!, 29 May 1926, p.61)

Cobb and Co. coach factory—Hay (1876-closed by 1899)

Back in 1876, "we see by the Hay Standard that Cobb and Co. are going to build a coach-factory at Hay, and employ about twenty tradesmen at the factory. The lime has to come from Victoria, and Castlemaine is to export a paint-shop '107 feet long by 36 feet wide,' as a part of the concern." (News And Notes, 15 Jul 1876, p.2)

By 1878, the factory was already well established. "The firm of Robertson, Wagner, and Co., more familiarly known as Cobb and Co ... have made Hay their depot or centre for extending their usefulness. Their commodious offices and factory are well built on one of the most valuable sites in Hay, and speak well for the advancement. The building consists of a show room 40 x35 ft.; wood shop 72 x 35 ft.; smith's shop 100 x 30 ft.; paint, trimming, and harness department, 73 x 30 ft. The whole building being 300 x 73 feet wide. An extra forge has been lately added. The whole building, with plant and material, has cost about £10,000. All the latest improvements such as patent attire compressers, which saves the cutting of tires, have been introduced ; the tire plate has been specially made to ensure a good straight-faced wheel. The vyces are on the lever principle and do away with the old style of screwing. The painting department is furnished with Masury patent presses which have the paint prepared and ready for use. The steam machinery which it is intended shortly to erect will drive hand and circular saws, turning lathe, drill, and grindstone. There will also be steaming apparatus for twisting timber to any shape. In going through the factory we were pleasantly surprised at seeing the quantity of ash and hickory in stock, and when noticing how perfect appliances, we scarcely wonder at their being able to turn out coaches and buggies so splendidly finished.

We noticed two neatly finished horse brakes, with harness—one for Mr. John C. Wallace of Priory, and the other for Mr Officer, of Zara. An eight passenger coach for Mr. Burton, of Swan Hill to run at Bairanald ; a double seated buggy for Messrs. Booth, Oak, and Browne, of Wirlong ; a hooded buggy for Messrs. Quinn and Curry, of Tarella, Wilcannia ; a hooded buggy just finished for Mr. J. E. D'Archhy ; a passenger coach for Mr. Charters is in hand, as also a double buggy for Mr. Berthon, together with several others we have not been able to get the names of. This is one of the most complete establishments in the colonies. It may not be out of place to mention that Mr. G. A. M'Gowan is again in his element as manager, and that the manufacturing department is under the foremanship of Mr. Thomas Johnson, many years with the firm at Castlemaine. Mr. Parker informs us it is intended to place a verandah in front of the office which will add greatly to the appearance of the building and comfort of travellers.—Standard." (Cobb and Co.'s Coach Factory, 23 Oct 1878, p.3)

However, by 1893, the factory suffered a major setback. "A disastrous fire took place at the coach factory of Messrs. Robertson, Wagner and Co. early on Sunday morning. About half past one o'clock the ringing of the fire ... As the night was a rather warm one, many of those who were unable to sleep soundly were soon on the move. At the time the alarm was given the fire had a good hold of the building, as it could be seen from all parts of town ... some member of the fire brigade were out with the reel and actively at work endeavouring to check the spread of the flames ... the water being pumped from the underground tank at Tattersall's Hotel ... In the part of the building situated on the north side there was a good deal of timber used for coach building and this was all destroyed ... The origin of the fire, as is generally the case, is enveloped in mystery ... Mr. Proctor, the foreman of the works, locked up the premises ... no one ... so far as is known was on the premises from that time until the fire was discovered ... the member of the brigade did good service ... Mr. John Witcombe, directed the operations of the brigade in a cool and prompt manner ... Mr. M. Reid, worked well throughout ... Mr. Proctor and Mr. Parker ... coolness and tact had an inspiring effect upon others" (Fire at Cobb and Co's Factory, 13 Dec 1893, p.2)

Despite such challenges, the factory left a lasting legacy. In 1908, an advertisement noted that "John Sandow, Coach and General Blacksmith ... commenced business ... employed for twenty years in Cobb and Co.'s Factory." (Advertising, 3 Apr 1908, p.3)

Finally, in 1919, the property once known as Cobb and Co.'s factory and offices was sold to the Hay Motor and Engineering Proprietary Ltd. "In the late seventies and early eighties this building was the scene of Cobb and Co.'s coach factory, harness making depot and showrooms, and in those years it contained more first class mechanics than have ever been assembled under one roof in Hay since then.

With the advent of the railway in 1882, and afterwards with the extension of railways to Cobar and the mallee districts of Victoria, the coaching traffic waned, gradually, but surely, and the necessity of maintaining a big staff at the factory became less and less, and eventually the business was given up.

We have no doubt that the new proprietors of the buildings have bought them with the intention of extending their present operations, and we will be very pleased if the old factory becomes once more a flourishing hive of industrial enterprise." (No Title, 2 Sep 1919, p.2)

Cobb and Co. coach factory—Bourke (Pre 1864-1899)

In 1888, Cobb and Co.'s Bourke factory was actively recruiting skilled tradesmen. "Wanted, one General Coachsmith, one Coach Bodymaker, and one General Job Woodman, for Cobb and Co's coach factory, Bourke ; must be first-class men. For full particulars apply to Messrs. Briscoe, Drysdale, and Co., 397, George-street, Sydney." (Advertising, 10 Sep 1888, p.4)

The following year, in 1889, the scale of the operation was highlighted in a local report. "Of the expansive industry which Messrs. Cobb and Co. have established in this town ... A visit to the factory would entirely astonish very many even those who have been living within the sound of its steam whistle ... Even apart from the various pieces of machinery, the enterprize of the firm is well demonstrated by the huge stock of material which is in store ... also all supplies of saddlery and of every article be used in connection either with vehicles themselves, or in riding and driving." (Messrs. Cobb and Co's Factory, 9 Nov 1889, p.4)

However, by 1895, the factory suffered a major setback. "Messrs. Cobb and Co.'s coach factory, Bourke, caught fire on Sunday morning, the blacksmiths shop and engine house being burnt. The total damage is estimated at £2000." (Cobb & Co.'s on Fire, 27 Nov 1895, p.2)

The factory was officially closed by 1899. "Cobb and Company's coach factory, which has been in existence at Bourke for many years, has been closed." (Current News, 27 Apr 1899, p.4) "On Saturday evening last the employees of Cobb and Co., whose factory in Bourke has just recently been closed down, invited Mr. John Myles—who for years had been their foreman, and, since the death of Mr. M. Morrison, their manager—to meet them at Mr. T. Green's Cambridge Hotel, where supper had been provided for the occasion. The tables in the long-room were covered with all the dainties imaginable, besides being decorated with flowers and evergreens, the work of Mrs. Green and her attendants. The Company being seated, His Worship, the Mayor, Dr. Faithfull, occupied the chair, and Mr. R. Jack, the Vice Chair, while 'our guest' sat on the left of the Chairman, and Mr. W. J. Brooks a representative of Cobb and Co, from Bathurst, sat on his right. The Chairman briefly referred to the object of the gathering, stating that the employees of the old firm had invited Mr. Myles to sup with them, as a mark of the esteem and respect they had for him, and to express their appreciation of his kindness and ability during the number of years he had been over them in the factory. (Cheers). He would call upon Mr. Jack to propose *The late firm of Cobb and Co*. Mr. Jack was well received, and in a brief speech he gave the toast.

He said he was sorry that the Bourke branch of the firm Cobb and Co had been closed, because there was no doubt the business men would feel it as well as the employees. The branches at Castlemaine (Victoria), and Hay (N.S.W.), had also been closed, but he hoped they would soon be re-opened. In Bourke, however, the industry would be kept going because Mr. Myles was entering into business himself in premises in Richard-street. He wished him success. He would ask them all to drink to the old firm. The toast was heartily drunk midst cheers.

Mr. Brooks responded sympathetically on behalf of Cobb and Co. Mr. T. Sellors then proposed *Our Guest, Mr. J. Myles*. He said he had been caught on the hop, as it were, but in asking them to drink Mr. Myles' health he felt that there would be no heel tape. He had travelled a great deal, all over America and the colonies, and he could assure them he had never worked under a better foreman than Mr. Myles (cheers) who had always stuck up for the worker and gave a fair day's pay for a fair day's work, and always acted justly to any man who worked under him (cheers). Speaking for himself, he had always been satisfied, and he felt that all the other men were satisfied also. He wished Mr Myles every success in his new venture (Cheers). The toast was most heartily given, with *For He's a Jolly Good Fellow*, and ringing cheers. Mr. Myles .... thanked them most sincerely ... he had been foreman at the Bourke Branch of Cobb and Co. for over five years ... he hoped soon to see the drought break up, and prosperity come over the town once more. (Cheers.) Mr. Myles, senior., said the fire had gone out of the boiler and the engine had stopped ...

Mr. George Honey, who had worked for the same for 35 years, said he had watched the growth of it all the time, and was sorry to now see that some of the branches were being closed ... others who worked for Cobb and Co. for many years, namely, Messrs. Bob Jack, W. Woodfield ... Mr. W. Woodfield responded. He said he had been connected with the trade since 1865, having worked for Cobb and Co. shortly after Mr. Honey. He thanked Mr. Bradley and the company for the manner in which they had received the toast ... Mr. Phil Chapman was asked to give *The Old Drivers*, which he did, briefly referring to such well known jehus as George Walsh, Thomas Doyle and others." (The City Coach and Buggy Work, 26 Apr 1899, p.2)

In 1908, the old factory in Bourke burnt. "Cobb and Co's. old coach factory was destroyed by fire back to the engine shed last night. A few hundred pounds worth of material was also destroyed." (Old Factory Burnt, 9 Apr 1908, p.2) "The premises, which contained quantity of chaff and vehicles, had been used as a coach factory, but had been closed down for a number of years." (Fire at Bourke, 9 Apr 1908, p.5) By November that year "J. P. Martin, the well-known Bourke auctioneer, announces the sale of Cobb and Co.'s factory, stables, buildings, vehicles and material at Bourke on Friday next, the 20th inst. He will bring to the hammer the whole of the stock, material, second-hand vehicles, boiler and engine, steam hammer, and a large quantity of other valuable machinery, as well as ironwork used in the manufacture of drays, waggons, buggies, etc. He will also offer the whole of the factory buildings, land and other property. Full particulars may be obtained from the auctioneer." (Cobb and Co's Factory, 18 Nov 1908, p.2)

Cobb and Co. coach factory— Charleville (1886-1920)

In 1897, Cobb and Co. offered a retrospective on their vehicle manufacturing history. "A short sketch of our history in connection with the manufacture of high-class road vehicles will no doubt interest you. We started manufacturing in Brisbane in the early 1860's for our own Coaching Business and the public generally. The great experience gained by actually using our own made traps for our own work will be readily seen and appreciated by you. We were able to personally and thoroughly test and prove every new design of construction, variety of timber, quality of paint and other material, and sift out all that were found wanting before introducing them in traps for the public. As our coach routes extended out West we commenced to notice that our vehicles built with the coastal seasoned timbers would not stand the dry inland climate, they would crack and gape at all joints. This became so serious at last that we decided to move our Factory to a suitable inland locality, and after considerable thought Charleville, nearly 500 miles inland, was chosen, and our whole plant and equipment moved to there in 1886.

We had another Factory in Bathurst, N.S.W., and the machinery and plant from there were also removed to Charleville at the same time, making jointly a substantial and up-to-date plant and a greatly increased staff of expert workmen. The effect of this move was immediately apparent, for we purchased large stocks of timber and seasoned it in the same hot dry climate in which traps when built were used, and the result proved extremely satisfactory. We still carry big stocks of timber to make sure that only thoroughly seasoned wood gets into the vehicles, and that is why coastal built traps cannot compete with our inland seasoned make for lasting and enduring qualities. We have profited considerably by our over half a century's experiences, and are able to give you the full benefit of those experiences in any work you entrust to us. We feel sure we are able to give you a vehicle at a price as reasonable as one landed from a coastal builder, with the added advantages of containing thoroughly seasoned timber and being built with a full knowledge of the work required of it. We maintain it pays to buy the BEST ... Yours faithfully, Cobb & Co. Ltd." (Cobb & Co.'s Catalogue of High Class Vehicles, 1897)

Later that same year, however, tragedy struck. A report from November 16, 1897 stated: "Another disastrous fire occurred here this morning, completely destroying Messrs. Cobb and Co.'s splendid coach factory and saw-mill. The loss is estimated at between £10,000 and £15,000. The immediate loss to the town will be severely felt consequent on nearly thirty employees being thrown out of work. The fire was first discovered by an employee named George Hooper, who resided quite close to the works, at about a quarter past 1 o'clock this morning. An alarm was immediately given, but, owing to the inflammability of everything in connection with the establishment, it was a foregone conclusion that the buildings, machinery, stock, tools, &c., would be destroyed. After some little delay, a hose was attached to the nearest fire plug, but the heat from the burning mass was so great that the hose could not be used with any effectiveness.

There was a moderate north-east wind, which blew the flames towards the State school. However, that building being some twenty yards away from the road the danger of its catching fire was slight.

A cottage occupied by the Hooper family, who were employees of the company, which was situated on the eastern side of the factory, and detached, had the furniture which it contained removed by the many willing hands present, and every precaution was taken to prevent the fire reaching the building which was saved. Not so, however, the office, a detached building on the south-western side, fronting Wills-street, which took fire soon after the alarm was given, but not before Messrs. Search and O'Leary, had saved the safe, containing all the books, &c. The company will be seriously inconvenienced by the disaster, having had six new coaches under way for completion before Christmas, besides a number of buggies to make to order. Mr. Thomas Gallagher, the company's manager, was to have left Tambo this morning en route to this town. The telegraph office there could not be called before the coach left, so that he will not get the news till his arrival at Augathella this evening. It is not known here the total amount the stock, machinery and buildings were insured for." (Disastrous Fire at Charleville, 18 Nov 1897, p.2)

By December 1920, the Charleville factory closed permanently. The local paper reported, "Much regret has been expressed at Charleville at the closing down of Cobb and Co.'s large factory on Saturday, which is a distinct loss to the town and district beside causing the unemployment of several workmen. It is hoped that the business may be sold, and the old establishes business carried on as usual. It is stated Cobb and Co. probably will not carry on more coaching after the present contracts are completed." (Cobb and Co's Factory, 20 Dec 1920, p.2)

In 1921, "Cobb & Co., Ltd., Brisbane, for the year ended June 30 shows a net profit of £3507 after providing for depreciations of horses and plant. The coaching portion of the business showed a loss of £2235, due to the feeding necessary during July, August and September last year. The directors say: *We are very pleased to state, however, that December 31 of the current year terminates all our mail contracts, and that we have only renewed contracts for three services which are of great assistance to the stores in delivering goods inwards and outwards.* The three contracts renewed carry a total subsidy of £1485 per annum, which is an increase of £225 a year. Sales of coaching properties (paddocks, cottages, &c.) were very satisfactory, resulting in a net profit of £1290, which makes a good offset against the loss sustained on the mail contracts. Several properties remain to be sold. Charleville factory was closed, and the plant and buildings disposed of at a gratifying figure the factory, land, and buildings showing a net profit of £935, and the plant £128. The stock was harder to dispose of. Final results showed a loss of £444, which has been, written off. The stores netted £4931 after the stocks had been searchingly inspected and revalued on falling market values. The stocks, etc., of the five stores constitute a valuable asset, and represent the profits of the last few years, the cash realised from the sale of the coaching and factory properties, and the new capital subscribed.

The report further says: *The change from the erratic and risky coaching business to the more stable and lucrative one of storekeeping may now claim to have been practically accomplished.* The directors take a hopeful view, and are of opinion that regular annual dividends should be started before the end of the current financial year." (Company News, 2 Nov 1921, p.5)

1926 – "THE HOOPER FAMILY ... A few, years ago there was a 'Back to Brisbane Week,' in which there was a procession of old-time vechicles, and in it was Cobb's coach, which was an improved model on the original coach. Charles Hooper supervised its construction at Charleville 26 years ago, and it is intended to have that coach housed at Canberra, along with other historical relics of the early days. The coach gives rise to a very interesting comparison, for it was the last built in Queensland, and on the other hand his father built the first in New South Wales. While in Charleville the late Charles Hooper was closely associated with the public life of the town, and was also a prominent rifle shot and cricketer. Deceased leaves a widow and a grown-up family." (Historic Family, 22 May 1926, p.6)

Cobb and Co. coach factory—Castlemaine

1872 – "WANTED, Coachtrimmer. Cobb and Co.'s factory, Castlemaine. Apply Aw. Johnston." On the same page "Lost, a magpie. Reward. Dr. Hewlett, Nicholson-street, Fitzroy." (Advertising, 9 Oct 1872, p.1)

Cobb and Co. coach factory—Kilmore

1908 – "MR BENJAMIN PROSSER, who has been a resident of Kilmore for over 50 years died on Monday night at the age of 85 years. Mr Prosser was foreman of Cobb and Co.'s coach factory in Kilmore in the early days, and was a church warden of Christ Church for over 45 years." (Items of Interest, 11 Aug 1908, p.4)

Cobb and Co. coach factory—Bendigo

Supporting evidence not yet located.

Cobb and Co. coach factory—Goulburn

Supporting evidence not yet located.

1870-1875 William Barnett, wheelwright & blacksmith, Gulgong
(American & Australasian Photography Company) – Courtesy State Library of New South Wales

ca. 1890-98 Cobb & Co Factory Lower William St, Bathurst, David Brown in Charge – Courtesy Bathurst District Historical Society

Cobb and Co factory in Bourke during flood – Courtesy National Archives of Australia

Cobb and Co. Coach Factory Charleville early 1900s – Courtesy National Archives of Australia

Chapter Seven

N.S.W. coaching routes–
News along the tracks ... just a snippet

Map of New South Wales

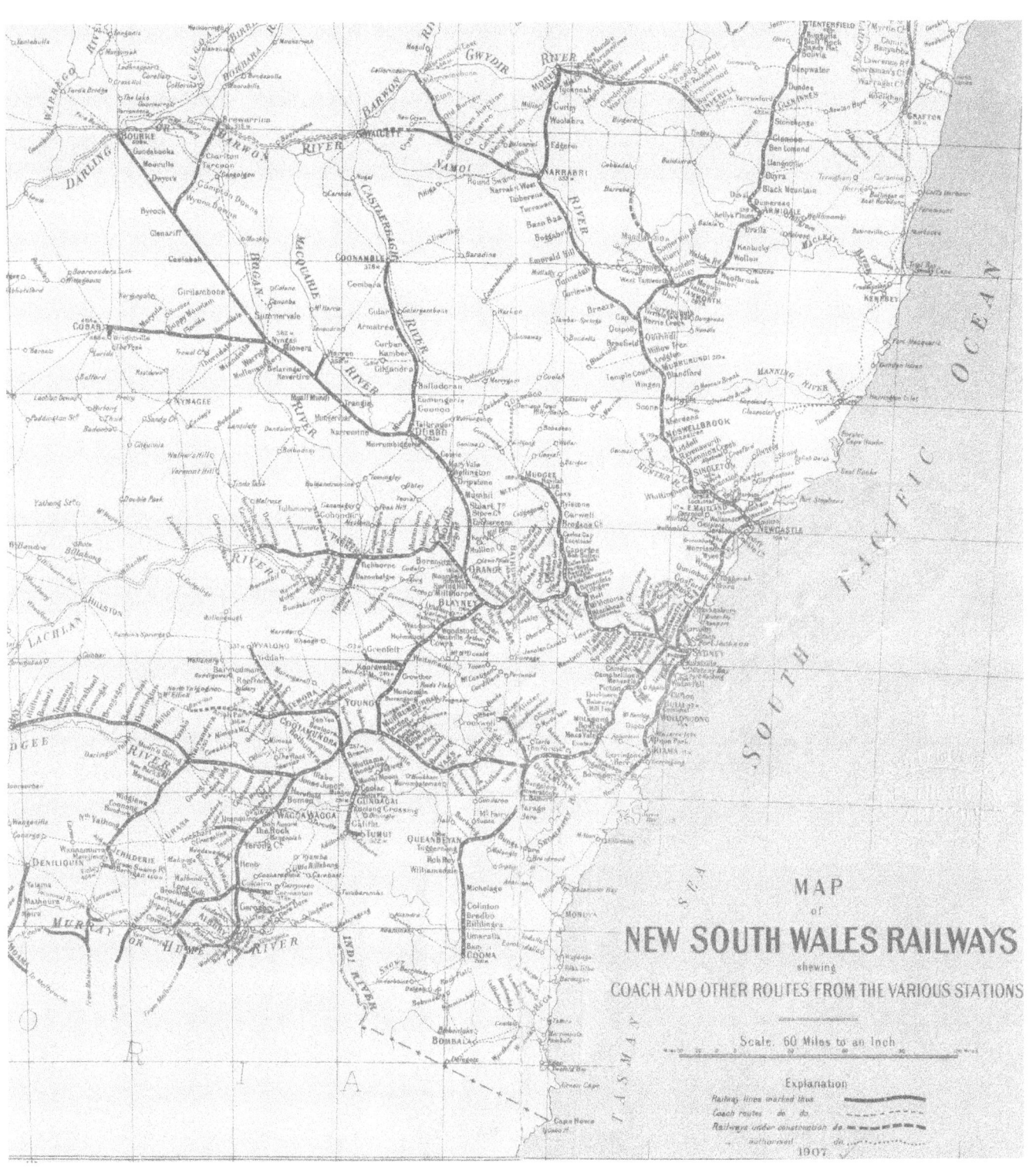

1907 Map of New South Wales railways [cartographic material] :
shewing coach and other routes from the various stations
– Courtesy National Library of Australia

The Rattle of the Coach

By Will Carter

Three times a week they listen
The bush folks far away
From city rush and rattle,
From all the busy battle,
Out where the sheep and cattle
Ever stray;
On Monday, Wednesday, Friday,
Impatient they approach,
And listen at the corner
For the rattle of the coach.

And thrice a week within them
The Bushmen's hearts are glad
When, oft, in gloomy weather,
When 'Blues' of evil feather,
Might send them altogether
Raving mad,
They wait around the corner,
And see the World approach,
And bring the Bush its message,
With the rattle of the coach.

1906 'The Rattle of the Coach' – The Sydney Mail and New South Wales Advertiser, 26 Dec 1906, p.1650
1931 'A Relic of the Past' – The World's News, 14 January 1931, p.9

News along the tracks, east of Bathurst

1862 – LOCAL AND GENERAL INTELLIGENCE "THE SYDNEY MONTHLY OVERLAND MAIL ... item of intelligence—the attractions of the Lachlan gold-field remain undiminished, this week's returns forming a large proportion of nearly 20,000 ounces that have been received at the Mint ... The Great Western Railway has been opened for traffic as far as South Creek, four miles from Penrith ... It is stated that Messrs. Cobb and Co., of Melbourne, are about to transfer their line of coaches to this colony, and to commence running between Sydney and the Lachlan diggings ... The arrival of the Northam, with the March mails, has been the most important event of the week ... In local matters there is little that calls for special reference, if we except the unpleasant fact that, as usual at this season of the year, coughs, colds, and catarrhal affections are greatly complained of ... Several school examinations have taken place during the week in the suburban districts. The results, in most instances, were considered very satisfactory ... The Corporation of Sydney are proceeding with commendable activity in the kerbing and repairing of the streets in the southern part of the city. Devonshire-street is now being kerbed and guttered to Elizabeth-street, an improvement which was much needed, especially in wet weather ... The vexed question as to the legality of the Sewerage rates, is about to be set at rest, by the decision of the Supreme Court ... The half-yearly meeting of the Bank of New South Wales was held on Thursday, when the profits for the half-year were declared at £83,605 17s. ...

A gold watch, valued at sixty guineas, was presented to Mr. W. J. O'Brien, proprietor of Tattersall's Hotel, on Monday night, as an acknowledgment of the kindness and hospitality shown by him to the All-England Eleven on the occasion of their visit to Sydney ... Great complaints have been made of the overcrowding of the Manly Beach steamers on Easter Monday ... The new lighthouse at the harbour of Port Stephens was illuminated for the first time on the 1st instant. The light is at an altitude of 126 feet, and is visible at a distance of seventeen miles in clear weather ... The unfortunate quarrel between the Newcastle miners and the Company has not yet been arranged. On Saturday last the men were on strike, having refused the terms which were offered, viz., an advance of three pence per ton for the top coal ... A telegram from the Lachlan states:—Some claims on Caledonian north lead have produced 20 oz. of gold to the dish ... The Indian mango has been grown successfully in the Botanic Gardens, Sydney. A specimen weighing one pound was cut from a tree last week ... The annual meeting of the Hunter River Vineyard Association was held on Wednesday afternoon, when some very superior specimens of wine were exhibited ... According to the last official report of Mr. Bruce, the cattle inspector, inoculation has been found very effectual in preventing the spread of the disease known as pleuro-pneumonia ... Cattle-stealing has been proceeding on an extensive scale at Liverpool Plains ... An ox, bred by Mr. Lee, of Bathurst, was killed at Parramatta recently, the carcase yielding a nett weight of 1308lbs., exclusive of the loose fat, weighing 115 lbs. The animal was entirely grass-fed ... The head and paw of a 'warrigal,' or native dog, were found lately in a state of petrification in a cave near Cooradigbee, in the Yass district, and are to be sent down to the Sydney Museum ...

A fine sample of beeswax, weighing 2½ tons, has been received in Sydney, from Liverpool, during the last few days. It is intended for shipment to England." (Local and General Intelligence, 18 Jun 1862, p.2)

1888 – SYDNEY NEWS "George Street on a Saturday night gathers the metropolitan multitude. Of late years several arcades have been made, running through from George Street to the streets behind. These covered ways are brilliantly illuminated at night, and thickly set with shops on either side, but the main street is the chief promenade. A visitor coming into the city from the railway station for the first time, might wonder what all the commotion is about ; but this is the normal condition of the street every Saturday night ... Anyone who wishes to study the physiognomy, the dress, the style and carriage of the people, may have his fill of opportunity here. From the Haymarket to King Street is one of continuous crowded promenade." (1888 Saturday Night in George Street, Sydney - Picturesque atlas of Australasia/edited by Andrew Garran, p.80)

1887 – PENRITH NEWS. "The Sydney Hunt Club had a meet on Saturday. A drag was laid through Hornseywood and the York Estate. The affair caused great excitement here. They afterwards went to Emu Plains and did some good work. There were one or two falls ... It is reported that the inquest on the 'Claremont ghost' will be further adjourned for more medical examination ... Suez mail per R.M.S. Ballaarat is due here on Monday next ... WHATEVER ELSE YOU FORGET. Remember to ask your grocer for Cadbury's Cocoa Essence—the purest and best cocoa, therefore the cheapest—4s." (Penrith News, 8 Aug 1887, p.5)

BUSHRANGERS "Mr. Richard Palmer ... was a driver for Cobb and Co ... Once he was bailed up by bushrangers, and on another occasion he was present when a bushranger was shot dead by a constable ... his coach was stuck up by bushrangers. Mr. Palmer had pulled up to water the horses; he had twelve women and two men aboard that day, and the usual mails. Captain Riley, who owned a station at Rylstone, was one of the male passengers, and the other was Mr. Bennett, Cobb and Co.'s manager at Wallerawang.

The coach was being driven along quietly when two rough-looking fellows, named Stapleton and Rose, jumped out of the bush and called out 'Bail up!' at the same time covering the driver and those on the box seat with revolvers. A third member of the gang, McGrath, was holding his mates' horses in the bush. Mr. Bennett was driving the coach at the time and he was ordered to drive on and follow the leader—Stapleton—and the other bushranger into the bush; Mr. Bennett hesitated, but Mr. Palmer, seeing the awkwardness of the position, took the reins and followed the bushrangers; he did not want to be shot, he explained. The coach followed the highwaymen about half a mile into the bush, and the passengers were then searched, the leader at the same time threatening that he would blow out the brains of anyone who attempted to move. The women were searched first—some of them had tried to hide their money in the curtains of the coach, but it fell out, and the bushrangers seized it. Whilst one robbed the passengers, the others had us covered with his revolver, says Mr. Palmer. As for me I never carried a pistol the whole time I was driving; it was no good trying that on, for if I had done so, and the bushrangers got wind of it, they would have shot me. For that reason few drivers carried arms ...

SAVED HIS WALLET. Captain Riley, who had just sold some property, had a wallet containing some hundreds of pounds. This he managed to slip, under cover of his overcoat, into Mr. Palmer's hand, and it was saved. The mail bags were rifled, and the driver told to move off. *Later, however,* says Mr. Palmer, *I drove the coach back to the spot and recovered what was left of the mails. The bushrangers had hoped to obtain gold, but as it happened, they just missed a big haul by being a day late.*" (Early Days, 24 Jul 1931, p.7)

1862 – LOCAL & GENERAL INTELLIGENCE "Numerous casualties have occurred during the week. On the evening of the 25th ultimo a fire broke out in the house of a person named Cobb, off Campbell-street. It was extinguished, however, before any material damage was done. On the same morning, a man named William Hayes, lately employed in the Railway Department, expired suddenly in the Cheshire Cheese public-house, Elizabeth-street. In the evening of the same day, a lad named Roddan, was drowned by falling out of a boat in Darling Harbour ... A fire broke out on Saturday evening in the house of a Mr. Anderson, in Clarence-street, but was fortunately extinguished before any material damage was done. It originated in the bed-curtains igniting while Mrs. Anderson was putting her children to bed. The bed and bedding and some few articles of furniture were destroyed ... an old and respected colonist, expired at his residence from concussion of the brain, caused by being thrown out of a vehicle on the previous Friday. A young woman, named Eliza Whitehead, died on Sunday evening under the influence of chloroform, administered for the purpose of performing an operation. The coroner's jury acquitted the doctor (Foulis) of all blame in connection with the occurrence ...

A boy named Hammond, aged twelve years, was recently found dead hanging to a tree near his parents' residence on the Derringullen Creek. He was suspended by a bridle with which he had been sent to catch and bring in a horse. It is supposed, from the position of the body, that he lost his life by accident while essaying some gymnastic feat ... On Easter Monday, a horse broke away with a dog-cart from the stables of Mr. B. Thomson, and, coming into collision with a gas post near the Union Bank, smashed the vehicle into fragments. A gentleman who was in the dogcart managed to jump out, and escaped with two or three severe bruises ... A young man named Joseph Smith, sixteen years of age, died on Sunday last, from the effects of a kick he received while attending on a race-horse at Randwick ... A man named John Daley had his leg broken on Tuesday evening, by the wheel of his dray passing over it. He was proceeding homewards, and fell from the shaft on which he was sitting ... A man named James Browning was killed at Quirindi on the 2nd instant, by his horse coming into collision with a tree, and on the following day Mr. Richard Chambers, postmaster of Wallabadah, met his death under exactly similar circumstances ... A man named John Lacey was found dead in the bush on Wednesday. He had gone out to fetch in wood, but not returning, search was instituted, and the body was found beside his cart, from which it is supposed he fell and broke his neck ... An infant named Cecilia Douglas, aged two years, died on Friday week, at Maitland, through eating off phosphorus from some wax matches she got hold of. Intelligence from different parts of the colony is to the effect that the late timely rains have been pretty general ...

Mr. James Farr, publican, of York-street, had his leg broken on Tuesday, by his horse coming into collision with a dray near the corner of King and Clarence streets ... Mr. George McKay, employed as time-keeper on the Southern extension line, was thrown from his horse on Thursday night week, and received a severe shaking. It is said that, while lying insensible from the fall, some rascal stole his watch from his pocket ... A young woman, named Mary Cronen, has been killed while on her way to Mudgee, by her horse running away, and dashing her against a tree ... A fine little boy, the son of Mr. Isaac Moss, of Brickfield-hill, died on Saturday from injuries received by being run over by a baker's cart ... Mr. George Small, of Kissing Point, had his leg broken recently through a horse running away with him, and coming into collision with another on which his brother was riding in an opposite direction. The bridle, it seems, broke, and the horse was thus rendered unmanageable ... A child, named Ellen Bowtall, died on Wednesday from injuries received by being knocked down by a horse on the Cook's River Road. The rider of the animal, a man named George Wallshin, was apprehended to await the decision of the coroner's jury ... Mr. George F. Codrington, M.D., late coroner for the Braidwood district, was killed on Saturday evening last, by his horse falling over some stumps in the roadway near Booth's public-house, on the way to Major's Creek. It would appear that the girths of the saddle broke in the fall, and that the unfortunate gentleman was thrown with great violence on his forehead. The accident was not discovered till the following morning" (The Sydney Monthly Overland Mail, 21 May 1862, p.5)

1862 – "DISTRESSING ACCIDENT.—On Saturday evening, Mr. Grovenor, of Cooma Cottage, met with an accident of a very distressing nature. He was watching a game of billiards that was being played at the Royal Hotel, when Mr. Milne who was engaged in it, not observing that Mr. Grovenor was behind him, passed the point of his cue over his shoulder, bringing it violently in contact with one of Mr. Grovenor's eyes. We understand that the injury is a very serious one, and the sufferer has experienced the most excruciating pain. Dr. O'Connor was sent for, and has afforded Mr. Grovenor all the relief that is in his power." (Local and General Intelligence, 18 Jun 1862, p.2)

1900 – "A SYDNEY-SIDE BLIZZARD. AN ANTARCTIC VISITATION. Some Phenomenal Experiences, Sydney, Saturday. The most remarkable weather known to the oldest inhabitant has been felt here during the last 24 hours. Rains whose force and volume have never been approached for more than 30 years have visited the region between the Blue Mountains and the coast, flooding the entire intervening country. The mountains and all the uplands are shrouded in snow drifts. Railway traffic is practically suspended. Trains are blocked in all directions by snow and water, while the telegraph lines have almost wholly collapsed. In the Bathurst, Orange, and Blayney districts, beyond the Blue Mountains, the snow storms have been so severe that all passenger trains have to be preceded by a pilot engine. From Rockley the strange fact is reported that an engine and brake van occupied eight hours in going 15 miles. At Bathurst passengers are sleeping in the trains, which are prevented from travelling by the snow, which in places is from 3 to 8ft. in depth." (Late Telegrams, 8 Jul 1900, p.1)

1870-1875 Part of a panorama of Sydney Harbour with Lavender Bay (centre), taken from Holtermann's house (American & Australasian Photography Company) – Courtesy Mitchell Library, State Library of New South Wales

1888 Saturday Night in George Street, Sydney – Picturesque atlas of Australasia/edited by Andrew Garran, p.80

1870-1875 Randwick Coach and Horses Hotel, corner Avoca & Albion Streets,
(American & Australasian Photography Company) – Courtesy State Library of New South Wales

1870-1875 James Leggatt, Smithfield (Butchery) branch, probably Home Rule (Cart says Gulgong)
(American & Australasian Photography Company) – Courtesy State Library of New South Wales

1870-1875 Road into Little Hartley (American & Australasian Photography Company)
— Courtesy State Library of New South Wales

1870-1875 Post Office, Hartley (American & Australasian Photography Company)
— Courtesy Library of New South Wales

Lithgow – Source unknown

1870-1875 Charles Pittitt (?), wheelwright and family, in front of bark hut workshop, Little Hartley (American & Australasian Photography Company) – Courtesy State Library of New South Wales

1870-1875 Flour mill and Kelk & Alford's store, Blayney
(American & Australasian Photography Company) – Courtesy State Library of New South Wales

George Rosser, Cobb and Company stagecoach in a country town;
There is a gas light in the background (Leonard R. Rosser) – Courtesy Museums Victoria

1870-1875 Carcoar Hotel and the Public School in Icely Street, Carcoar
(American & Australasian Photography Company) – Courtesy State Library of New South Wales

1900 Looking towards Holy Trinity, Kelso – Courtesy Bathurst District Historical Society

1870-1875 Ironbarks, N.S.W. (later named Stuart Town)
(American & Australasian Photography Company) – Courtesy State Library of New South Wales

1870-1875 Patrick Coyle's Clubhouse Hotel, incorporating the booking office and terminal
for Coyle's Bathurst Coach Service, later taken over by Cobb & Co., Hill End
(American & Australasian Photography Company) – Courtesy State Library of New South Wales

News along the tracks, west of Bathurst

1870 – LOCAL AND GENERAL INTELLIGENCE "The Australian ... Pastoral and Agricultural Prospects. THE fine weather which we had for a fortnight, at a time when the long continued rains had awakened apprehensions that seedtime would pass without an opportunity of getting the land ploughed for wheat, naturally leads us to the consideration of the present prospects of the country districts. In many a locality the question still is, Shall we go to the labour and expense of putting in another crop on the spot from which the floods have swept off all that was there? From the table-lands of Orange and New England there is the invitation to come up and take possession of land beyond the reach of floods ...

And at the same time the English newspapers abound in comments on the change of opinion which has begun to take place in the mother country in reference to Australian preserved meats. The practical conclusion to which all their facts point is not difficult to make out. The direction that enterprise should take is becoming more and more clear ... before long there will be a constantly increasing demand for Australian meat in the mother country and Europe ... A considerable portion of the land subject to floods, being of the richest kind of pasture offers the best facilities for fattening purposes and farmers on the river banks will do well to increase the number of their live stock, and to devote to pasture some of the land hitherto occupied by crops liable to be swept away by floods. The superabundant rain of the autumn, whatever losses they may have occasioned in some localities have made the grass all over the colony grow with a luxuriance almost unexampled ... There is every reason to expect that the spring will open under very favourable auspices ; and to hope that abundant crops may reward the labour of the farmers, and compensate, to a great extent, for the losses of the autumn. Without disparaging the suffering and anxiety to which so many of our fellow-colonists have been subjected, we may even now congratulate them on prospects which promise speedily to wrap the memory of all that is painful about the experience of the early part of the year in a grateful cloud of prosperity." (The Australian Town & Country Journal, 18 Jun 1870, p.8)

1892 – LACHLAN NEWS "The new Hay boiling-down establishment commences operations this week ... Mr. Wynberg, agent for the company, has been around here buying up sheep for the works, and he has succeeded in purchasing some thousands at from 1s. 6d. per head. Mr. P. Smith, another agent, is in the Hillston district doing the same, and has carte blanche to buy all the sheep he can. It is said the machinery, when in full working order, is capable of putting through 10,000 carcases per week. Some squatters and selectors here grumble at the prices offered, and refuse to sell; others are disposing of their fat stock freely ...

Mr. F. Small, the Hillston comic singer, was engaged breaking in a young cow, when the wild animal kicked him severely on the mouth. Results : Lips badly spoilt and several teeth, gone. It is to be hoped that the catastrophe may not interfere with his voice ... Last Wednesday was the hottest day of the season; the thermometer registered 100 deg. in the shade at noon.

At 3.30 p.m. the wind suddenly blew a hurricane from the south, bearing on its wings black clouds of dust that darkened the sun. The fine sand forced its way through every small crevice till floors and furniture were covered thickly with it, giving the housemaid a deal of extra work next morning. It has been beautifully cool ever since ... Although the Lachlan has been running high for months past (it has fallen 6ft.) yet a deal of fish of different sorts have been caught. One, a cod, was recently caught which weighed 35lb ... Upon the late hot forenoon a fire originated, through some unknown cause, in one of the paddocks at Narringa. Of course all haste was made to put it out but this could not be done till some 60 acres of grass had been burned, and had it not been for a road that baulked the fire it might have ran for miles ere it could have been got out. Fortunately, it was extinguished before the afternoon gale arose." (Later Lachlan News, 9 Dec 1892, p.17)

1862 – BUSHRANGERS "COACH ROBBERY AT THE LACHLAN.—One of Cobb and Co.'s passenger coaches was stuck-up last Monday morning, near Forbes. Many of the passengers were bound for New Zealand when they started, but they were relieved of their valuables, and bound to gum-trees by the robbers. There are two roads leading towards Bathurst— the mail coach took the other road, and escaped. It is supposed the robbers had designs upon the mail, as it contained all the letters, &c., for England. As yet no clue to the robbers has been found.—*Ovens Constitution*, Oct. 1." (The Civil War in America, 3 Oct 1862, p.7) While in 1863 "The coach that left Forbes yesterday was stuckup ... the Cassilis mailman was stopped, a few miles from Mudgee, and robbed of the mail ... robberies are fearfully prevalent ... Cobb and Co.'s coach was stopped by five men, armed and craped, and with the passengers, seventeen in number, robbed of £200 and other valuable property" (Advertising, 19 Aug 1863, p.5) and in 1864 "On Sunday morning last, before daylight, Mr. Barnes, the driver of Cobb and Co.'s coach, was fired at by two men, one on each side of the road, about nine miles from Forbes, because he did not stop when ordered. Happily the brigands were on foot, and could not follow the coach." On the same page "The correspondent of the Yass Courier writes that the man Ben Hall has organised a new gang, and that he is now at the head of not less than seven well mounted armed men ... The bushranger Vane, lately sentenced to fifteen years at Cockatoo, arrived in Sydney on the 22nd instant, having been brought down from Bathurst in charge of a strong party of police under the command of sub-inspector Roberts. A large number of persons assembled at the terminus for the purpose of seeing this unhappy young man, who has gained such an unenviable notoriety in the annals of crime ... A man named Christy Bowler, an accomplice of the bushranger Gilbert, is in the hands of the police." (The Sydney Monthly Overland Mail, 21 May 1864, p.5)

1864 – BUSHRANGERS "BEN HALL NEAR BATHURST. Considerable excitement was produced in town on Thursday, from a report that was circulated that Ben Hall and his companions had visited Fitzgerald's Mount, which is situate but some twelve miles from Bathurst. On inquiry, we found that the report was quite correct. It appears that one of Cobb and Co.'s stage coaches, on reaching Fitzgerald's Mount, on the way down from Carcoar to Bathurst, was stopped by three men, who proved to be Ben Hall, a very young man named Dunlevy, and an old man, who, it seems, has for some time accompanied Hall in his depredations.

The trio darted suddenly from the bush, and issued the usual order of a bush robber to 'pull up.' In seeming surprise, Hall accosted the driver with, *Halloa, Peter! I'm always sure to meet you when I stick up a coach.* He then asked for the mail bags. Peter replied, *I don't drive the mail now.* The rejoinder was, *Well, we can't let you go on ; you must come with us.* Coach and driver were then taken into the bush. Mr W. Flanagan, coming up on horseback, was detained as a matter of course, and also a Mr Lewis, who was on his way to Carcoar; and, from inquiries, the robbers learned that the mail would not be long before it came up.

On arriving at the spot, the mail was challenged and detained. The mail bags were cut open, the letters torn, and what money could be found taken. Whilst under guard in the bush the driver of the stage coach was asked by the old man bushranger what time it was. Peter put his hand to his watchpocket, but some one present mentioned the time of day, and the watch was suffered by its owner to remain where it was. The hoary-headed sinner observed this, and afterwards reminded the wary driver that he had neglected to tell him what time it was. Supposing, naturally, that the old man intended to have his watch, Peter took it from his pocket, and prepared to deliver it. Hall, however, interfered, and prevented the transfer. The robbers then took their departure, having observed every civility during their operations. The drivers came on to Bathurst, and gave information of the affair. Police were started out in pursuit; but up to the time of going to press, no news had arrived either of their route or their proceedings.—*Free Press*, July 9." (Ben Hall Near Bathurst, 16 Jul 1864, p.5)

1895 – "LADIES' COLUMN. USEFUL INFORMATION. Small doses of salt will check hemorrhage of the lungs or stomach ... To relieve hiccoughs at once take a lump of sugar saturated with vinegar. Toothache may be relieved by the application of cotton saturated with ammonia ... To Detect the Adulteration of Flour.—Take up a handful of it and squeeze it together. If it is pure it will appear in a lump, but if it is adulterated with chalk or Whiting it will crumble directly ... To prevent Mould on Ink.—Home made ink is apt to become mouldy if not very carefully prepared. This, may be prevented by adding a few drops of oil of cloves, to the ink before it is bottled ... To Protect Gilt Frames from Flies.—Pour a quart of boiling water on half-a-dozen large sliced onions. Cover it and let it stand for two days, then strain and brush the gilding with the liquor, and flies will not touch it ... The skin of a boiled egg is said to be the most efficacious remedy that can be applied to a boil. Peel it carefully, wet and apply to the part effected. It will draw off the matter and relieve the soreness in a few hours ... A writer in one of the medical journals says he has found the application of a strong solution of chromic acid, three or four times a day by means of a camel's hair pencil, to be the best and easiest method for removing warts. For a scald or burn, apply immediately pulveried charcoal and oil. Lamp oil will do, but linseed is better. Cover the surface with molasses, and then cover thickly with flour, is another good remedy, as is also to coat burn with mucilage ...

Weaning should never be sudden, but should be accomplished very gradually, one or two bottles of some suitable food being given once or twice daily instead of nursing. The change being gradual does far less injury to mother and child ... To Freshen Salt Butter.—Place the butter in a basin, and pour over it some freshly skimmed milk. Work it about with butter spoons until all the salt is out of it. Pour away the milk, wash once with water, make into pats, and serve ... Ink for Tracing Drawing.—Take half a teaspoonful of blue stone, ground to powder, and a quarter of a teaspoonful of brown sugar.

Mix together, then add sufficient water to make it of the consistency of ink. Use with a quill pen or a fine camel-hair brush ... To Restore Black Leather.—Mix a tablespoonful of brown sugar with the same quantity of gin, and then add gradually sufficient ivory black (powdered) to make it into a paste. Beat an egg well, and then add it to the paste. Stir together and then apply it to the leather ... To Toughen Glass.—New glass should never be used until treated so that it is rendered, as near as possible, unbreakable. Place tumblers, decanters, etc., in a large pan, pack them round with hay, and then with cold water. Place the pot on the fire and bring it slowly to boiling point. Then remove from the fire and stand it aside until cold ...

HOW TO KEEP IN GOOD HEALTH ... A sponge bath of cold or tepid water should be followed by friction with towel or hand ... Don't work, immediately after eating ... Be moderate in the use of all liquids of all seasons ... See that your sleeping rooms and living rooms are well ventilated, and that sewer gas does not enter them ... Brush your teeth at least twice a day, night and morning ... How do women manage to kill time asked some inconsequent and guileless man, and a woman promptly answered by giving a description of her own duties for one year ... Number of lunches put up, 1157 ; meals ordered, 963 ; desserts made, 172 ; lamps filled 328 ; rooms dusted 2269 ; children dressed, 786 times ; visits received, 897 ; visits paid, 167 ; books read, 88; stories read aloud, 234 ; games played, 329 ; church services attended, 125 ; articles mended, 1236 ; articles of clothing made, 120 ; letters written, 426 ; hours in music, 204 ; hours in Sunday school work, 208 ; sick days, 44 ; amusements attended, 10 ... put up 75 jars of pickles and preserves ; made seven trips to the dentist, polished silver ..." (Ladies' Column, 27 Apr 1895, p.3)

1913 – "MISCELANEOUS HINTS. Tar may be removed from the hands by rubbing with the outside of fresh orange or lemon peel and drying immediately. The volatile oils dissolve tar so that it can be rubbed off ... Cayenne pepper is excellent to rid cupboards of mice. The floor should be gone over carefully, and each hole stopped up with a piece of rag dipped in water and then in cayenne pepper ... Before arranging maidenhair fern in vases, soak it for two hours in cold water; then singe the ends of the stems with a match. Ferns thus treated will last three times as long, and keep quite green and fresh for several days ... To render dustbins perfectly sanitary burn a couple of newspapers or two or three handfulls of straw in them each time they are emptied. Let the flame rush out, and it will remove every trace of grease or damp from the iron, and render the dustbin as healthy as a new one, and quite free from any unpleasant smell ... Handkerchiefs and white clothes that have become yellow may be whitened in the following simple manner: After they have been washed in the usual way, lay them to soak overnight in clear water, into which cream of tartar has been put. A teaspoonful to a quart of water is the right proportion. When ironed they, will be as white as snow." (The Household, 29 Aug 1913, p.13)

1872 Cart bogged in what was originally a gold digging outside William Meares flooded Criterion Store, Hill End
(American & Australasian Photography Company) – Courtesy Mitchell Library, State Library of New South Wales

1870-1875 Robert Robinson, postmaster, in the door of Gulgong Post Office
(American & Australasian Photography Company) – Courtesy State Library of New South Wales

Cobb and Co. Coach – Courtesy of The Sovereign Hill Museums

1870-1875 Robert W. Heard, saddler, Gulgong
(American & Australasian Photography Company) – Courtesy State Library of New South Wales

Miner's tent-house, Hill End (American & Australasian Photography Company)
– Courtesy Mitchell Library, State Library of New South Wales

1870-1875 Family and bark hut house, Hill End (American & Australasian Photography Company)
– Courtesy State Library of New South Wales

ca. 1890 Bowenfels house (Lithgow Blast-Furnace Group) – Courtesy Flickr

1870-1875 Whitewashed cottage with corrugated iron roof
(American & Australasian Photography Company) – Courtesy State Library of New South Wales

1870-1875 Single storey Georgian-style house with corrugated iron roof, ironwork balustrade and formal symetrical paths and garden beds (American & Australasian Photography Company)
– Courtesy State Library of New South Wales

1870-1875 Mine head & group of gold miners, Gulgong area
(American & Australasian Photography Company) – Courtesy State Library of New South Wales

1870-1875 Family in front of Blunt's Commercial Hotel, including stabling and paddocks, Lucknow
(American & Australasian Photography Company) – Courtesy State Library of New South Wales

1870-1875 Gold mine, rig and bark hut, Lucknow
(American & Australasian Photography Company) – Courtesy State Library of New South Wales

1870-1875 Orange, Byng Street, Charles Stockwell, innkeeper, and his Commercial Hotel with Royal Mail coach outside
(American & Australasian Photography Company) – Courtesy Mitchell Library, State Library of New South Wales

1870-1875 Patrick Fahy's Steam Engine Hotel, Orange
(American & Australasian Photography Company) – Courtesy State Library of New South Wales

1870-1875 Post Office (and Courthouse), Wellington, N.S.W.
(American & Australasian Photography Company) – Courtesy State Library of New South Wales

ca. 1873 Orange, Summer Street, Dalton Bros, the Post Office, Coroner's and
County Clerk Offices – Courtesy National Library of Australia

News along the tracks, north of Bathurst

GOLDFIELDS "Turon River ... Memories of golden days ... pioneer miners ... urged by the lust for gold ... acres of ancient mining cuts" where Chinese "silently and systematically extracted the gold, and sent much of it home to China, often surreptitiously packed away in consignments of the bones of their deceased compatriots, in order to evade the Customs authorities." (Sofala, 1 Mar 1935, p.8)

1862 – BUSHRANGERS "(To Cobb and Co., Bathurst.) THE MUDGEE MAIL STOPPED. The down mail with four passengers was stuck up 5 miles from here, all the bags were opened and the cash taken. The cheques and drafts were left. Start the mail again in an hour." (Mudgee, 5 Nov 1862, p.2)

1870 – GOLDFIELDS "Parties of diggers are daily passing through Mudgee, on their way to try their fortunes at the new rush at Gulgong. There must be over 1000 people on the field now, and 'the cry is still, they come.' Most of the new arrivals have the appearance of being thoroughly practical diggers, who mean downright hard work." (Miscellaneous Items, 9 Jul 1870, p.4)

1872 – HILL END NEWS "Tenders will be received at this Office ... from persons willing to contract for Erection of a Post and Telegraph Station at Hill End ... Plan, specification, and form of Tender may be seen, and further particulars obtained, at the Colonial Architect's Office, Sydney, and at the Court House, Hill End. Henry Parkes." (Erection Of Post And Telegraph Office, at Hill End, 25 Jun 1872, p.1639)

1873 – GOLDFIELDS "Australian News in English newspapers. To the editor of The Herald. Sir—I enclose a paragraph cut from the Mining Journal published in London on November 30, 1872, which I think shows how little New South Wales is known in England. In it the Hill End gold mines and the tin discoveries are reported in such a manner as to imply that they are situated in the colony of Victoria ... It is almost a decisive proof of the necessity for the Government of the colony making some effort to disseminate accurate information as to our resources. I have the honour to be, Sir, your obedient servant, Jno. W. Creed ... *Melbourne, October Tin-Mining enterprise is steadying down. There are as yet few dividend-paying concerns; but the hope is great, the best paying mines being generally its measure. Transactions in gold shares have been less numerous, and limited almost to the Hill End cemeteries. The rich claims of Beyers and Holterman's, Carrol and Beard's, Hixson's, Creighton and Beard's, Paxton's, Rapps, and Krohmann's, all continue to be favourite ones. Tin companies have experienced a decline, so many obstacles occur to bringing the mineral to market. About 220 tons have reached this port during the month, and much has been sold by auction, at prices varying from £76 to £84 10s. per ton. Since I last wrote, some beautiful diamonds have been found at Bathurst, and a deposit of opal of rare excellence has been found near Rockhampton.*" (Australian News in English Newspapers, 13 Mar 1873, p.3)

1875 – SOFALA NEWS "Post and Telegraph Office Burnt Down. The Post and Telegraph Office, at Sofala, was burnt to the ground on Sunday night ; but the loss of property was not very great. Several other properties were damaged.

The fire originated in a Chinaman's store, next to the Post and Telegraph Office. Mr. Smith, the post and telegraph master, lost everything. An inquest is to be held." (Sofala Post and Telegraph Office Burnt Down, 22 Jun 1875, p.2)

1878 – "FATAL COACH ACCIDENT NEAR GULGONG. The Sydney Herald's correspondent thus writes :—*One of those unfortunate accidents which it is rarely my duty to record, occurred here on Sunday afternoon, the 8th instant, between this town and the Home Rule, resulting in the death of a young lady named Emily Jane M'Guire, who was en route to fill the office of teacher at the public school. It appears the mail, upon leaving Mudgee, had two lady passengers, the deceased (Miss M'Guire), Miss Vile, and a male passenger named J. A. Courtis, who sat upon the box with the driver. Arriving at the Home Rule, the owner and driver requested the above gentleman to hold the reins while he delivered the mails, and he consented to do so ; but while the driver was engaged, he left, having requested a Chinaman to hold the horses while he retired for a few minutes. The flapping of the curtains, it is supposed, startled the horses, and they went away at full speed. Miss Vile made a clean jump from the coach, and fortunately escaped, with the exception of a few braises. The horses at a rapid rate crossed the bridge, and, when within one mile, a young man named Allen, who was in pursuit, caught them up, calling to the young lady to sit still, but all to no purpose; she made a jump from the coach, falling in such a manner that her neck was broken. Every assistance was rendered, but of no avail; life had passed. The horses proceeded at their leisure, and were stopped about half-way between the two towns. On Monday, Mr W. J. Henningham, coroner, Mudgee, held an inquest upon the body, and the evidence of the witnesses was similar to the statement given above. The verdict of the jury was accidental death, caused by the jumping from a coach, but that great blame is attached to the driver in not having a competent person left in charge during his absence, and to Mr J. A. Courtis in leaving the coach, after proffering his services to attend till the drivers return.*" (Fatal coach accident near Gulgong, 18 Jun 1878, p.4)

1881 – LOCAL INTELLIGENCE & WEATHER "Gilgandra ... The oppressive heat during the past month has been without exception the hottest we have had for years. A mere existence—104 and 105 in the shade every day ... We are almost at a standstill in business matters at present ... MAILS—We get two a week from Sydney. The Coonambleites are applying for an extra one ... POST OFFICE.—Our post office is now managed by a most trustworthy officer, Mr. E. W. Austin, who performs the double duties of postmaster and groom for Cobb and Co., under the superintendence of Mr. John Barry. This gentleman, it will be remembered, did the Jehuship for His Grace the Duke of Manchester." (Gilgandra, 26 Feb 1881, p.38)

1900 – "SNOW IN MUDGEE ... now heavily falling in Mudgee ... Snow-balling has started, and it bids fair to be a repitition of the scene on June 2nd, 1896, the date of the record fall. Mount Victoria, Sunny Corner, and other places report heavy falls." (Snow in Mudgee, 6 Jul 1900, p.15)

1903 – LOCAL INTELLIGENCE & HEALTH "There are two cases of typhoid fever in the hospital ... A case of diphtheria, which occurred in Mudgee the other day, was undoubtedly due to a hidden defective drain ... After inquiry it has been decided not to move the Gulgamree post office from its present site at Mr. Rayner's ... When Pasha Barry was Cobb and Co.'s manager, they had £600 a year for Mudgee to Gilgandra mail. Today the contract price is £240 annually ... A wandering bull caused quite a commotion in Market-street on Wednesday afternoon. The inquisitive bovine was very anxious to get into the bar of Langbridge's Hotel." (Local Brevities, 8 Jan 1903, p.13)

1914 – LOCAL & GENERAL INTELLIGENCE "Mr. Barry, who lived in Mudgee for many years, where he managed the business of Messrs. Cobb and Co., when that firm ran coaches out as far as Walgett, is now comfortably settled down to end his days in Wellington. The old 'Pasha' never looked better.

He is spending a great amount of money in improving the Club House Hotel, Wellington, which he owns. 'Pasha' holds some of the best property in and around the western town. The hotel property includes some cottages and three or four acres of ground in the centre of the town. This old Mudgee pioneer has done well in land speculations. He bought 20 acres on the banks of the Macquarie River a little while ago, and could sell it at 200 or 300 per cent, profit now. He also purchased 117 acres of land close to the town, and for it has been offered two or three times the original purchase money. As he does not require cash, he is content to hold on to his land. Many Mudgee people will be glad to learn that the veteran is doing so well ...

Dr. Harris, the popular Gulgong medico, is working up a magnificent practice in the old mining township. The people of the town and district are getting into the habit of relying upon his undoubted skill and expert knowledge. The genial doctor comes from a 'medical' family. He has a couple of sisters and several brothers in the same profession, while his father was in his day one of the best known medical men in the Newcastle district ... Mr. J. W. Duesbury, for years a member in the firm of Messrs. T. H. Marks and Co., Mudgee, took a trip to New Zealand with the team of New South Wales cricketers. The old Mudgeeite is an intimate friend of Mr. M. A. Noble, who accompanied the team. Mr. Duesbury, being a heavy man, went in for a good deal of walking while in the Dominion, in order to keep down his condition. In his enthusiasm he must have overstrained himself, for when he returned to Sydney he had to seek medical advice, and the doctor told him that he must take things easily, owing to the fact that he had strained his heart slightly ... The boring plant that recently came to Mudgee (being the first of its kind to arrive here) was as attractive to young Mudgee as the average travelling circus. Kids swarmed round the plant like, bees, and pestered the life out of the men in charge with questions as to what it was, and where it was going ... Mr. E. L. Gaffney, who is school teacher at Mount Lambie, via Rydal, writes to tell us that they have been having a good deal of snow over that way lately. Lambie is only seven miles from the misnamed Sunny Corner. Several falls have been experienced during the past month, the last being five or six inches deep" (Local Brevities, 23 Jul 1914, p.29)

1926 – "EVENTS TO COME ... BAZAAR AND FETE AT DUNEDOO A grand bazaar and fete will be held in Lyceum Hall, Dunedoo, on February 9, 10, and 11, 1927. Proceeds in aid of R.C. Church; RACES AT COLLAROY The Collaroy Race Club will hold a race meeting on January 3, 1927; DANCE AT PYRAMUL A dance in aid of the local cricket club will be held in the Pyramul Hall, on Boxing Night, (Monday) December 27; RACES AT COOLAH The Colah Race Club will hold a meeting on January 26, (Anniversary Day.) £50 prize money. Full particulars on application to sec. E. R. Weaver; SOCIAL AT PIPECLAY A social in aid of Buckaroo School equipment fund will be held in the Pipeclay School of Arts on Saturday January 1st; SOCIAL AT COBBORA A social will be held on Boxing night, (Monday Dec. 27,) at Cobbora, in aid of the local cricket club; TROTTING MEETING AT MUDGEE The Mudgee Trotting Club will hold a meeting on Saturday, January 1, 1927. Prize money totals £150 and the programme consists of six events; SOCIAL AT COBBORA A social will be held in the Cobbora Hall on Friday January 21, in aid of the Dunedoo Convent; GULGONG SHOW The annual Gulgong Show will be held on Tuesday and Wednesday, March 8 and 9; MARKET DAY, DANCE AND SPORTS AT ULAN A Market Day and sports will be held at Ulan on New Year's Day.

A plain and fancy dress social at night. Proceeds in aid of Church of England; TENNIS TOURNAMENT AT MUDGEE A grand tennis tournament will be held at Mudgee, Victoria Park courts on January 1, and 3, 1927. Entries close on Dec. 24, with Mr. H. Barton, hon. sec. Mudgee; MUDGEE SHOW The next annual Mudgee Show will be held on Thursday, Friday and Saturday March, 3, 4, and 5; BICYCLE SPORTS Bill Bamford is promoting another day's bicycle sports to be held in the Victoria Park, Mudgee, on Saturday Jan. 15. The Mt. Frome cup handicap, the prize for which is a cup valued at £5/5 presented by the Mt. Frome lime workers will be the chief event. A good afternoon's sport is promised. Programmes on application, from Bill Bamford, Mudgee; GRAND BALL AT ELONG A grand ball will be held at Elong in the Pioneer Hall on New Year's Eve (Dec. 31) in aid of the Cancer Research Fund; SPORTS AT LEADVILLE A day's sports will be held at Leadville on Saturday January 1. Programme and particulars obtainable from Mr. A. Robertson, Secretary; BALL AND RACES AT HILL END The Hill End Race Club will hold a meeting on Friday Decem. 31., (New Year's Eve.) The programme consists of 8 events and £28/10 prize money. Entries close with the secretary (Mr. A. Ross) on day of races. Grand Ball will be held in the Royal Hall at night; BALL AND SPOILS AT CRABOON Sports will be held at Craboon on Monday January 3, 1927. A ball will be held at night. T. H. Clarke, Craboon P.O. is the hon. sec.; WALLERAWANG RACES The Wallerawang Race Club will hold a meeting on Wednesday January 26. Entries close with the Sec. (J. Heel) on Monday January 17. 'Phone 24; RACES AT BARADINE The Baradine Turf Club will hold a race meeting on Friday Dec. 31, and Saturday January 1. 1927. Full particulars on application to the Sec. Mr. T. C. Masman. 'Phone 18 Baradine; RACES AT CASSILIS The Cassilis Race Club will hold a race meeting on Decem. 27; SOCIAL AT PIPECLAY A social will be held at Pipeclay School of Arts on Monday Dec 27. (Boxing Night) in aid of the institution; HOGMANAY AT DUNEDOO Hogmanay will be celebrated in the Lyceum Hall, Dunedoo, on New Year's Eve in aid of the Dunedoo Presbyterian. Church building fund; SOCIAL AT LUE A grand social in aid of the Church of England building fund will be held in the Lue Hall, on Dec. 26. (Boxing night.) Fordham's jazz band; SOCIAL AT HOME RULE A social will be held at the Home Rule Hall, on Monday, Dec. 27, (Boxing Night,) proceeds in aid of the Home Rule Cricket Club; SOCIAL AT APPLETREE FLAT A social will be held in the Appletree Flat Assembly Hall, on Boxing night, Dec. 27. Proceeds in aid of the institution; DANCE AND SPORTS AT PYRAMUl A sports meeting will be held at Pyramul, on the sports ground on January 26, (Anniversary Day.) Pedestrian races for girls and boys, throwing at wicket, etc. A dance will be field at night; SPORTS AT GULGONG A day's sports will be held at Gulgong, under the auspices of the Athletic Club, on January 26th (Anniversary Day). The programme consists of cycling, pedestrian, motor car, and miscellaneous events. Entries close with the secretary (H. Evans) on January 16; RACES AT COONABARABRAN The Annual Cup Meeting, of the Coonabarabran Jockey Club, will be held at Coonabarabran on Tuesday and Wednesday January 11 and 12. The prize money totals £264. Nominations close with the secretary Mr. W. E. Oakes. 'Phone 95." (Events to come, 23 Dec 1926, p.17)

1872 Winter snow storm, Clarke Street, looking south from Tambaroora Road, Hill End, New South Wales (Charles Bayliss 1850-1897) – Courtesy National Library of Australia

1870-1875 Mark Mathews, wheelwright and carriage maker, Mayne Street (next to the Lachlan Brewery), Gulgong (American & Australasian Photography Company) – Courtesy Mitchell Library, State Library of New South Wales

1870-1875 Looking east on Mayne Street along the southern side toward Medley Street, Gulgong
(American & Australasian Photography Company) – Courtesy State Library of New South Wales

John Bax, Mudgee Cobb & Co. - Source unknown

1870-1875 Daniel Pope's Bakery, Gulgong (American & Australasian Photography Company)
– Courtesy Mitchell Library, State Library of New South Wales

1870-1875 Detectives Powell & Hannan and their office, Gulgong
(American & Australasian Photography Company) – Courtesy State Library of New South Wales

1870-1875 Giovanni Piesenti's Cafe de France, (later 'Colonial Wines'), Gulgong
(American & Australasian Photography Company) – Courtesy State Library of New South Wales

1870-1875 Alexander Cameron and his three motherless children outside his Crystal Fountain (drinks store),
(also the office of the Tambaroora, Mudgee & Gulgong Mining & Prospecting Co. and a branch of the Argus newspaper),
Gulgong (American & Australasian Photography Company) – Courtesy Mitchell Library, State Library of New South Wales

1870-1875 Clarke Street scene, Hill End, looking north from George Hodgson's iron,
timber & wine merchant business, with Merlin's photographic laboratory cart in the background
(American & Australasian Photography Company) – Courtesy State Library of New South Wales

1870-1875 Road making and ditch digging outside Monie's Hill End Hotel,
Curtain's Barber Shop and Harris' Duke of Cornwall Hotel, Hill End
(American & Australasian Photography Company) – Courtesy State Library of New South Wales

MUDGEE.

For Auction Sale by
HARDIE & GORMAN

IN CONJUNCTION WITH Messrs CROSSING AND COX,

on the GROUND MARKET St.,
OPPOSITE ROYAL HOTEL, AT MUDGEE,

ON THURSDAY MAY 15TH 1890.
AT 12 O'CLOCK NOON

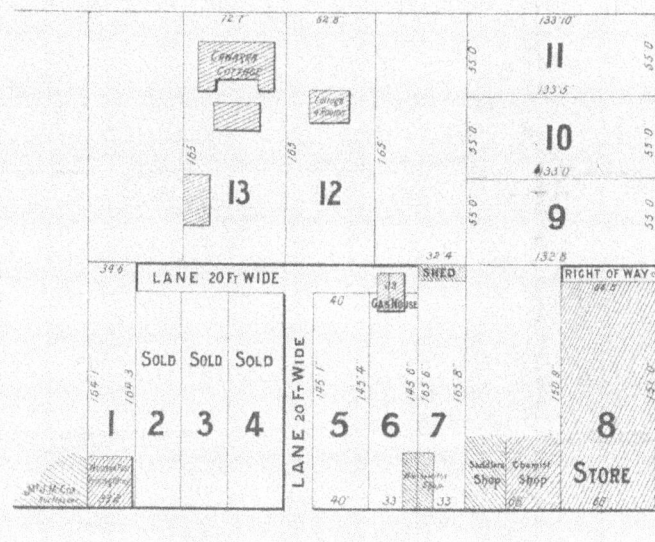

— TERMS OF SALE —
10 PER CENT. DEPOSIT, 10 PER CENT.
IN 3, 6, 9, 12, 15, 18, 21, 24, 27, 30 MONTHS FROM DAY OF SALE
BY PROMISSORY NOTES, WITH 6 PER CENT INTEREST.

1890 Mudgee : for auction sale/by Hardie & Gorman, in conjunction with Messrs. Crossing and Cox, on the ground Market St., opposite Royal Hotel at Mudgee – John Sands, Sydney, Lith.

News along the tracks, south of Bathurst

1863 — "A JEREMY DIDDLER.. Within the last few weeks, Goulburn has been honoured by a visit from a gentleman of the name of Edward Francis Clarke, who gave himself out as a nephew of Mr. William Clarke, of the well-known firm of William Clarke and Sons, gold brokers, Melbourne. Mr. Clarke took up his quarters at the Commercial Hotel, and stayed there for several weeks. On Saturday last, however, he announced his intention to leave for Sydney, and asked for his account, which was handed to him accordingly to the tune of about £21. Not having any loose chance, some of which he said he might require, he paid the bill with a cheque on the Bank of New South Wales for £25, and received about £4 in change. Having settled this matter to the satisfaction of himself and his landlord, he proceeded to Cobb and Co.'s office to book his place to Sydney. The fare £3, he paid by another cheque on the Bank of New South Wales, Goulburn, for £6, receiving £3 in change from Mr. Robertson, the agent. On Sunday morning he left by the coach, deeply regretted by the numerous circle of acquaintances be had formed at the Commercial. Monday being the Anniversary Day, was a bank holiday, and of course the bank was closed. On its reopening on Tuesday, however, the cheques were duly presented, but were met, not with funds, but by the statement that the drawer had no account at the bank, nor ever had. The result was that both the landlord of the Commercial and Mr. Robertson, found that they had been thoroughly duped. Information was at once given to the police, and a warrant was immediately issues for Clarke's apprehension. We believe, however, that as yet he has not been taken into custody, although there is good reason to conclude that he has not succeeded in leaving the colony.—*Goulburn Chronicle*. January 31." (Moruya Regatta, 3 Feb 1863, p.2)

1870 — FLOODING RAINS "Mr. John Horton, of Goulburn, who claims to be the oldest surviving driver of Cobb and Co,s coaches, gives some of his recolections ... After making a trip from Tarcutta, Mr. Horton delivered his mail at Gundagai and remained in the town for two hours. While there he met a dealer who had just returned from a trip to Young, where he had disposed of a large quantity of bacon and cheese. The dealer was on his way home to Tumut, and although advised against the undertaking, the Tumut man determinedly set out to take his horse and cart across the flooded creek. The horse had not gone far when it was caught in the current, a large crowd of people watching the animals plight from the banks of the creek. First to act was Mr. Arthur Rankin, then manager of a Gundagai bank, who subsequently settled at Lockyersleigh, near Goulburn. He took a boat into the stream and secured a hold on the reins, but was unsuccesful in his efforts to get the horse to the bank. Horse and cart were swept downstream for a distance of about 150 yards, both ultimately disappearing in the flood waters.

The following day a horseman made two successful crossings of the creek, and was essaying his third trip when the horse was washed off its feet by the curent. When the flood waters had receded some days later the missing horseman and his mount, dealer's horse and cart, and Mr. Horton's horse (mentioned in the first article) were found together against the root of a tree 300 yards down the creek.

Resuming his coach run when the weather had cleared Mr. Horton had to collect about half a ton, of mail which had been held up at the South Gundagai Post Office. Two weeks later brought an illness, which resulted in him retiring from the service of Sheehan and Garry, his place being taken by an old Sydney driver named Billy Payne, who at that time was residing in Gundagai.

FIFTY MILES A DAY On recovering from his illness Mr. Horton accepted a position as driver for a man named Potter, who had the mail contract between Adelong and Tumut, this necessitating a 50 miles trip daily in daylight. After holding this job for three months he began work for Mr. James Roberts, being engaged in driving from Yass to Young. The roads on this section were in appaling condition, Mr. Horton recalling an instance where a loaded team took a week to travel a mile. As the condition of the roads prevented him from running to schedule, Mr. Horton soon tired of his position and returned to Goulburn. Within a fortnight of his return he was offered a job by Mr. Colin Robertson, manager of Cobb and Co.'s Goulburn branch, and gladly accepted, taking over the Goulburn-Yass run in succession to Fred Gilliam, a brother of George Giliam of Ashton's circus fame, who was compelled to resign from Cobb and Co. owing to ill health. Mr. Horton commenced driving with Johnny Dailey, at that time one of the State's veteran coach drivers. That was in 1870, the winter proving to be one of the wettest sesons experienced for years. Lake George was almost overflowing and the coaches did not have a dry trip for almost five months.

One trip from Goulburn to within three miles of Yass occupied 17 hours, the fact that O'Brien's Bridge was completely under water preventing the coach from reaching Yass that night. The passengers—three police constables, and a lady on her way to Albury—were compelled to spend the night at a hotel on the Goulburn side of the bridge. The bridge presented a sorry spectacle the following morning, the flood waters having washed away about 6ft. of the approach on the Yass side, and the decking was buried, beneath tons of debris. The arrival of a two-seater buggy enabled the lady passenger, with the mails and luggage to be transferred across the river. One of the constables walked into Yass and returned with the down mail for Sydney and Mr. Hurley, then M.P. for Campbelltown. The iron bridge at Yass had been washed off its piers and lay at the bottom of the river.

MADE THE GRADE With one passenger aboard, the coach commenced its return trip to Goulburn, but on arrival at Gunning it was found that the creek had flooded and the water reached along the main street to as far as the Telegraph Hotel. Asked if he would be willing to make the trip through the water, Mr. Hurley replied that he was agreeable if Mr. Horton considered the undertaking would not incur any great risk. The sergeant of police issued a warning against attempting a crossing, but was told that the mail had to be in Goulburn by 10.15 a.m., and the journey, which was watched by a large crowd of people was commenced. There were four good horses in the team, the two leaders being about 16 hands high. The coach succeeded in getting through and a cheer went up from the spectators, Mr. Horton reached Goulburn only a quarter of an hour behind schedule, Mr. Hurley complimenting Mr. Robertson, the coach proprietor, on Mr. Horton's performance." (Cobb and Co. Coachman, 21 Nov 1932, p.4)

1895 – "QUEANBEYAN ... ELECTION. A correspondent wires :—Mr. Walter Harcourt Palmer, the freetrade and labour candidate, addressed the electors yesterday at Canberra and Gininderra, and at each place had splendid receptions. His chances of election are considered certain by a great number ... SYDNEY ... POLITICAL. A large number of electors of the King Division, including many members of the federal party, met this morning and decided to invite Sir Henry Parkes to contest the King Division, guaranteeing all expenses. They have a requisition signed by 600 electors to be presented to Sir Henry this afternoon. The probability of this contest is causing considerable stir in electioneering circles ... SHEEP SALES. At the sheep sales today biddings were brisk and prices much better ... LONDON PUNISHING A THIEF. A man who had robbed a lady of her purse in the Strand was captured by several people, dragged to the Thames embankment, ducked in the river, and then handed over to the police." (Latest Intelligence, 11 Jul 1895, p.3)

1900 – "THE LACHLAN IN FLOOD. Alarming reports have been received from Forbes, where the Lachlan River is raging like a torrent. Two flood-boats have been sent to Goulburn to assist the people flooded out by the rising of the Mulwarrie River. After the stream at the latter place had resumed ordinary dimensions, the dead bodies of horses, cattle, pigs, poultry, and the body of a man named George Tyler White, 81 years of age, were found. White had been living an isolated life in a solitary hut. To escape the rising flood he had climbed to the top of a high wall, on which he had placed a signal light. The light was seen, but before rescue could reach him, the cold overcame him and he fell into the flood below and perished. ON THE SOUTH COAST. Reports from Moruya state that heavy floods are raging, in consequence of seven inches of rain having fallen. During last night a bridge over the stream near the town was washed away, and other casualties are reported. At Yass 63 people are taking shelter in the Church of England school, and others in the court house. At another place a whole family took refuge in a tall gum tree. A boat manned with rescuers came very near capsizing among the water-buried branches of submerged trees. The whole family of nine were ultimately saved, but they are now in a very pitiable condition, owing to the severity of their exposure. PLAGUE SUBSIDING AT SYDNEY. Sydney, Saturday. No fresh cases of bubonic plague have been reported since Sunday." (Late Telegrams, 8 Jul 1900, p.1)

1906 – ADELONG WEDDING BELLS "A wedding of some interest was celebrated in the Methodist Church, at Adelong, on Thursday, April 5th, the contracting parties being Mr. Edward Thompson, of this town, and Miss C. J. Taylor (Jennie), eldest daughter of the late Mr. Hezekiah Taylor (Mine Manager, of Mount Boppy), and Mrs. Taylor, of Cornishtown. The Rev. W. A. Burns performed the ceremony. The church was beautifully decorated for the occasion by the ladies of the congregation. The bride, who was given away by her brother, Mr. Tom Taylor, wore a handsome gown of white voile trimmed with kiltings, Brussels lace, and rosettes of white ribbon, and the customary wreath and veil, and she carried a shower boquet. She also wore a gold curb chain and padlock bangle, the gift of the bridegroom. The bridesmaids were three sisters of the bride— Misses Effie, Lena and Marjorie Taylor ... The bridesmaids carried boquets tied with pale green ribbon streamers and wore gold brooches the gift of the bridegroom. Mr. A. V. Bellamy was 'best man.' The 'Wedding March' was beautifully played by Miss Ayres (organ) and Miss Young (violin). The wedding breakfast was served at Tremayne Cottage, the residence of the bride's mother, after which the party drove to Mount Horeb to witness the departure of the happy couple for Sydney, where the honeymoon will be spent. Rice and confetti were in joyful evidence ... The bride was the recipient of many handsome wedding presents ... On Tuesday, 3rd April, the members of the congregation gave Miss Taylor a kitchen tea, at which she received many useful articles for use in her new home ... Rev. W. A. Burns (minister), Mr. White (Superintendent) and Mr. Trudgeon (on behalf of the choir) spoke in eulogislic terms of Miss Taylor's many good qualities, and wished, her all happiness in the new life upon which she was entering. Mr. Tom Taylor, on behalf of his sister, thanked them for their kindness and good wishes. Miss Taylor had been for many years employed by Mr. A. E. Merryfull, and her aptitude for the business won for her high enconiums. She had filled the role of chief grocer in the store for a long time, and resigned from the position at the end of March to enter the bonds of matrimony. We wish the happy couple all joy, happiness, and prosperity in their future career in life." (Adelong, 13 Apr 1906, p.2)

1908 – "ACCIDENT TO A SLUICER. (From our own Correspondent.) A serious accident occurred yesterday to a miner named James Atkins, working on Francis' sluicing claim, at The Sounding Rock, on the Abercrombie River. He was working in an open cutting when about 15 cwt of dirt fell upon him. He was badly cut and bruised about the body, but no bones were broken. A doctor from Carcoar attended the sufferer last evening, and holds out every hope for his recovery. Some years ago Tom Atkins, brother of the injured man, was killed by a fall of earth while working in another cutting close to where the accident happened, and he himself had only just fully recovered from a serious crushing, which at one time gave the doctor grave doubts of recovery." (Trunkey, 27 May 1908, p.4)

1932 – QUEANBEYAN NEWS "With the death of Mr. John James Breen at the residence of his only daughter Mrs. Tuttle, at Enmore, at the age of 82 a romantic link with the past has been severed. He was born in Queanbeyan, and spent his life in the district until he moved to Sydney. He was one of the last of the surviving drivers of Cobb and Co.'s coaches, with the run of the mail between Goulburn and Cooma. In attempting to cross the Molonglo River while in flood he was washed down stream, and lost both coach and horses and with great difficulty saved his own life. He served as an alderman in the municipal council ... TEST TEAM OF 1881. Colonel Alfred Spain has had in his posession for more than half a century a linen handkerchief upon which are printed photographs of the Australian Test Team of 1881. Those figuring in the central group are—W L Murdoch, T Horan, F Allan, G H Balley, J Conway, A Bannerman, C Bannerman, J Blackham, F R Spofforth, D W Gregory, W Midwinter, T W Garrett, and H F Bovie. In the corners of the handkerchief appear the separate photographs of Spofforth, Blackham, Murdoch, and C. Bannerman." (A Cobb and Co. Coachdriver, 6 Dec 1932, p.6)

1870-1875 Arthur Street, Trunkey, looking north towards Bathurst
(American & Australasian Photography Company) – Courtesy State Library of New South Wales

1870-1875 Looking south along Arthur Street, Trunkey from the Commercial Hotel
(American & Australasian Photography Company) – Courtesy State Library of New South Wales

ca. 1871 Goulburn (American & Australasian Photography Company) –
Courtesy Mitchell Library, State Library of New South Wales

1870-1875 Market Street, Goulburn, looking from Dickson's Commercial Hotel towards
Auburn Street – Courtesy State Library of New South Wales

1880-1889 The Temora gold field, the miners' Sunday afternoon – Courtesy National Library of Australia

Holtermann shooting party camp in bush (American & Australasian Photography Company) – Courtesy Mitchell Library, State Library of New South Wales

ca. 1908 T. J. Williamson and his Soda cart, Yass, New South Wales – Courtesy National Library of Australia

Shearers, near Harden (Olliver & Forsyth) – Courtesy National Library of Australia

Chapter Eight

Abercrombie House, Bathurst N.S.W.

It began with the Stewarts

"The following lines written by Rev. John Graham, of Craven Chapel, London, on visiting the monument of General Stewart, are almost equally applicable to the general's son, who is buried at the same picturesque spot." (Story of the Bathurst Pioneers, 25 Nov 1922, p.13)

Where shall we bury father?" His sons and daughters said.
Shall, we take him to old Scotland To sleep with kindred dead?

No! but on yonder hill top. Enshrined, his dust should lie
'Neath the sky he loved to gaze on, The blue Australian sky.

From that brow, sublime and silent, He would oft the beauties trace
Of mountain, vale, and river; Let it be his resting place.

Upon that lofty hill top The obelisk shall rise,
And from the far Blue Mountains Shall meet the traveller's eyes.

While the eagle haunts that hill top, And silence broods around,
On the summit sleeps the pilgrim Till the final trumpet sounds.

Abercrombie House, owned by the Morgan Family – Courtesy Christopher Morgan

The Morgan Family

2023 "ABERCROMBIE HOUSE ... an Australian heritage treasure in Bathurst, New South Wales ... home of the Morgan Family for more than half a century ... the Cobb and Co. coaches travelled on the west and southwest roads that went straight through the middle of this property in the roaring days!" (2023 Christopher Morgan, Abercrombie House)

"The property, as established by Major-General William Stewart in the 1820s, took up the entire Parish of Mount Pleasant which was 15,000 acres running up against the western edge of the City of Bathurst. The Ophir Road, The Mid Western Highway and the Mitchell Highway all went through the property—Cobb & Co. coaches were running along all of those roads. At the centre was the village of Evans Plains on the Mid Western Highway to Blayney, which had several inns and coaching stops. There was also a small village called Dunkeld on the Mitchell Highway at the point where the road begins its climb up from the Bathurst Plains, which had been a bullock wagon resting place since the earliest years of the Bathurst settlement, and which had an inn through much of the 19th century. The south west corner of the Mount Pleasant Estate property ran south almost to Fitzgerald's Valley and the house 'Bathampton', which is where Rutherford's family moved to from 'Hereford'. 'Hereford' and 'Bathampton' were both constructed by the builder David Jones and his brother the carpenter William Ellis Jones—who also built Abercrombie House (at that time known as The Mount/Stewarts Mount/Mount Pleasant).

Currently, a Cobb and Co. coach (on loan from Mr. Ray Green) has been placed into the carriage garage on the southern side of the 1876 basalt Stables Building. The stables are currently being restored to include an interpretive display, along with period items, tack and harness." (2023 Christopher Morgan, Abercrombie House)

The Stewart Family from Strath, Caithness, Scotland

"STEWARTS AND THEIR ANCESTORS ... It may not be generally known that the Bathurst Stewarts have the same ancestor as the present King of England. Her Majesty, Queen Victoria, who died in 1901, was the twenty-second in descent from Alan, First High Steward of Scotland, who died in 1177, and from whom are descended a branch of the family known as the Stewarts of Appin, to which branch the subjects of the present sketch belong. Major-General William Stewart, who died in 1854, was also twenty-second in descent from the said Alan." (Story of the Bathurst Pioneers, 18 Nov 1922, p.13)

"MAJOR-GENERAL WILLIAM STEWART, MOUNT PLEASANT, BATHURST AND BENDICK MURRULL ... was born in the Highlands of Scotland where his family held an estate in Caithness, in 1769. Donald Stewart, his grandfather, was 'out' in the 'Forty Five' fighting for Prince Charles Edward ('Bonnie Prince Charlie' of Highland hearts and song). William Stewart entered the army as Ensign, by purchase, in the 101st Regiment, 10 March 1794, and his promotions bear date as follows: *Lieutenant (1795), Captain (1799), Major (1805), Lieutenant-Colonel (1801), Colonel (1819), Major-General (1830)* ... Colonel Stewart and his Regiment served as portion of the Army of Occupation, in France, until the Allied troops evacuated it in 1818. [The foreign services of this officer commenced in the West Indies, under General Sir Ralph Abercromby, in March, 1796. (Memoir of the Late Major-General Stewart, 15 Apr 1854, p.2)] He received the Gold medal for Albuera. The 3rd Regiment was ordered to New South Wales, and arrived here in August 1823 ... From the 1st December, 1825, upon the departure of Governor Brisbane, to the 18th December, 1825, upon the arrival of Governor R. Darling, [Colonel Stewart] performed the duties of Acting Governor of the Colony ... in 1826, embodied a mounted police troop ... and a member of the Land Board ...

About this time the British Government were making great reductions in the strength of the Army and Navy, and found it difficult to provide adequate compensation to reduced officers and men for the services ... It was therefore decided by Government that they should receive 'free' grants of land in these new territories, in sufficient quantity to reward them according their rank, length of service, and subject to residence upon them ...

Amongst those who had been promised first choice in 1827 was Colonel Stewart ... he selected 3,200 acres on Evan's Plains Creek, in the western side of the Parish of Mount Pleasant, County of Bathurst, as his primary grant, which was set apart for him. In addition he was allowed to lease a considerable area surrounding his grant, and subsequently purchased it at 5/- and 12/ per acre. This was the first large land grant made on that side of the river, upon which there was not then a single private habitation erected, except a Government stockyard on Princess Charlott's Creek, west of Mt. Pleasant, and another on Queen Charlott's Vale Creek, under the Bald Hill ... in 1832, [Stewart] retired on half-pay, after 38 years meritorious service in four quarters of the globe." (Early Settlement and Settlers of Cowra, 22 Apr 1932, p.3)

1833 'STRATH' RESIDENCE–MAJOR-GENERAL WILLIAM STEWART

"He returned to New South Wales, and in the same year was joined by his family ... took up his residence on his Mt. Pleasant grant at Bathurst, when he built a substantial house, since known as 'Strath' ... the occupant of 'Dananbilla,' 16,000 acres; 'Bendick Murrell,' 12,000 acres, on Bendick Creek; and 'Crowther,' 14,360 acres, on Crowther Creek. Major-General Stewart died at his residence, 'Mount Pleasant,' Bathurst, on 8 April 1854, aged 85 years. He was buried on an elevated knoll, or hill, in the centre of his estate. A solid granite obelisk, rising to a considerable height, and to be seen from a long distance, has been erected by members of his family to mark his resting place, bearing a suitable inscription. He left a family of one son [James H. Stewart] and three daughters." (Early Settlement and Settlers of Cowra, 22 Apr 1932, p.3)

'STRATH' RESIDENCE–THE GHOST

"Everyone has heard of the 'Strath Ghost.' It is as well-known as the 'Spectre of Tappington,' or 'Fisher's Ghost' of Campbelltown. Of course, like all other folk lore traditions, it has different versions, but the indisputable basic fact remains that scores of people are convinced that there is at 'Strath', a mysterious apparition that no one has ever yet been able to account for or explain. 'Strath,' it may be mentioned, is the name of the original home of the late General William Stewart. It was built by him on the banks of the Macquarie River, some five miles from Bathurst, about a hundred years ago. The writer of these notes has had no personal experience of ghosts, and can only speak from hearsay. He recently asked a member of a well-known family, who had lived at 'Strath' for the greater part of his life, whether he had ever seen the 'ghost.' The reply was, *I have never seen it but I have heard it scores of times. It goes through the house in the night, apparently slamming doors and smashing crockery. It seems to drive up to the front door at a furious pace, and when the door is opened there is nothing there.* It is related that a dour old Presbyterian minister was once staying at 'Strath,' and was very angry with his host for speaking of the ghost as if he really believed in its existence. *I am surprised,* he said, *that you, a Christian man, should repeat such nonsense ; please let us change the subject.* Next morning Mr. Stewart, who was up very early, found his guest sitting under one of the river oaks, where he had apparently been for some time. He inquired the cause of his friend's discomfiture, and received the following answer: *Never ask me what I saw and heard last night, for I can tell it to no mortal man!* The ghost is said to appear immediately before the death of a member of the family.

We do not either accept or discard those stories. We simply give them for what they are worth. We believe 'Strath' is vacant at the present time, and no doubt anyone who would like to spend a few nights there, with a view to solving the mystery, could easily obtain permission to do so." (Story of the Bathurst Pioneers, 25 Nov 1922, p.13)

1883 'Mount Pleasant' Residence—James Horne Stewart

James joined his father in Australia. "Mr. J. H. Stewart was born in Edinburgh on the 5th September, 1825, and came out with his mother to join his father ... Advancing in years, Major-General Stewart then determined to dispose of his Scotch estates, which lay not more than twenty miles from the house of the historic John O'Groafs, opposite the Orkney Isles, and settle down for the remainder of his life at Mount Pleasant. In 1850 Mr. J. H. Stewart paid a visit to the old country, and on his return was made the recipient of all his father's property. In the following year all the sheep on the estate were attacked by scab, and very serious losses ensued ; so next year Mr. Stewart determined to work his land upon the system of tenantry, which he has continued ever since. In 1854 Mr. Stewart's father died, at the ripe old age of 85 ... In 1883, Mr. Stewart removed from the residence which his father had built [Strath] and assumed the occupancy of the mansion which occupies a position on the brow of a most picturesque knoll and commands the admiration of all passers-by.

The residence is built of granite, obtained from the hill side below Major-General Stewart's tomb, relieved by freestone. The style of architecture is Elizabethian ; the building consists of two storeys, with basement and attic, and contains 40 rooms. Everything for the mansion was supplied by Mr. Stewart, and it is almost impossible for him to estimate the exact cost, but the sum of £22,000, which he actually paid out of pocket will give some idea of the wealth which has been lavished by the Squire of Mt. Pleasant on the home. Everything about the place presents an appearance of splendor and homeliness. From a window in the attic a magnificent view of the surrounding country is obtained ... Immediately around the house ... Flower beds and shrubberies are laid out in numerous enclosures, clumps and rows of evergreens wave their cooling branches in the warm Spring afternoon ... Inside the residence the fittings and furnishings are the result of exquisite taste, despite their costliness. The appurtenances to the residence are all that could be desired, and the stable with carriage-house and coachman's residence thoroughly in keeping with all the other buildings. Close by the residence a very extensive orchard ...

With the exception of 800 acres for his own private use, Mr. Stewart has the whole of his magnificent estate rented to tenants. At one time the names of 117 tenants appeared on the books, but gradually as the smaller holders went away their interests were bought up by the more substantial farmers, and at the present time there are not more than 50 in occupation of the land. And not only this ; some of the farms, through bad seasons and low prices, are at the present time entirely vacated. The leases of Mr. Stewart's tenants; run from terms of 10 years up to 15 years. On the whole they are spoken of by him as a thrifty and industrious lot of people, and little or no trouble exists between landlord and tenants regarding the right or claims of each other ... The fences are kept in excellent order ; the improvements are on the whole very substantial ... Mr. Stewart is fully alive to the responsibilities which devolve upon him in his possession of the wealth which he commands." (Pictures from the Plains, 11 Oct 1890, p.2)

In 1918, "Mr. J. H. Stewart, of Mt. Pleasant estate, in the Bathurst district, one of the best known properties in New South Wales, has reached his 93rd year, having exceeded the age of his father, the original owner of the estate, by eight years ...

The family history is a real romance. The surviving Mr. Stewart's father distinguished himself with the British forces in the campaign against Napoleon in Spain ... he was awarded a heavy gold inscribed medal by the Duke of York, and this trophy Mr. J. H. Stewart now has in his possession at Bathurst ... the Stewart family, including the present Mr. J. H. Stewart, then aged ten, who had been left in Scotland, put off in a 33-ton sailer, and, after leaving port and returning twice, entered upon the voyage, which took seven months to complete. The family remained in Sydney for a few years, but in 1833 went to Bathurst, and took up permanent residence at the Mount. The palatial residence—claimed as one of the finest and most distinctive country homes in the whole of Australia—was not then in existence, the old home being a well-built brick structure [Strath], still standing on the bank of the Macquarie. This was built by convict labor, as were the old composite walls that line the picturesque road passing the mountain in a well patronised thirteen-miles circular trip from Bathurst itself. The present big building was put up by the present owner after the old officer's death in 1854, at an age of 85 years. The material, blue-grey granite, was taken from one huge boulder found on the estate." (Father Fought Napoleon, 17 Sep 1918, p.7)

While "Mrs. W. B. Rankin, in her memoirs, writes:—*On the 30th July, 1858, we started on our long journey over the Blue Mountains. Mrs. Stewart who has just returned from Scotland, formed one of our party, and her presence added greatly to the enjoyment of the journey. The railway was then finished as far as Parramatta, and we spent the first night at the Woolpack Inn. We left next morning with a team of four good horses. I cannot remember the names of all our stopping places. Pulpit Hill was one of them, and the Weatherboard another. We stayed a night at Hartley Vale, and also at Bowenfels. We arrived at Bathurst on August 2. A cold wind was blowing across the plains, and we thought, the climate worse than an English winter. Here I parted from Mrs. Stewart, but this was only the beginning of a lifelong friendship, and I shall never forget her many acts of kindness and affection.* The house now known as 'Strath' was there in 1837 ... Only one-third of the original portion remains, the rest having been taken down in the [18]seventies. It is now used as a holiday residence by Mrs. Sydney Jamieson, granddaughter of the General." (Story of the Bathurst Pioneers, 18 Nov 1922, p.13)

In 1906, Mr. J. H. Stewart wrote to The Bulletin from The Mount, Bathurst, stating the following: "You again give a very erroneous account of the manner in which my late father acquired this property, Mount Pleasant, This is the true statement. My father reached Sydney in May, 1825 ... He brought with him an order from the Imperial Government for 3000 acres of land in any part of the colony. This quantity was only 1000 acres more than was usually given to those settlers who could deposit £1000 to their credit in some bank in Sydney for a few days necessary to secure the grant. My father got his 3000 acres from the Duke of York, as a reward for military services in the Peninsular War. General Darling left the colony soon after my father's arrival, and he acted as Governor until Sir Thomas Brisbane reached the port. But it was not until 1827 that he made his selection near Bathurst. I have in my possession a letter to him from the Governor, requesting him as a personal favour to run up and make his selection to facilitate settlement. He made a hurried trip across the mountains, and took up his 3000 acres on the west side of the parish of Mount Pleasant, along Evans Plains Creek, but not including Monument Hill, where his remains now rest. In 1828 he was sent with his regiment to India ; but before leaving he secured a lease of the remaining portion of the parish, containing about 12,000 acres. On arrival at Calcutta he was appointed Commandant at Meerut, where he remained for four years, and in 1832, when he was raised to the rank of Major General, he left the army on half pay, and returned to look after his grant at Bathurst. He then purchased the 9000 acre block where the monument on the hill and the mansion house now stand, adjoining his primary grant, at the upset price of 5s per acre.

It was not until 1838 that he secured the 2400 acre block at the south side of the parish, for which he paid 12s per acre."

- By 1920, Mr. James Horne Stewart was recognised as the district's largest landholder and its oldest resident. He "lived in the darkest days of the country, when men were flogged for petty offences, and when such crimes as sheep stealing were only expiated by death. By his demise another link of the dark past is broken and Bathurst loses one of its most interesting and best known identities ... It is some nine years ago that the late Mr. Stewart was honored by his tenants and presented with an illuminated address, and Mrs. Stewart received a silver tea and coffee service ... Here are the deceased words: - *My father was a greater man than I could ever possibly have been, and I am very anxious to keep his memory green ... in 1825 [the 3rd Regimant of Buffs] were despatched to Sydney. My father brought out with him the appointment of Lieutenant-Governor, and he was appointed Acting-Governor during an interval between the departure of Sir Thomas Brisbane and the arrival of Sir H. Darling. The former had left five men condemned for sheep stealing, and my father did not believe in the death penalty for that offence; consequently, he reprieved them. He afterwards used to say that this was the most satisfactory act he had ever performed ... he was appointed Major-General, and he at once left the army on half-pay, and returned to Bathurst. As soon as his agent in Scotland heard of this he packed us all away from Strath, my father's property in Caithness, and we landed in Sydney in May, 1835. My father then decided to settle near Bathurst, where he died in 1854.* The Stewart mansion at Mt. Pleasant is one of the most palatial in the western district. Its surroundings are amongst the most beautiful and the situation ideal." (The Stewart Estate, 14 Jan 1920, p.2)

Late in that year, "Probate has been granted of the will of the late Mr. James Horne Stewart, of Mount Pleasant, near Bathurst, who died on January 13 last, leaving to his widow and children an estate of the net value of £36,979, of which £15,248 represented realty and £9285 shares in mines in New South Wales." (Late Mr. J. H. Stewart, 25 Aug 1920, p.9) While "the testator, who died in January last, appointed his sons Athol William Wolfe Stewart and Albyn Athol Stewart—the latter renounced probate—executors and trustees of his estate. He left £300 to Charles Dean in recognition of long and faithful service. Testator bequeathed the residue of the estate to his widow and children." (Late Mr. J. H. Stewart, 26 Aug 1920, p.10)

Mount Pleasant' Residence–Athol William Wolfe Stewart

1905 – "WEDDINGS. Stewart— M'dougall. The marriage of Mr Athol Wolfe Stewart, eldest son of Mr J. H. Stewart, of The Mount, Bathurst, with Miss Frances Helen M'Dougall, daughter of J. T. M'Dougall, of Buccarumb Station, Dalmorton, was solemnised at the residence of the bride's aunt, Mrs G. P. Bowman, of Kiadue, Elizabeth Bay, on Tuesday afternoon, April 18, by the Rev. J. Kinghorn, of North Sydney, in the presence of a number of the relatives of the bride and bridegroom. The bride was given away by her cousin, Dr. Rignold Bowman, of Parramatta, and Mr Arthur Bowman acted as best man. Miss Kathleen Suttor was bridesmaid.

The guests present at the ceremony were : — Mr and Mrs Stewart, of The Mount, Lady and Miss Allen, Sir William and Lady McMillan, Mr and Mrs Percy McArthur, Mr. Arthur Allan, Mrs G P Bowman and Miss Bowman, Dr. and Mrs Bowman, Mrs G A Mansfield, Mr and Mrs Leslie Rouse, Mrs Boyce and Miss Capon, the Misses Myril, Helen and Muriel Bowman, Dr. Jamieson, Mrs Kinghorn, Miss Kite, and Mr and Mrs Albyn Stewart. The presents were numerous and costly." (Weddings, 1 May 1905, p.3)

1912 – "MOUNT PLEASANT. Sale of a Noted Bathurst Property Held by the one Family since Government Grant First Issued over 80 years ago. Hain and Searight, Sydney, (in conjunction with E. H. Taylor and Coy., Bathurst) report, having effected the sale of this noted estate, comprising 11,078 acres freehold lands, on account of Mr. Athol Stewart, the purchaser being Mr. A. C. Reid ... It is the intention of the purchaser to subdivide the property." (Mount Pleasant, 9 Mar 1912, p.5)

"Mr. A. C. Reid ... arrived in town on Sunday night, accompanied by Mr. Searight, of Hain and Searight, the well-known station auctioneers, Sydney, and spent Monday in going over the estate with Mr. Miller, and interviewing as many tenants as possible. It is Mr. Reid's intention to offer the property for sale in suitable areas, but wishes first of all to consult with the present tenants, with a view of finding out what portions they may desire to purchase. The survey work has been entrusted to the firm of John Miller and Co., and Mr. Miller himself has been asked by Mr. Reid to go into all details with the tenants.— Bathurst Times." (The Mt. Pleasant Estate, 3 Jul 1912, p.2)

After 90 years the Mt. Pleasant subdivision occurred. "Says the 'Bulletin':—After being held for nearly 90 years in close grip, Mount Pleasant, near Bathurst (N.S.W.), is to be cut up and sold in small farms." (After 90 Years, 8 Nov 1913, p.3)

In 1924, Mr. Stewart's health drew public attention: "Mr. Athol Stewart, of 'The Mount,' underwent a successful operation in St. Vincent's Hospital this morning." (Personal, 10 Jul 1924, p.2)

While the paper noted: "CHARITY WORKER'S DEATH, Bathurst ... Mrs. Helen Stewart, wife of Mr. Athol Stewart, of The Mount, and prominent worker for charity, died on Sunday. She was a member of the local branch of the Country Women's Association." (Charity Worker's Death, 18 Oct 1927, p.16)

Local Intelligence & Memories–In & Around Mount Pleasant, Bathurst

1842 – "MARRIED. At Bathurst, on the 14th instant, by the Rev. Colin Stewart, the Reverend Kirkpatrick Dickson Smythe, of Bathurst, to Elizabeth, second daughter of Major General Stewart, of Strath, Caithness, Scotland, and of Mount Pleasant, Bathurst, New South Wales." (Family Notices, 19 Jul 1842, p.3)

1852 – "STRATH COTTAGE. TO BE LET, from the first day of June next, with kitchen, stable, coach-house, &c., attached, and paddocks containing about eighty acres, situated on Mount Pleasant, about two and a half miles from town. Rent—£65 per annum." (Advertising, 10 Apr 1852, p.3)

1853 – "TO BE LET, From the 1st of July, Strath cottage, with the outhouses and large paddock adjoining, abutted on the Macquarie River, about three miles from Bathurst. Apply at Mount Pleasant. June 15th, 1853 ... James Stewart. Notice. The public are hereby informed that the road to Kings Plains, known as 'Rodd's New Line', is not a highway, so far as that portion which passes through this estate is concerned, and as steps will shortly be taken to stop it completely, all persons are warned against using it as a public road. James H. Stewart. Mount Pleasant, 15th June 1853." (Advertising, 18 Jun 1853, p.3)

1870 – "JOTTINGS BY THE WAY BATHURST. But let us pay some attention to the neighbourhood of the western capital. The Glanmire Brewery—yes—Mr. Baillie (obliging man) will drive over ; in doing so we cross the Denison bridge ; let us stop and look at it. Spanning the Macquarie in three bays of about 112 feet each ... Iron having an eccentric habit of expanding by heat and contracting by cold, allowance is made for this weakness by disconnecting the girders over the saddles and giving them free and fair play for expansion, contraction and deflection. The old bridge being now demolished ... A run of seven miles, brings us to Mr. Coombes's gate, on the Sydney Road, and another quarter mile to his house on rising ground, from which by an easy descent we come to the brewery ... The Glanmire brew is an honest beer, genuine malt and plenty of hops ; give it an unmistakeable home-brewed flavour ... Kelso is a village suburb of Bathurst, on the opposite side of the Macquarie River. It boasts the oldest church in the district, the present incumbent, the Rev. Mr. Lisle, having been in residence thirty eight years. There is also a good school ...

'Carwinyan' at the back of Kelso, is the pretty cottage residence of J. B. Richards, Esq., land agent, in Bathurst ... and from the verandah a capital view is obtained of Mr. Webb's fine residence, and Mr. M'Phillimy's in the vale ... Some distance down the river from Carwinyan is Mr. Rotton's estate of Blackdown, on which two things are to be observed, the boiling-down establishment, and the nature of the Macquarie Riverbanks ...

The great Mount Pleasant estate bounds Bathurst on the west, the nucleus of which was a maximum grant from the Crown of 2000 acres, concerning which a 'yarn' is current in Bathurst, which has no foundation in fact. The property, by purchase, now comprises 15,000 acres, reaching within a mile of the town, and being the parish of Mount Pleasant. It was not many years ago a sheep-walk, but being thrown open for agricultural settlement, was rapidly taken up, and there are now nearly one hundred resident tenants. Every encouragement for permanent settlement has been afforded. Two public schools have been opened, a steam-mill, stores, blacksmiths' shops erected, and a reading room built, where papers and periodicals are supplied by the proprietor, and where the young people meet for mutual improvement, by debates and penny readings. Two villages have been laid off and sold, at each of which, there is a post-office and church or chapel.

The principal portion of the estate, 'Evans's Plains,' is named after the surveyor, who was sent up by the Government in 1820 ... 8000 acres are farmed, and 7000 acres reserved for commonage, until required for farms, the timber being the tenant's also. Maize, barley, and potatoes are grown, but wheat and hay are the staple products, many adding dairies to their work, while others make time by cartage. Reaping machines, double-furrowed ploughs, and improved farm implements, are being introduced, and the Adelaide wheat stripper, was first introduced in this neighbourhood. It threshes the grain, partly cleaning it as it travels, and when the large compartment beneath is filled, the grain is drawn out on to a tarpaulin in the field, and being put once through the winnower and bagged, is ready for the mill. When the railway is completed to Bathurst, the metropolis will be largely supplied with grain from this part of the country.

The obelisk raised to the deceased general stands conspicuous to the country round, on the summit of Mount Pleasant, some 300 feet above the river and the Killeshiel Creek, and by no means pleasant to ascend, being thick with loose trap boulders and spauls. The obelisk is plain, square, blunt-pointed and having a marble tablet facing the north-east, containing in brief the history of the illustrious dead. It runs thus:—*Erected to the memory of Major-general Stewart, late Colonel in His Majesty's 3rd Regiment of Buffs, and first proprietor of this estate, who died on the 8th April, 1854, at the advanced age of 84 ... In private life, he was universally esteemed as a useful and honourable member of society; he constantly proved himself a ready friend of the poor, and then, like a shock of corn fully ripe, and in lively faith of Our Blessed Saviour's atonement, he departed this life. He was universally and deservedly regretted. This obelisk has been raised as a faithful token of affectionate remembrance by his surviving children—Arise and depart, for this is not your rest ...*

Opposite the quaint old battlemented brick mansion of the general's and across the river, is the 640 acre farm originally owned by Captain Piper, and called 'Westbourne' ... In the opposite direction, and a small distance up the Vale Creek, stands the well planned and splendidly furnished residence of Mr. Edmund Webb. This house has what many buildings are spoiled for the want of—a spacious hall—Mr. Webb's hall is twelve feet wide, narrowing to ten feet beyond the arch ... We will now say our arithmetic.

The amount of land selected at Bathurst, under the Land Act of 1801, is 46,081 acres, 34 perches, and the total number of acres under cultivation in the police district of Bathurst, is 43,648 acres—viz., Wheat—for grain, 24,720 acres, for hay, 404 acres ; maize—for grain, 2941 acres, for green food, 56 acres ; barley—for grain, 1075 acres, for green food, 372 acres, for hay, 89 acres ; oats—for grain, 2819 acres, for green food, 34 acres, for hay, 5669 acres ; rye, 110 acres, millet, 5 acres, potatoes, 1288 acres, sorghum, 13 acres ; sown grasses for green food, 196 acres, for hay, 396 acres ; vines, 58 acres, gardens and orchards, 272 acres, 'all other,' 131 acres ... On the Electoral Roll there are for Bathurst, 1111 ; for East Macquarie, 2545 ; for West Macquarie, 951. The population of the city is about 5000." (Jottings by the way, 15 Jul 1870, p.4)

1899 – "WEDDING AT MOUNT PLEASANT. Yesterday afternoon at Mount Pleasant the residence of Mr. J. H. Stewart, Miss Florence Beatrice Landseer Morris, only child of the late Captain Arthur Morris, of Sydney, and Mr. Albyn Athol Stewart, second son of Mr. J. H. Stewart, were wedded. The ceremony was performed in the drawing-room, which was artistically decorated with white flowers and soft-tinted greenery. The Rev. James Kinghorn, of St. Stephens, celebrated the union in the presence of a large and distinguished gathering. The bride, who looked charming, was attired in a rich ivory corded silk dress with delicate trimmings, the sleeves and yoke were of tucked chiffon and orange blossoms, at the skirt which was trained, was nicely trimmed with ruche of chiffon and ribbon, finished with a beautiful chiffon sash. She also wore a handsome orange blossom wreath and carried a choice bouquet. She was accompanied as bridesmaids, by Miss Roslyn Stewart and Miss B. McMillan, of Sydney who wore costumes of white muslin and lace and carried pretty pink bouquets. The bride was given away by Mr. Stewart, and Mr. Athol Stewart (brother of the bridegroom) acted in the capacity of groomsman. The breakfast was held in the large dining hall and the toasts to the happy couple were enthusiastically honored. The presents, which very numerous and likewise of great value, were laid out in the library and were greatly admired. After the breakfast had been partaken of, the happy couple left for Dulcie Vale, where portion of the honeymoon will be spent, the travelling dress of the bride being a brown coat and skirt and white hat and vest. The bride's dress came from the establishment of Messrs. E. Webb and Co., and was designed by Mrs. Fitzgerald.

Among the visitors were:—Hon. F. B. Suttor and Miss Suttor, Mr. and Mrs. Jago Smith, Miss V. Smith, Dr. and Mrs. Machattie, Dr. and Mrs. Moore, Miss Kite, Dean and Mrs. Marriott, Rev. A. J. Webb, Miss Webb, Mr. and Mrs. Reading, Mr. and Mrs. G. Suttor, Miss Sutherland, Miss Kennedy, Mr. Britten, Mr. and Mrs. James Ranken, Mr. and Miss M'Phillamy (Orton Park), Rev. and Mrs. Kinghorn, Mr. and Mrs. Lindsay (Strath), Mr. and Mrs. Arthur Allen (Sydney), Mr. and Mrs. Jack Allen, Mr. Mrs. and Miss McMillan, Miss Bassett, Dr. W. P. Bassett, Mr. Arthur Bowman, Mr. Harley McKenzie, Dr. Sydney Jamieson, Mr. and Mrs. J. B. Nicholson, Mr. and Mrs. James Nisbet, Mr. Gilbert Orr, and Mr. and Mrs. J. P. McArthur." (Wedding At Mount Pleasant, 22 Feb 1899, p.3)

1914 – "WEDDING. HARDIE—LINDSAY. St. Stephen's Presbyterian Church was the scene of a fashionable wedding last night, the parties being Mr. John A. Hardie, A.M. Inst., C.E., eldest son of Mr. John Hardie, M.A., and Mrs. Hardie, of 'Colonsay,' Paisley, Scotland, and Patsie Violet, daughter of Mr. and Mrs. R. M. Lindsay, of 'Strath,' Mt. Pleasant. Rev. J. H. Robertson officiated. The bride, who was given away by her father, wore a draped gown of ivory satin charmeuse, with bodice of lace and ninon, and girdle of silver tissue, finished at end with roses of the same shade.

Her tulle veil (kindly lent by Mrs. Hugh Busby) was arranged over a pleated band of silver tissue, with a small bunch of orange blossoms over each ear. The bride carried a bouquet, which, with a gold expanding bracelet watch, was the gift of the bridegroom. The bridesmaids were Miss Peggy Lindsay (sister of the bride) and Miss Doris Koeboke. Both were dressed in grey floral ninon, with blue sashes, looped near the foot with bunches of pink bebe roses and forget-me-nots. A bunch of forget-me-nots was also worn in the belts. Their caps were of blue tulle with broad bands of blue velvet, finished over the ears with tiny bunches of forget-me-nots. Three little girls, Jean Busby, Anne Jamieson, and Betty Stewart, in dainty frocks of white muslin and insertion, with blue belts and rosettes, acted as trainbearers. All carried bouquets of pink roses and carnations, which, with their brooches, were the gifts of the bridegroom. The bride's mother wore lilac crepe-de-chine with black belt, and hat with white feathers. The best man was Mr. James Hardie, of Sydney, cousin of the bridegroom, and Mr. Donald Smith filled the role of groomsman. Messrs. A. Blackett and A. Maxwell acted as ushers. After the ceremony, Mr. and Mrs. Lindsay, the bride's parents, entertained the guests at 'Strath.' Mr. and Mrs. Hardie subsequently left for Sydney on their honeymoon. The bride's travelling dress was a coat and skirt of sand-colored resilda, and white hat trimmed with black tulle and wheat ears, with blue velvet bow. The presents made up a valuable collection, including many cheques."(Wedding, 8 Jan 1914, p.2)

1915 – "WEDDING AT MOUNT PLEASANT. A quiet but interesting wedding took place on Thursday last at the residence of Mr. W. Stewart, of Mount Pleasant, the contracting parties being Mrs. E. Hucker, of Lake Bolac, and Mr. Malcolm Davidson, of Westmere. Both parties are well and favourably known throughout the district in which they reside. The Rev. A. McLeod, of Wickliffe, conducted the ceremony, and after the wedding breakfast, at which the usual toasts were honoured the happy couple drove to Willaura to catch the afternoon train to Ballarat and Geelong, where the honeymoon is to be spent." ([?] at Mount Pleasant, 4 Nov 1915, p.2)

1921 – "REMINISCENCES OF BATHURST by Rev. T. J. Curtis ... The old homestead at Mount Pleasant had towering above it a lofty hill, 'The Mount,' chiefly, composed of granite and crowned with a monument of granite, beneath which the mortal remains of Major General Stewart found sepulture, and afterwards those of his son. Some considerable time after his father's death Mr. Stewart erected the splendid mansion of solid granite which thereafter constituted his and his family's residence, the whole of the stone having been quarried from 'The Mount.' He took great pride in the richly carved solid oak furniture with which all the rooms of his mansion were filled, and the complete and magnificent collection of ancient armour which found place in the spacious hall. During a fortnight spent by me on clerical duty at Bathurst a few years ago I was the honoured guest of Mr. and Mrs. Stewart for a few days, and Mr. Stewart told me that the furniture and armour had formed, part of the exhibit at the Great Exhibition at the Garden Palace, Sydney, afterwards burnt down, and he had purchased them for a great sum ... The history of the mail coaching days on the main roads of the State is idyllic. While I was a citizen of Bathurst, the Sydney mail was run, first by Henry Rotton, then by Crane and Roberts, and afterwards by Cobb and Co. until the completion of the railway, and from first to last the service was efficient and frequently thrilled with adventure. For many years two and a half days were consumed on the journey; then—under Crane, and Roberts— the mail commenced to run through in twenty-four hours, travelling all night, and so it continued under Cobb and Co. to the end. In those days my visits to Sydney generally happened about twice every year, and on one occasion my experience on the mountains was memorable. Chris. Browne, one of Cobb's crack drivers, had mounted the box at 'The Weather Board' (an inn on the Blue Mountains) about dusk, and, gathering up the reins of the five thoroughbred greys (all Cobb's horses were thoroughbred), cried 'Hooplah!' as they sprang into their collars and bounded away.

Behind them was an immense red and gold leather-springed coach, containing eleven passengers under its hood, and all be curtained and strapped up, for it was a freezing night. I was on the box beside the driver. Suddenly the leaders, taking fright at a white horse attached to a spring-cart trotting up the road, swerved off the track, up an embankment, and into the lightly timbered bush, taking, of course, the rest of the team and the coach with them. The driver lost his balance and fell off the box; I tried, but failed, to grab the reins, and so, on the principle of discretion being the better part of valour, jumped off. Near by was the driver, on his feet, unhurt. The horses, already mad with fright, were plunging on through the scrub in the direction of a deep culvert, in the most imminent immediate peril of dire disaster. Another minute and the sound of crash and confusion fell on my ear, telling me that the inevitable had happened. Chris. Browne and I reached the culvert at top speed, and there found the coach capsized, with its eleven passengers imprisoned within its strapped curtains—perhaps with their necks broken, though we heard some groans. Then some of the straps gave way, releasing several of the passengers, apparently unharmed. The horses had all been thrown off their feet, and were desperately struggling in a tangle of harness. We managed to get the horses released, and then the rest of the passengers. Meanwhile the driver had hastened back to the 'Weather Board,' and soon returned with the groom and some fresh harness. Then, together, we managed to get the coach upright on its wheels, and found that though one of the axles was bent it would still run, and what was infinitely better, none of the passengers or horses was injured, and the harness needed but little patching up. The substantial hood of the coach had sufficiently borne the shock and strain of the capsize to protect the passengers from injury. And so it came about that, thanking Providence for our miraculous deliverance, we sped onward, and reached Sydney only two or three hours behind time." (Reminiscences of Bathurst, 27 Jul 1921, p.16)

1922 – MEMORIES "Mrs. Stewart was possessed of a remarkably sweet and kindly disposition, which won for her the love and esteem of all classes of the community. Her sister. Lady Wigram Allen, is said to have been her counterpart, and to have had the same attractive and unselfish nature. Her daughter, Mrs. Sydney Jamieson, has inherited many of her mother's characteristics. She says, *I love the old days and ways, and have many manuscripts and letters which belonged to my father. There is one from Governor Brisbane to my grandfather, asking him to dinner at Government House, Parramatta, at 6.30, and to stay the night, as it was too far from Sydney to come and go in the same day! There are letters from Governor Darling and Surveyor Oxley, about the taking up of land at Bathurst, which quite dispose of the fine old hoary tale that the General went to tho mount, and claimed all that he could see! There is a letter from grandfather to Captain Piper, welcoming him to his new home at Westbourne and sending him a lot of legs of mutton to convert into hams! I seem to live in the past, when I go back to Bathurst. Miss Jane Piper and Mrs. Busby told me many stories of the early days. I should like to write down what I know of almost forgotten things connected with the old homes at Westbourne, Saltram, and Rainham. Such stories as that of the bushrangers camping at Sawpit Creek, and the police riding after them in the moonlight, and my father, hearing their horses turn in at the old house gate, and mistaking the pursuers for the pursued, waiting with his gun, behind the turreted brick wall to get a shot at them. Fortunately he discovered his mistake just in time. And Captain Piper, giving his grand dinner at Westbourne, hospitable to the last. And Mrs. Piper, sitting near the door, lest the convicts should run away with her silver spoon! Captain Raine, who built Rainham, where Mr. Neil Stewart was married to Miss Murray, a relative of Lawson the explorer, was one of the early pioneers. There is a brooch at Rainham with a history. Ask Mr. C. Boyd to show it to you. The early history of Bathurst would supply ample material for a thrilling romance!* The present mansion at the Mount, now the residence of Mr. Athol Wolf Stewart, was built in 1878. The original Crown grant was 3200 acres, afterwards increased by purchase." (Story of the Bathurst Pioneers, 25 Nov 1922, p.13)

1922 – "FIRST POSTAL REGULATIONS. The original document is in the hand writing of General Stewart, and is dated 1820. The method was discontinued in 1832. In 1824 James Smith and Thomas Fullor established the first conveyance from Parramatta to Bathurst, undertaking to do the journey in four days. The fare was 20/, and letters 1/ each. The first regulation provided for a Postmaster-General to be appointed in Sydney, and a General Post Office to be erected in the most convenient and public situation, which can be selected on the verge of the harbor, so as to ensure prompt communication with all vessels arriving in, or departing from Sydney Cove; and deputy-postmasters to be appointed for Parramatta, Windsor, Liverpool, Campbelltown, Cawdor, Newcastle, Port Macquarie. The principal superintendent to act in that capacity at Emu Plains, and the Commandant's clerk, or the chief constable, at Bathurst, under the Commandant's special charge. Other regulations provided for the despatch of mails to various points in New South Wales by coach and horses and for the relays to facilitate the distribution of letters, etc." (Story of the Bathurst Pioneers, 25 Nov 1922, p.13)

1912 – SHOW "Although the weather was hot on Thursday, the Mount Pleasant Agricultural, Horticultural and Floricultural Society's annual show attracted a large gathering, and the gate takings were better than last year's. Thursday's was the fifty-first show of the society ... art exhibits, needlework, children's work ... fruit, vegetables, dairy produce, flowers and cereals ... exhibition of cattle and sheep ... As usual, the fixture attracted a large number of city people, most of whom motored to Mount Pleasant ... horses in action ... there was an excellent array of blooms in all varieties ... pigs ... poultry ... That an able committee, under the guidance of Mr. F. Thomson as chairman, had been at work was shown by the way the arrangements were carried out. Mr. H. W. Harms as secretary did his arduous work well." (Mount Pleasant Sale, 30 Nov 1927, p.2)

The end of the Stewart era at 'The Mount'

1927 – "LATE MRS. ATHOL STEWART. BATHURST, Tuesday. The death occurred on Sunday of Mrs. Athol Stewart, of The Mount, Bathurst, a prominent citizen, widely known for her philanthropic and charitable work in this district. Mrs. Stewart was president of the ladies' auxiliary of the district hospital, and a prominent official of the Country Women's Association. The remains were taken to Sydney for cremation, and the burial will take place at The Mount on Thursday." (Late Mrs. Athol Stewart, 19 Oct 1927, p.16)

1927 – AUCTION SALE. "Bathurst. Preliminary notice. A most important auction sale will be held on Tuesday and Wednesday, 29th and 30th November, each day at 10.30 A.M. Prompt. Under instructions from and for and on account of Athol Stewart, esq., In consequence of his immediate departure for england. The whole of the valuable furniture, costly appointments, and household effects, contained in the family mansion, known as mount pleasant (a few mile from Bathurst). Further particulars of this important sale will appear in later advertisements. James R. Lawson, auctioneers. 236 Castlereagh-street, and clements and mccarthy, Bathurst, auctioneers in conjunction." (Advertising, 5 Nov 1927, p.4)

1927 – "MOUNT PLEASANT SALE The two-days sale of Mr. Athol Stewart's effects at Mt. Pleasant commenced yesterday. There was a good attendance, and the auction was conducted by Mr. Maxwell Lawson of Messrs Jas R. Lawson, Sydney and Mr. C. Holman. the well-known salesman for Messrs Clements and McCarthy, Bathurst. Bidding was brisk throughout and good prices were realised. About 740 lots, including the whole of the outside implements, and articles were disposed of, leaving the interior appointments and the furniture to be sold to-day. The sale will be resumed at 10.30 o'clock this morning." (Mount Pleasant Sale, 30 Nov 1927, p.2)

1927 – "THE SALE AT STEWART'S MOUNT Yesterday the sale of furniture and effects under instructions of Mr. A. W. Stewart, of Mt. Pleasant, was continued before another large attendance. Generally speaking bidding was brisk, and the sale was most successful. Amongst the lots sold yesterday were: Grandfather clock, £29, Mrs. John McPhillamy ; Bluthner piano, £57/10 ; marble top desk, £22, Mrs. S. Jamieson ; two bevelled glass mirrors, £24, Mrs. S. Jamieson ; small Davenport, £11 ; pair of bronze ornaments, £26, Mrs. Barry, Royal Hotel. The china ware sold from £5 to £8. The sale will be continued at 10 a.m. today, when 250 lots will be disposed of." (The Sale at Stewart's Mount, 1 Dec 1927, p.2)

1927 – "THE MOUNT. A DESERTED MANSION. BY 'BATHURST BURR.' The historic mansion home of the Stewart family, pioneers of the west, at Mount Pleasant, Esrom, near Bathurst, which has been in uninterrupted occupancy of the family for nearly a century, is now untenanted ; the whole of the magnificent, and mostly unique, household furniture, together with all outside requisites, being disposed of recently at auction. Known as 'The Mount,' and constituting one of the finest homes in Australia, the stately stone mansion is full of associations with the early days, and was last occupied by Mr. Athol Stewart. It is a perfect type of Scotch castle, and is a copy of the ancestral home of the Stewart family in Scotland ... Major-General Stewart ... built himself a house, which still stands opposite the present mansion, which was built by his son, the late J. H. Stewart, in 1878." (The Mount, 10 Dec 1927, p.13)

1942 – "STEWART MANSION AS WOMEN'S HOSTEL Mr. and Mrs. Athol Stewart have given their mansion at Mount Pleasant, Bathurst, to the Women's Land, Army for the duration, the Director of the W. L. A. (Mrs. Aileen Lynch) has announced. The home will be used as a central hostel for land workers and will eventually provide accommodation for 150 girls. The cost of preliminary renovations will be defrayed by Mr. Max Edgell, who already has 30 girls working on one of his properties. The first 30 girls will go into residence at Mount Pleasant shortly." (Stewart Mansion as Women's Hostel, 5 Oct 1942, p.2)

1946 – "THE STEWART VAULT ... Remains of other members of the family are buried in it. These include Mr. J. H. Stewart, son, and his wife. The body of Major-General Stewart; was taken up the mount by bullock dray. The body of his son was conveyed by a car, driven by Mr. A. T. Tipping, a retired Bathurst garage proprietor, now residing somewhere in the Metropolitan area." (Legends of Mt. Pleasant, 27 Jul 1946, p.5)

MANSION "Mount Pleasant ... a granite mansion, which is the admiration of the people of Bathurst. A place, grand enough to please the most, ostentatious, a place artistic enough to satisfy the tastes of the most fastidious ... The descendants of such sturdy pioneers form the backbone of the country, and Bathurst district seems to be particularly rich in that direction. In addition to the Stewart clan, old families are represented by tho decendants of such well-known names of Cox, Hawkins, Kite, Mills, Ruble, Ranken, Rotten, Lee, Sutton, McPhillamy, Icely and others." (Mount Pleasant, 20 Feb 1925, p.4)

Abercrombie House'—The Morgan Era

And let's not forget "the Morgan family who have spent the last 50 years restoring and maintaining the magnificent house and its outbuildings and grounds, and sharing it with the community." (www.abercrombiehouse.com.au) The mansion is now named 'Abercrombie House'.

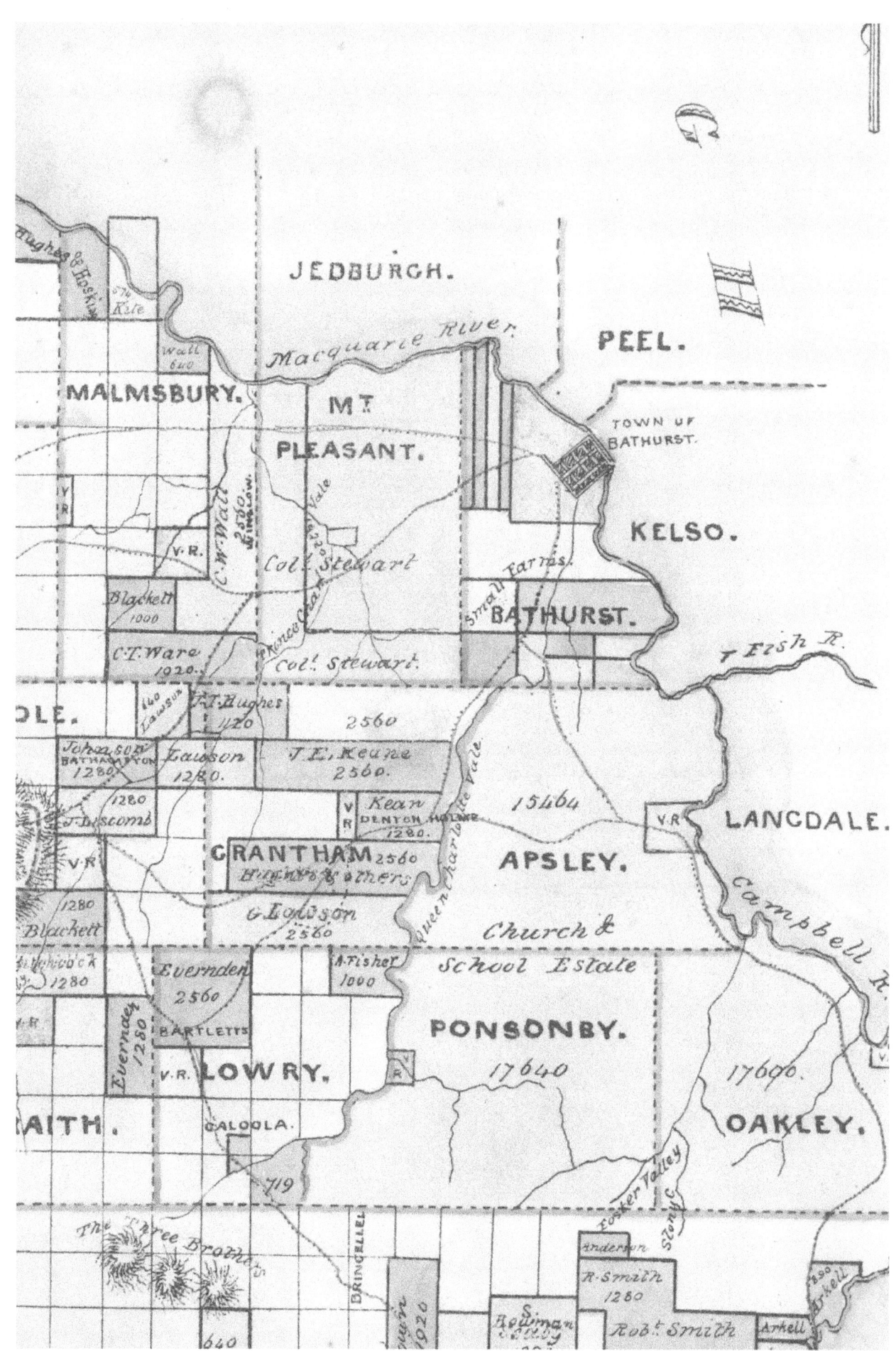

1846 W. Baker, et al. Baker's Map of the County of Bathurst [Cartographic Material]) – Courtesy National Library of Australia

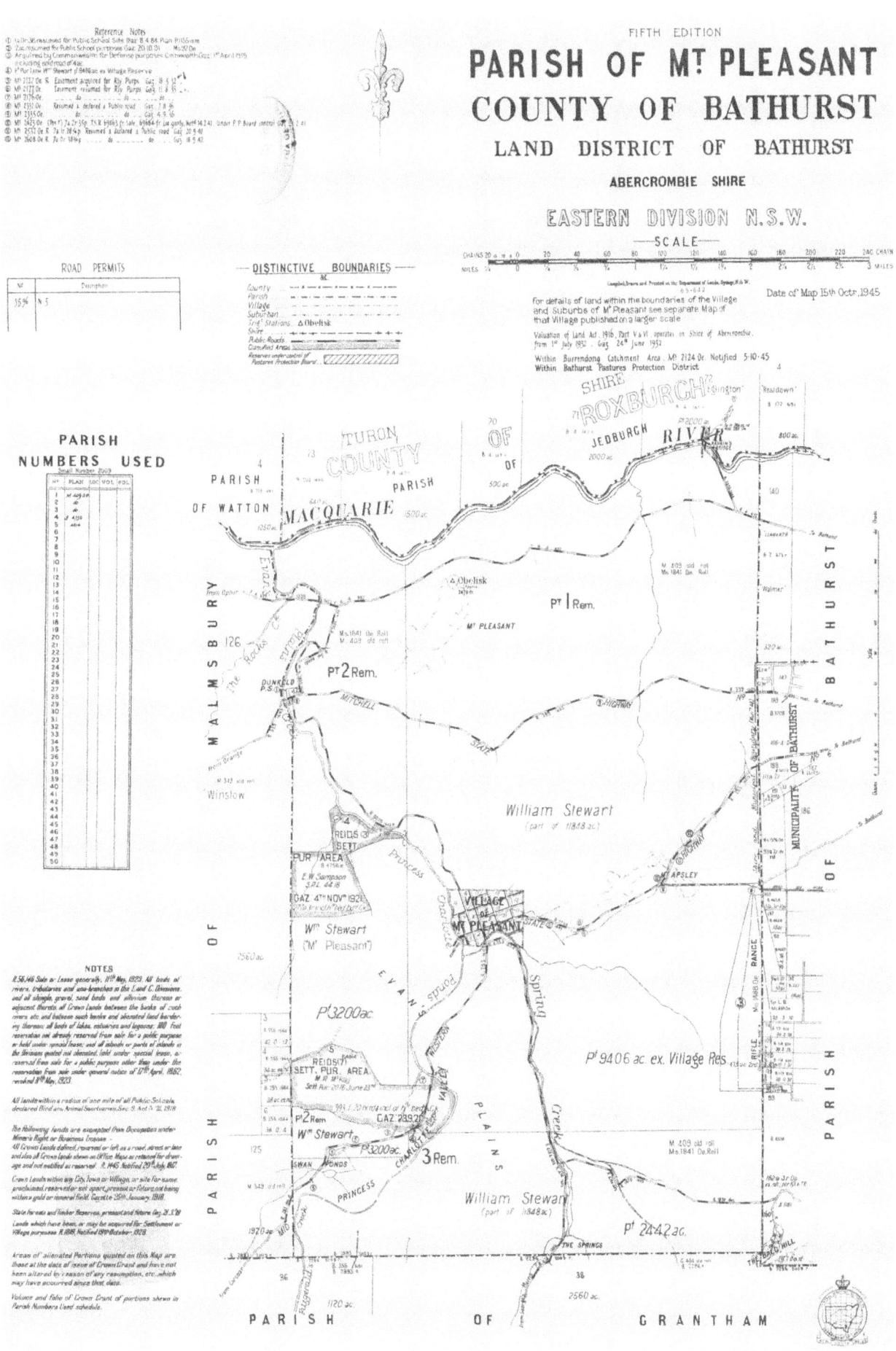

1945 Parish of Mt. Pleasant, County of Bathurst: Land District of Bathurst, Abercrombie Shire, Eastern Division N.S.W. (Department of Lands, Sydney) – Courtesy National Library of Australia

Major-General Stewart, 1815 – The Daily Telegraph (Sydney), 25 Nov 1922, p.13

1853 General Stewart's farm, 5 miles beyond Bathurst on the road to the diggings (Mt. Pleasant), NSW (G. F. Angas) – Courtesy National Library of Australia

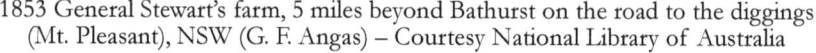

'Strath', Bathurst, erected by Major-General Stewart, "The house now known as Strath was there in 1837 ... Only one-third of the original portion remains, the rest having been taken down in the [18] 'seventies. It is now used as a holiday residence by Mrs. Sydney Jamieson, a granddaughter of the General." – The Daily Telegraph (Sydney) , 18 Nov 1922, p.13

'The Mount' [now known as Abercrombie House], Bathurst, erected by the late Mr. J. H. Stewart (James Horne Stewart) – The Daily Telegraph (Sydney) , 18 Nov 1922, p.13

1912 Stewart Family children at Mt. Pleasant – Courtesy Bathurst District Historical Society

ca. 1895 Abercrombie House – Courtesy Christopher Morgan

2023 Abercrombie House Stables – Courtesy Christopher Morgan

2023 Abercrombie House Stables, coach on loan from Ray Green – Courtesy Christopher Morgan

Cobb and Co's horse-drawn coaching comes to a close ...

1915 "VEHICLE ACCIDENT AT BATHURST. As the result of their horse taking fright at a motor lorry, Sir. and Mrs. John Storey and a child 8 years old are now in the Bathurst hospital. The horse played up at the sight of the motor, and capsized the vehicle, in which the family sat, and the six occupants were thrown out. Mr. Storey sustained a fracture of the leg, and the child received a similar injury ; while Mrs. Storey is suffering from concussion. The other children escaped uninjured." (Vehicle Accident at Bathurst, 23 Aug 1915, p.4)

1922 "MOTOR TRANSPORT. POPULARITY INLAND. REDUCING COSTS. The motor transport industry is making great progress throughout New South Wales, because farmers, merchants, and traders are beginning to realise the motor is a far better proposition than the horse, as greater distances can be run ... Transport is probably the oldest business in the world, and plays an important part in modern commerce, and as we have shown, is one of the biggest overhead expenses that have to be met. In many cases business men find that a large percentage of the profit they are entitled to is lost on transport. There is no particular reason why this should be the case if the transport problem is taken seriously, and if this is done it is possible to make it a profit-making factor in the business. Many things have to be considered in the transport question, the most important being the purchasing of an efficient vehicle, likely to have a long life, and run with a minimum of 'wear and tear,' cheap to maintain, reliable at all times and with a plentiful supply of spares in the country and a guaranteed service." (Motor Transport, 2 Dec 1922, p.20)

"No motor, be it ever so swift and sure, can ever be to the old Australian half as attractive as the coach with its sterling team, its sound equipment, and its splendid driver. There were bad times, too, and, after all, the old-timers will admit that the railway carriage admits less cold, rain, and icy winds, that there is more leg room, and food is rather more varied, though more hurriedly dispensed. But, one is a little sorry for travellers by the new order of things. They will never know the exquisiteness of a moonlit drive in winter through frost, or the exhilaration of the long rush downhill in the morning to a sleepy mining town, the stately march of forest and plain and hill along the old roads, and the glimpses of the old time settlement, and the friendly public house of wonderful meals, banished these many years by railway and motor." (Exit Cobb's, 5 Sep 1924, p.3)

"The romance of road-coaching in Australia ... abounds with incident and accident by flood and fell, by field and forest. Over miles of drought-stricken plains, through leagues of raging bush-fires, amid incessant rains and through the raging waters of swollen rivers, Cobb's coaches plunged along, beneath blazing sun-heat and in blinding storm, in heat and in cold, in midnight darkness and the crash of elemental war. The three great lamps have glowed in the blackest night as beacons of hope and messengers of civilisation, Cobb's mail-coach typifying a red link between the active world of affairs and the expatriated dwellers of the far Out-back." (A Pioneer of the Coaching Days: The Late James Rutherford, 20 Sep 1922, p.26)

"The passing of that old coach at Surat [Queensland] is the end of a gallant chapter in Australia's past ... Great names are associated with Cobb and Co.'s services, such as those of the late James Rutherford, of Bathurst, and the late Walter Hall, of Sydney. Though it is years now since the railways; and then the motor cars, displaced many of the old coaches, there was, up to recently, a wide net-work of these services spread all over out-back Australia. A fine service it was, full of peculiar Australian characteristics, casual, happy-go-lucky in many ways, marked by good fellowship, good humor, courage, and an immense patience with the weather, the vicissitudes of the road, and the extraordinary development of out-of-the-way human traits. What has become of all those splendid drivers and horsemen of old Cobb and Co.? Gone where we all must go—Daily Telegraph." (Exit Cobb's, 5 Sep 1924, p.3)

"Around the name of Cobb and Co. will ever linger memories of the most romantic period in Australian history—the roaring days of the 'Fifties, the days of the bushrangers, the days of historic adventure by flood and field, the days of the sternest pioneering ..." (Sydney Mail, 20 Apr 1921, p.10)

Appendices

Appendix 1: Supporting evidence for many Cobb and Co. proprietors

1854

"Freeman Cobb, of Brewster, Massachusetts; John Murray Peck, of Lebanon, New Hampshire; James Swanton, of Omar, in New York State; and John B. Lamber, of Leavenworth, out in the far west of those days, Kansas." (a [?] Drive, 31 July 1937, p.4)

"Cobb's three original partners —I would like to correct in one or two particulars ... the names of Cobb's three original partners ... were John Lamber, James Swanton, and John Murray Peck (my father) ... Within twelve months Lamber retired, and Arthur Blake came into the partnership, he and my father (Peck) managing the road and the outside business, Mr. Swanton the buying and supplying the fodder, which was an important business in those days, large quantities being imported from California, and hay from Tasmania at £37 10s per ton while Mr. Cobb managed the financing and Melbourne office." (Old Coaching Days, 10 Jun 1922, p.7)

"Mr. Lovell Smith, who is compiling a history of the coaching days, stated that the founders of Cobb and Co. were Freeman Cobb, James Swanton, John Murray Peck and John B. Lambert. This fact had frequently been misstated." (Motor Show, 6 May 1925, p.14)

1856

"NOTICE.—The Undersigned, intending to leave this colony, requests that all Unsettled Accounts, and Claims of every description, be presented at the Booking Office, No. 23 Bourke-street east, on or before Thursday next, 22nd inst., for settlement, after which date they will not be recognised. Freeman Cobb. Melbourne, May 16th, 1856." (Advertising, 19 May 1856, p.7)

"Notes and Queries. COBB AND CO. .. Correspondents, I notice, are inquiring when and where Messrs. Cobb and Co.'s coaches started? In answer to this question I have a distinct recollection of these coaches in Victoria in 1854. The entire plant—coaches, horses, stabling in various parts of the colony were owned by Thomas Davies, who in 1856, I think, or early in 1857, sold the lot for £60,000. The running of the coaches for a few years by Davies was well done, and the best of horses were used, costing up to £4/ a piece, but Mr. Davies, who was a true gentleman and valuable friend, did not succeed in making any adequate returns for himself. I do not remember who had the sobriquet of Cobb and Co., next or before Mr. Davies. It came from America, of course—Yours, QUEENSLAND." (Notes and Queries, 12 Sep 1885, p.19)

1857

"Grand Gift Enterprise ... Under the Management of the following Committee of Gentlemen ... Thos. Davis (Cobb and Co.) ... in consequence of a number of Gentlemen having taken the Unsold Tickets, he is able to carry out his original plan of distribution—First Gift (1,000) One Thousand Pounds, Second Gift" (Advertising, 27 Apr 1857, p.8)

"THE Co-partnership existing under the firm of Messrs Hoyt & Potter, coach proprietors, is by mutual consent this day dissolved. All claims against & all bills due the above firm will be settled by A. B. Covington, Cobb & Co's office. Signed, HENRY HOYT WARREN POTTER. Witness, A D. Shepard, Dated, Ballarat, August 31st, 1857" (Advertising, 1 Sep 1857, p.4)

"Notice.—Mr. Thomas Davies, having disposed of his entire interest in the Telegraph Stage Lines, both on the Melbourne and Castlemaine, and Geelong and Ballaarat Roads, to Alexander Walker, Esq., of Melbourne. In retiring from the business begs to tender his thanks to the public for the support hithorto granted him, and on behalf of his successor, who will ably sustain the reputation of Cobb and Co.'s Telegraph Lines, to ask a continuance of patronage. (Signed) Thomas Davies. 23 Bourke-street, Melbourne, September 19th, 1857." (Advertising, 26 Sep 1857, p.8)

"Tenders are Requested for the Lines Of Coaches, known as Cobb and Co.'s Telegraph and Estafette Lines, running between Geelong and Ballaarat, and between Melbourne and Castlemaine, Maryborough and Sandhurst. One-third of the purchase money at least must be paid in cash, and the balance by approved bills, at dates not exceeding three and six months. A cash tenderer in full will have preference. Parties may either tender for the one or both lines. Full particulars can be learned on application to the undersigned, with whom tenders are to be lodged. Tenders will be opened at Twelve noon, on Wednesday, 21st inst. The highest or any tender will not necessarily be accepted. Alex. Walker, Cobb and Co., Telegraph Coach Office, 23 Bourke-street, Melbourne, 8th October, 1857." (Advertising, 10 Oct 1857, p.8)

"Cobb & Co.'s Coaches, 24th October, 1857. All claims against the undersigned as proprietor of the Telegraph Line of Coaches to be sent in within ten days from this date, or they cannot be recognised. Alexander Walker, 23 Bourke street." (Advertising, 2 Nov 1857, p.1) 30 Dec 1857 "we have this day disposed of our entire interest in the Lines of Coaches now running on the Castlemaine, Sandhurst, and Maryborough roads, and known as Cobb and Co.'s Telegraph Lines, to Messrs. Swanton, Blake, and Co., who will continue running as usual. All accounts against said lines prior to date will be liquidated at our office. Watson and Hewitt. Per H. Butler. December 28th." (Advertising, 30 Dec 1857, p.3)

"Mr. A. Hewitt, a son of one of the principals of Watson and Hewitt, stated that his father entered the business in 1857, and pioneered the Gippsland service in 1863. He then went to South Africa, and started services to the gold diggings. Freeman Cobb also went to that country." (Motor Show, 6 May 1925, p.14)

1858

"We beg to inform the Public that we have this day disposed of our entire interest in the Lines of Coaches now running on the Castlemaine, Sandhurst and Maryborough roads (known as Cobb and Co.'s Telegraph Lines) to Messrs Swanston, Blake, and Co, who will continue running as usual. All claims against said lines to be sent in within one week from this date, otherwise they will not be liquidated. Watson & Hewitt, Per J. F. Sweeney, Castlemaine Hotel, Dec. 28, 1857." (Advertising, 1 Jan 1858, p.2)

"This day disposed of our Lines of Mail Coaches, plying between Melbourne and Ballaarat and Geelong and Ballaarat ... to Messrs. F. B. Clapp and Co. ... Watson and Hewitt." (Advertising, 19 Jan 1858, p.8)

"Cobb and Co's Telegraph Line of Mail Coaches ... Melbourne, Sandhurst, Maryborough, Ararat, and Pleasant Creek ... Swanton, Blake & Co ... A. L. Blake, Manager. ON and after this date the business heretofore carried on under the name Swanton, Blake, and Co., will be conducted under the style of the 'Victoria Stage Company.'—A. L. Blake, Manager." (Advertising, 23 Aug 1858, p.4)

1859

"NOTICE.—The undersigned, being about to leave the district, requests that all persons to whom he is indebted will send in their accounts to Mr. O. B. Clapp, M'Ivor Hotel, Maryborough, by the 1st March, otherwise they will not be recognised. W. H. BRAYTON." (Advertising, 1 Mar 1859, p.4)

"Victorian Stage Company partners ... Arthur Lincoln Blake (Head manager of business at Melbourne), Charles Culwell Gardiner, Jacob Rogers, Peleg Whitford Jackson, George Loop Woodworth, John Francis Britton, Levi Rich, Oliver Blake Clapp, Christopher Ives, John Murray Peck, James Joseph Blake formed 1st December 1857 ... Very soon after the business was launched by the purchase of Watson and Hewitt's line of coaches from Melbourne to Castlemaine ... Very soon after the business was launched the plaintiff [McCormick] and Mr. A. L. Blake had violent personal differences, which enlarged into differences on the policy of the partnership. The rest of the firm sided with Mr. Blake, and supported him in excluding the plaintiff ... from all practical interference in the business beyond his sharing in a very considerable income produced by it Mr. Blake and the other partners wished to establish new lines, which Mr. McCormick opposed." (Advertising, 19 Sep 1859, p.2)

"The Victorian Stage Company having taken the Livery Stables at the Castlemaine Hotel, horses entrusted to their charge will receive every attention. Civil and attentive grooms. The best oats and hay constantly kept: Charges moderate. P.S. Passages secured to Launceston, V. D. L., per screw steamers 'Royal Shepherd,' and 'Black Swan,' leaving Melbourne every 5 days. Apply to J. F. SWEENEY." (Advertising, 17 Oct 1859, p.2)

"NOTICE.—All CLAIMS against, and all Debts due to, the VICTORIAN STAGE COMPANY up to the 30th November, inst., must be SENT IN to the head office, No. 23 Bourke-street east, on or before the 16th December, proximo, as the partnership expires on the 30th inst. by effluxion of time. Victorian Stage Company, per A. L. BLAKE, Manager." (Advertising, 25 November 1859, p.3)

1860

"NEW YORK LIVERY and LETTING STABLES. 90 Bourke-street east, adjoining the Royal Mail Hotel and Cobb and Co.'s new booking office, and opposite the Theatre Royal. Saddle horses for ladies and gentlemen, buggies, barouches, carryalls, chaises, waggons, tiburies, dog-carts, trotting-sulkies, cabs, and light comfortable Coaches for picnics, excursions, &c. Livery for horses by the day, week, or month, on reasonable terms. Baits. Private sale-yards of the Victorian Stage Company for matched and single horses, of which a number are constantly on hand. Persons visiting the Theatre Royal may have their horses carefully attended to, and brought to the door of the theatre at close of the performance, or at five minutes' notice. Baits, or not, as desired. All the above-named vehicles are new. The horses have been selected for the express purpose of letting and comprise light showy hacks, and carriage horses, strong roadsters for journeys, fast trotters, and slow steady animals for family use. Parties having homes at this establishment may have them brought to their residence by leaving their orders with the manager. The proprietor, formerly a partner in the Victorian Stage Company, desires the favour of a call from all old friends and patrons of the line. F. J. ROGERS, Proprietor. J. M. BRADLEY, Manager" (Advertising, 16 Apr 1860, p.8)

"PROSPECTUS of the AUSTRALIAN STAGE COMPANY. Capital, £75,000, in 15,000 Shares of £5 each, Preliminary deposit of £1 per share to be paid on application, and the remaining sum of £4 per share within 14 days of allotment, or deposits will be forfeited. Operations will be commenced as soon as the amount of 8,000 shares are subscribed and paid up. In the event of the required number of shares not being subscribed for, the Directors undertake to return the deposits in full. Provisional Directors : William Randle, Esq., Melbourne. Cyrus Hewitt, Esq., Melbourne. William Williams, Esq., Melbourne. Matthew M'Caw, Esq., Melbourne. John R. Ricards, jun., Esq, Melbourne. John Halfey, Esq., Melbourne. A. L. Blake, Esq., Melbourne. F. B. Clapp, Esq., Melbourne. G. B. Perkins, Esq., Swan Hill. William Woods, Esq., Sandhurst. Thomas Ogilvie, Esq., Geelong. J. D. Robinson, Esq., Geelong. Hugh M'Phillimy, Esq., Geelong. C. C. Skarratt, Esq, Geelong. T. A. Lascelles, Esq., Geelong. J. T. Fallen, Esq., Albury. David Jones, Esq., Ballarat. Walter Craig, Esq., Ballarat. Alexander Kelly, Esq., Ballarat. Frederick Taylor, Esq., Castlemaine. Edward Cay, Esq., Castlemaine. B. Butterworth, Esq., Castlemaine. Caleb Anderson, Esq., Castlemaine. Charles Croaker, Esq., Portland. B. H. Fernald, Esq, Pitfield. William Malcolm, Esq., Hamilton. Joel Tompkins, Esq., Raglan. Oliver Cooper, Esq., Ararat. J. L. Huntley, Esq., Belfast. Francis Tozer, Esq., Warrnambool. With power to add to their number. Bankers—Bank of New South Wales. Solicitor—W. H. Gatty Jones, Esq. Secretary—W. Kent Hall, Esq.

"NOTICE.—We, the undersigned, hereby give notice, that we have WITHDRAWN our NAMES from the published LIST of DIRECTORS of the AUSTRALIAN STAGE COMPANY, and ceased to have any connexion therewith since the 22nd ult, Dated June 8, 1860. BENJAMIN BUTTERWORTH. CALEB ANDERSON. EDWARD CAY. F. TAYLOR" (Advertising, 11 Jun, 1860, p. 8) Advertised the same week "Introduction of Australian birds into Britain.—Gentleman desirous to aid in Mr. Edward Wilson's plan of introducing the AUSTRALIAN MAGPIE and LAUGHING JACKASS into BRITAIN are requested to SEND BIRDS of those species to the undersigned, who will be glad to arrange for their transmission to Europe. Ferd. Mueller. Melbourne Botanical and Zoological Gardens, January l8." (Advertising, 12 Jun, 1860, p. 3)

"WE, the undersigned, do hereby give notice that the PARTNERSHIP hitherto existing, between us, under the style of the VICTORIAN STAGE COMPANY, EXPIRED by effluxion of time on the 25th of June ult. All claims against the said company up to that date must be sent in to A L. Blake, the manager, in Melbourne, or to one of the agents mentioned below on or before the 21st of August, or they will not be recognised. The names of the agents are as follows :—J. F. Britton, Sandhurst ; P. W. Jackson, Castlemaine ; J. M. Connoll, Digger's Rest ; C. D. Pollock, Maryborough ; H. T. Millie, Shamrock Hotel, Ararat ; A. Montegani, Creswick's Creek ; E. T. Foley, Ballarat ; James Hay, M'Ivor ; Wm. Jones, Echuca. (Signed) ARTHUR LINCOLN BLAKE. PELEY WHITFORD JACKSON. JOHN FRANCIS BRITTON. OLIVER BLAKE CLAPP. CHRISTOPHER IVES. JOHN MURRAY PECK. CHARLES CULWELL GARDINER." (Advertising, 21 Jul 1860, p.3)

1861

"NOTICE.—The PARTNERSHIP hitherto existing between ALEXANDER W. ROBERTSON, WILLIAM B. BRADLEY, WALTER R. HALL, WILLIAM F. WHITNEY, EDWARD MOORE, and FRANK MAY, and trading under the name of the Bendigo Stage Company, has been this day DISSOLVED, by mutual consent, that is so far as said Alexander W. Robertson is concerned, who retires from the firm, having disposed of his interest in the same to the above named W. B. Bradley, W. R. Hall, W. F. Whitney, Edward Moore, and F. May, who will still continue to carry on the business as heretofore. ALEXANDER W. ROBERTSON. WILLIAM B. BRADLEY. WALTER R. HALL. WILLIAM F. WHITNEY. EDWARD MOORE. FRANK MAY. Witness—B. G. Teasdale." (Advertising, 1 Feb 1861, p.8)

"Notice.—The Business heretofore carried on under the style or title of F. B. Clapp & Co. Will in future be known as The Australian Stage Company. E. T. FOLEY, Agent." (Advertising, 28 Jan 1861, p.1)

"Cobb and Co's Leviathan Coaches ... Australian Stage Company ... C. Russell, Manager, Geelong and Melbourne; A. C. Brunig, Manager, Ballarat" Advertised on the same page "To Lovers of Cleanliness. You may get your head cleaned for 1s ; hair cut for a bob ; face cleanly shaven and washed with lavender water for 6d.—at Professor Antonio Lopas's. All may come." (Advertising, 15 Mar 1861, p.1)

"Notice.—The partnership heretofore existing under the style of the Bendigo Stage Office having expired by effluxion of time, and the plant being disposed of to Messrs. Watson and Hewitt, the coaches of the above firm will cease running after the 30th inst. All accounts due to or by the firm to be rendered at this office within 15 days from date. W. R. Hall, W. F. Whitney, W. B. Bradley, Edward Moore, Frank May. 48 Bourke-street east, March 28, 1861." (Advertising, 28 Mar 1861, p.3)

"The Undersigned having sold their line of Coaches to Messrs. Robertson, Britton, and Co., request that all accounts against them be sent in immediately to their office Lonsdale street west. Watson and Hewitt 3 June, 1861." (Advertising, 4 Jun 1861, p.1)

"Cobb's Coaches—We understand that Messrs. Watson and Hewitt, who have for so long been the proprietors of Cobb's Telegraph Line of Coaches, have disposed of all their interest in the line to Messrs. Robertson, Britton, and Co, both the principal partners in which firm have long been connected with coaching enterprise in Victoria. An advertisement, which appears in our columns, requests that all accounts against Messrs. Watson and Hewitt, in this district, may be sent in to Mr. C. D. Pollock, M'Ivor Hotel, Maryborough, for liquidation." (Advertising, 7 Jun 1861, p.3)

Matthew Veal, proprietor Smythesdale Line of Coaches (Advertising, 14 Jun 1861, p.1)

"Permit me, Sir, to inform you ... mail contract for this year to Clapp and Co ... In the present year 1861, John M'Phee is the contractor for the Mail service, No. 132, Keilor road to Ballaarat, and for No. 143, Ballarat to Avoca, both of which contracts have been purchased from him by the Australian Stage Company, and carried by them. That they purchased the plant off Mr M'Phee, and paid him as consideration for the mail service on the condition that he should not tender for those mails in 1862, unless at such a figure as they might think proper. This information I had from M'Phee himself in the presence of two other gentlemen ... I am besides informed that Robertson, Britton and Co, who are present carrying out the contract of Watson and Hewitt, on the Castlemaine road, have been in negotiation with him for the line Castlemaine to Creswick, &c. ... Australian Stage Company, of which Russell and Warren are partners ... (Signed) WM. BROWN, Mail Contractor, Geelong." (Advertising, 20 Nov 1861, p. 6)

1862

"Mr. G. O. R. Fenner, of St. Kilda, writes with reference to the partners in Cobb and Co.:—The city agent was A. Butler ; his brother was agent at Geelong, C. Miller at Castlemaine, J. Crowley at Sandhurst, J. Blake at Maryborough, J. M. Peck at Ballarat (afterwards the Ballarat agent was E. J. Brayton). John Wagner was superintendent in Melbourne. Neither E. Brayton nor W. Brittin was in the firm. After Mr. Hewitt's death A. W. Robertson and John Wagner became partners with Mr. Watson, and subsequently Walter Hall and E. James. The title of the firm then became Robertson, Wagner, and Co." (Notes & Answers, 4 May 1918, p.25)

"Cobb to the Lachlan.—We understand that in a few days, a large portion of, Messrs. Robertson, Britton and Co.'s stock will be transported overland to Sydney, for the purpose of opening regular communication between that city and the Lachlan. The conveyances at present running on that route are of a very primitive order, and will soon have to retire before the excellent coaches, magnificent horses, and first class Jehus, who acknowledge the way of the ubiquitous Cobb." (Castlemaine Police Court, 28 May 1862, p.2)

1865

"The first coaches ran in 1865, when Mr. H. Barnes, who died in April of this year, one of the oldest drivers and road managers of the firm, came to Brisbane to inspect, and shortly after brought the first turn-out, consisting of 16 coaches in all, made at the Bathurst factory of Cobb & Co. The first line was from Brisbane to Ipswich, Mr. Barnes opening the line with a team of twelve horses, he being strapped to the box. The writer of this notice well remembers travelling by coach to Ipswich in 1873. The vehicle was a 36-passenger coach, and was punted across the river at what was then known as Oxley Point (now Chermside). No luggage was carried, that being conveyed by the river steamers Settler, Shamrock, Glide, and other boats which used to ply between Brisbane and the confluence of the Brisbane and the Bremer. Cobb & Co. in Queensland was a separate concern from that in the south, although worked in conjunction, and Mr. Rutherford states that the partnership was at first split up as follows:—Mr. James Rutherford, half share; Mr. H. Barnes and Mr. John Robertson each one-quarter. The first stables were in Albert-street, Brisbane, on the site now occupied by Messrs. Fleming & Sons ironmongers. A big fire occurred in the late '60s, and new premises were obtained where the Queensland Machinery Co.'s premises now stand, and later on at the junction of Queen-street and Petrie Bight, where is now Joliffe's showroom and near Uhl's saddlery works. Both of these were old employees of Cobbs and shareholders." (The Gensis of Cobb & Co., 15 Sep 1917, p.11)

1866

"PENOLA. (From our own correspondent.) January 17, 1866. The weather here has been, very hot and sultry, the thermometer at times ranging over 100°. Messrs. Meigs and Anderson, the present spirited mail contractors from here to Hamilton have just placed one of the best class of Victorian coaches on the line ; and in consequence of their having nearly the whole of the Western District mails, passengers have now the advantage of booking right through to their destination, without chance of detention. It is to be hoped they will meet with the support they deserve. When shall we get our Adelaide mails conveyed in the same enterprising manner ?" (Penola, 20 Jan 1866, p.2)

1867

"In the juries of four court, yesterday, before Mr Justice Williams, the sitting was occupied with two cases in which official assignees were concerned. The first, that of Courtney v. Bennett and another, was to recover a sum of £375 paid to the defendants, as solicitors for Cyrus Hewitt, and on account of the sale of a number of his coaches, horses and harness before his insolvency. The jury awarded £109, being the amount claimed, less certain moneys owing to the defendants, and others paid by them on Hewitt's account. The case of Boland v. Shaw was to recover from an official assignee the value of some furniture seized and sold due by the insolvent for rent ... The causes for trial before juries of four will be divided on and after Wednesday next between the Chief Justice and Mr Justice Williams, the former taking the odd numbers on the list." (The News of the Day, 6 Aug 1867, p.5)

1868

"An extraordinary journey was made yesterday by Messrs. Robertson, Wagner, Geo. Watson, and James, proprietors of the Beechworth line of mail-coaches. The party, in buggy drawn by two horses (with changes) made the extraordinary trip of 163 miles, from Wangaratta to Melbourne, starting at four a.m., and reaching Melbourne at seven p.m By far the greater part of the journey was over bush roads, and Mr. George Watson drove all the way. The result shows the quality of Australian horses, and also the capacity of the driver. It may be added the patty stopped not unfrequently to refresh the cattle, and had a far from hasty dinner at Avenel, on the road." ('Tuesday, January 14, 1868', 14 Jan 1868, p.5)

"Judgments have been signed in the Supreme Court against the Queen in favour of Elizabeth Wingate Grant, for £80, and £6 1s. 3d. costs; Alex. W. Robertson, George John Watson, Willian James, and John Wagner, for £132; and £6 1s. 6d. costs; John H. W. Pettiit, £52 10s., £6 6s. 4d. costs. (The Gippsland Times, 7 Jul 1868, p.2)

1860s

"Jimmy Nicholas ... groom, driver, agent, manager, part owner, and finally, I was practically sole owner of Cobb and Co., Limited in Western Australia ... I merely mention this, to show that what I am about to say in regard to the different owners of coaching, that I have known in Australia is just what I personally saw of them. I have only heard of the original Mr. Cobb, who did some coaching in the early days of Victoria, also of different other early day coaching owners, but the most of these early day men, if not all, did not stick at the business anything like the time that the six men I am going to mention did, and neither did they do one-fiftieth part of the coaching these men have done. Their names were— Alick and John Robertson, John Wagner, Walter Hall and James Rutherford. A sixth man, Mr. Whitney, was connected with the firm, but I never saw him, and think he must have gone out of the business before my time. They were, I think, all Americans, and no doubt Rutherford, Wagner and Hall were supermen, who would have been great at any calling they took up. The two Robertson brothers were more of the office-type— good financiers, but not nearly the ginger in them the other three men had. I think they all came across from America to get to the Victorian goldfields. They had had coaching experience already in America with Wells, Fargo and Company, and I take it that when they saw the possibilities coaching offered in Victoria they at once grasped it, and were soon the King Cobbs of Australian coaching, a position they retained for many years. They all became very wealthy. They bought and formed some splendid sheep stations in the different States, and were largely interested in mining, especially in that very rich Queensland mine, Mt. Morgans. Mr. Hall died worth over a million, and the others followed on pretty closely, I think. They are all dead now and have been for some years. Somewhere in the [18]sixties they dissolved the partnership in Victoria. Jim Rutherford and Walter Hall took New South Wales as their base of operations, and traded as 'Cobb and Co., Rutherford and Hall, Proprietors, Sydney.' The two Robertson brothers and Jack Wagner retained the Victorian portion and traded as Cobb and Co., Robertson and Wagner, Proprietors, Melbourne.' The two firms were known as Victorian Cobb and New South Wales Cobb. Victorian Cobb did nearly all Victorian coaching. They crossed the Murray at Echuca and ran all that western portion of New South Wales out as far as Tibooburra, some 700 miles from Echuca. Sydney Cobb did the balance of New South Wales, and were largely interested in the Queensland Cobb and Co., which was I think, another registered company." (Coaching in the Commonwealth, 17 May 1925, p.9)

"When the doldrums fell on Victorian gold mining, in the [18] sixties, and the gold boom commenced in New Zealand, many of the coaches were shipped to Dunedin, and 'Cobb and Co.'s Telegraph Line of Coaches' started its picturesque career in the Dominion." (The Coaching Days, 10 Mar 1932, p.7)

1871

"Dissolution of partnership.—Notice is hereby given, that the partnership heretofore existing between the undersigned, as station owners and coach proprietors, in the colonies of Victoria, New South Wales, and Queensland, has been this day dissolved by mutual consent. Dated 15th day of August, 1871 A. W. Robertson, J. Rutherford, W. B. Bradley, Wm. F. Whitney, John Wagner. Witness—Alf B. Malieson, solicitor and notary public, Melbourne." (Advertising, 23 Dec 1871, p.3)

1872

"THE UNDERSIGNED, now and for many year past trading in New South Wales and Queensland's Mail Contractors, Coach Proprietors, and Station Holders, under the name, style, and firm of 'COBB and CO.,' hereby give NOTICE that they have no interest, or connection with, the line of omnibuses running in Sydney, having the name of Cobb and Co. painted on the doors. Dated this 20th December, 1871. James Rutherford. Walter R. Hall. William B. Bradley. William F. Whitney. Colin Robertson." (Advertising, 1 Jan 1872, p.1)

1874

"NOTICE is hereby given, that Mr. William Brown Bradley has retired this day from the partnership known as 'Cobb & Co.,' and that the said partnership will henceforth be carried by James Rutherford, Walter Russell Hall; William Franklin Whitney, and Colin Robertson. Witness our hands this 9th day of January, 1874. J. Rutherford. W. R. Hall. Wm. F. Whitney. Colin Robertson. W. B. Bradley. Witness,—George Pinnock." (NOTICE is hereby given, that Mr. William Brown Bradley has retired this day from the partnership known as Cobb & Co., 13 Jan 1874, p.76)

1876

"NOTICE is hereby given, that the partnership heretofore existing between the undersigned, as Coach Proprietors and Factors, and also as Station Holders and otherwise, under the style of 'Cobb & Co.,' has this day been dissolved by mutual consent ; and that the said business of the said partnership in all their branches, be in New South Wales and Queensland, will be carried on in future under the same style or firm by the said James Rutherford, Walter Russell Hall and William Franklin Whitney, by whom all the liabilities of the said firm will be discharged, and who will take and receive all the assets and debts of such firm, their receipts being sufficient discharges therefor. Dated this sixth day of May, A.D. 1876. James RUTHERFORD. W. R. HALL. WM. F. WHITNEY. COLIN ROBERTSON. A. W. ROBERTSON. Witness to the signatures of James Rutherford and Colin Robertson—A. PARRY LONG, Solicitor, Sydney. Witness to the signatures of W. F. Whitney, A. W. Robertson, and W. R. Hall—ALFRED H. PRINCE." (Advertising, 10 May 1876, p.6)

1881

"Qld SHAREHOLDERS in the BUSINESS. The first Queensland Cobb and Co., Limited, was incorporated in August 1881. The capital was £50, 000 in 500 shares of £100 each. The registered shareholders were W. R. Hall (Sydney), £9000 ; J. Rutherford (Bathurst), £10,000 ; F. Shaw (Brisbane), £2000 ; I. T. Barthelomew (Goganga), £1000 ; T. Gallagher (St. George), £600 ; C. M. Kirk (St. George), £1000 ; F. C. Shaw (Bogantungun), £1000 ; H. W. Shaw (Emerald), £900 ; H. B.

Taylor (Tambo), £1000 ; R. M'Master (Aramac), £400 ; J. Coyle (Roma), £200 ; W. J. Richardson (St. George), £200 ; L. Uhl (Brisbane), £200 ; J. Coyle (Charters Towers), £1000 ; W. Jenkins (Mangalore), £100 ; John Bock (Cunnamulla), £400." (For the Man on the Land, 13 Dec 1920, p.5)

1885

"Notice is hereby given that the partnership lately subsisting between us, the undersigned, James Rutherford, Walter Russell Hall, and William Franklin Whitney, carrying on business as coach proprietors, mail contractors, railway contractors, &c., under the style or firm of 'Cobb & Co.,' has been dissolved by mutual consent, as from the 15th day of October, 1885, so far as regard the said Walter Russell Hall, who retires from the firm. All debts due to or owing by the said late firm will be received and paid by the said James Rutherford and William Franklin Whitney, who will continue to carry on the business under the present style or firm of 'Cobb & Co.' As witness our hands, this 18th day of January, 1886. J. Rutherford. Witness to the signature of James Rutherford,—B. Hughes, W. R. Hall. Witness to the signature of Walter Russell Hall,—B. Hughes, Wm. F Whitney. Witness to the signature of William Franklin Whitney,—B. Hughes." (New South Wales Government Gazette, 29 Jan 1886, p.748)

1888

"DUNKELD. (From our own correspondent.) July 31. Coaching days in Victoria are now almost memories of the past, in consequence of the extended railway system throughout the colony. My recollection carries me back to the good old times early in the fifties when Cobb and Co. monopolised the passenger traffic between Hamilton and Ballarat, when Meggs and Anderson carefully and fearlessly tooled their conveyance with that indomitable pluck and endurance characteristic of the Yankee. Sometimes the obstacles met with were rather of a formidable character. A large tree would often be found lying across the coach track, completely blocking it. When passing through thickly timbered country much watchfulness had to be exercised to escape falling branches and trees. Indeed in most coaching journeys great care, courage and nerve were required on the part of the drivers, as well as coolness and decision, in overcoming the difficulties and dangers of the road ; but what could be more delightful than a drive through the bush on the box seat of a coach enlivened by the racy anecdotes and native wit of an American jehu? What a contrast to the present monotonous, but more rapid journey in a well appointed carriage behind the iron horse ? Not only did Cobb and Co. enliven the road, but commercial travellers, bullock teams et hoc genus omne contributed their quota to an exciting, wholesome and profitable trade now mopped up by railway transit. Any thing that will relieve the dull monotony of our bush towns is welcome. We therefore duly appreciated a visit from the Wickcliffe footballers last Saturday." (Dunkeld, 2 Aug 1888, p.4)

1889

"Mr J. Noble Wilson (The Ballarat Trustees Executors and Agency Company, Limited) reports the sale of Mr. A. Grant's cottage and freehold, Pleasant street, to Mr James Darby, at a satisfactory price. Also, on account of Messrs Vines and M'Phee (Cobb and Cos.), their premises, M'Kenzie street, to Mr Alexander Bell, for the sum of £500. Several purchasers for central shop and cottage properties unsupplied." (Advertising, 31 Aug 1889, p.3)

1894

"Carriage from Temora to the field is £3 10s per ton, but I think it will fall to about 30s after the roads get better. The coach fare is £1 each way. Cheap enough if the accommodation were good, which it is not. If Robertson, Wagner and Co. had taken a few of their spare coaches and a hundred horses to Temora, they would have done well. Sydney Cobb's manager was on the field the other day, and there is a probability of that firm putting on a line of coaches. Every conceivable description of conveyance is to be met with on the road between Wyalong and Temora, from a 20-bullock team to a wheelbarrow." (The Wyalong Goldfield, 3 Apr 1894)

"Cobb and Co. MR. W. F. WHITNEY, who died at Combing Park, Carcoar, a few days ago, was one of the original members of the great firm of Cobb and Co, the others being Messrs. A. W. Robertson, John Wagner, W. R. Hall, W. B. Bradley, and James Rutherford." (Cobb and Co., 14 Nov 1894, p.2)

1898

"The next to take over the business was Robertson and Britton, in whose interest the business was conducted for the next two years, when Mr Britton sold his interest, and Mr John Wagner entered into partnership with Mr Robertson, since which Robertson, Wagner Co. have controlled and owned the business." (Reminiscences of Cobb and Co., 26 Jan 1898, p.4)

1922

Queensland "Mr. E. Palmer, contractor for the mail from Charleville to Augathella and Tambo, will take over the coaches from Cobb and Co. on Saturday, having purchased all the plant and horses of Cobb and Co., as that firm is retiring from the coaching business in the West." (Interstate, 7 Jan 1922, p.29)

1908

"In 1861 the firm decided to extend their operations to New South Wales, and for that purpose took into partnership Messrs. James Rutherford, Walter Hall, Franklin Whitney, W. Bradley, and R. Brunig ... Mr. Brunig, mentioned as one of the party who came over in 1861, from Victoria to New South Wales, went out of the partnership before the firm purchased Crane and Roberts' interest in the southern districts. He had become timorous of the opposition that was opposed to the new firm by Crane and Roberts, and was compelled to sell his interest to the other members of the firm, and shortly afterwards left the Colony for the United States of America." (The Contributor, 25 Nov 1908, p.1405)

1929

"COBB & CO., IN VOLUNTARY LIQUIDATION. Notice is hereby given that Creditors in the abovenamed Company are required, on or before the 30th day of September, 1929, to send their names and addresses and particulars of their Debts or Claims to ALFRED UHL, 484 Queen-street, Brisbane, Liquidator of the said Company, and, if so required by notice in writing from the said Liquidator, are, by their Solicitors or personally, to come in and prove their said Debts or Claims at such time and place as shall be specified in such notice, or, in default thereof, they shall be excluded from the benefits of any distributions made before such Debts or Claims are proved. Dated at Brisbane the Twenty-seventh day of August, 1929. Alfred Uhl. Liquidator." (Advertising, 31 Aug 1929, p.3)

Appendix 2: Overview of Cobb and Co.'s Coaching lines in New South Wales

Sources are listed under 'Advertising' in the Reference List.

1862

Expansion further into New South Wales from Victoria:

28 Jun 1862 Cobb and Co's Telegraph Line of Coaches—Lachlan via Orange ... Cobb and Co's Office, Bathurst. James Rutherford. Manager N.S.W.; 22 Jul 1862 Cobb and Co's Telegraph Line of Royal Mail Coaches—running in connection with the Government Railways, from Penrith, Campbelltown ... Bathurst, Orange, Lachlan, Mudgee, Berrima, Goulburn, Yass, Lambing Flat ... Company's Office, Royal Hotel, George-street [Sydney]. W. R. Hall, Agent; 15 Oct 1862 Cobb and Co's Telegraph Line of Royal Mail Coaches—Penrith and Sydney, Paramatta, Forbes via Orange, Forbes via Carcoar and Cowra, Lambing Flat via Cowra, Orange, Mudgee

1863

13 Jul 1863 Cobb and Co's Telegraph Line of Royal Mail Coaches—Berrima, leaving Picton ... on arrival of train from Sydney ; 16 Jun 1863 Cobb and Company's Telegraphic Line, of Royal Mail Coaches—connection with the Government Railways from Penrith and Campbelltown ... Hartley, Bathurst, Carcoar, Cowra, Orange, Wellington, Forbes, Mudgee, Berrima, Goulburn, Gunning, Yass, Gundagai, Tarcutta, Albury, Lambing Flat, and intermediate stages ... Company's office, Royal Hotel, George-street. W. R. Hall ; 21 Aug 1863 Cobb and Co.'s Coaches.—Penrith to Bathurst, fare £1

1864

11 May 1864 NOTICE. Cobb and Co.'s Telegraph Line of Coaches—Day Coach for Bathurst will start from Beatson's Hotel, Penrith, at 6 a.m. Passengers must leave Sydney by the 5 p.m. or 11.30 p.m. trains the evening before. W. R. Hall ; 23 Dec 1863 Conveyance of Post Office Mails from the 1st January next ... 12 Cobb and Co ... Address Sydney ... Railway Station and Post Office Penrith, Hartley, Bathurst, and Orange. Current fare to be paid for every seat required by Government, other than those for Postal Inspectors and Mail Guards; 16 Cobb and Co. £2 10s. to be paid for every seat required by Government, other than those for Postal Inspectors and Mail Guards ... Orange, Murga, Forbes; 39 Cobb and Co ... Bathurst, Peel, Sofala; 17 Cobb and Co ... Picton, Goulburn, Yass; 23 Dec 1864 Conveyance of Post Office Mails from the 1st January next ... 14 Cobb and Co ... Address Sydney ... Railway Station and Post Offices Penrith, Hartley, Bathurst, and Orange; 18 Cobb and Co. £2 10s. to be paid for every seat required by Government, other than those for Postal Inspectors and Mail Guards ... Orange, Murga, and Forbes; 22 Cobb and Co ... Orange, Stony Creek, Ironbarks, Black Rock, Wellington, and Montefiores; 39 Cobb and Co ... Bathurst, Peel, and Sofala ; 15 Cobb and Co ... Picton, Goulburn, and Yass

1865

22 Dec 1865 Conveyance of Post Office Mails from the 1st January next ... 15 Cobb and Co ... Address Sydney ... Railway Station and Post Offices Penrith, Hartley, Bathurst, and Orange. Current fare to be paid for every seat required by Government, other than those for Postal Inspectors and Mail Guards ; 22 Cobb and Co ... Orange, Toogong, Murga, and Forbes ; 26 Cobb and Co. 40s. to be paid for every seat required by Government, other than those for Postal Inspectors and Mail Guards ... Orange, Stony Creek, Ironbarks, Black Rock, Wellington, and Montefiores ; 45 Cobb and Co ... Bathurst, Peel, and Sofala ; 57 Cobb and Co ... Bathurst, Evans Plains, Blayney, Carcoar, and Cowra ; 16 Cobb and Co... Picton, Goulburn, and Yass

1866

18 Dec 1866 Conveyance of Post Office Mails from the 1st January next... 13 Cobb & Co ... Address Sydney ... Penrith and Orange ; 14 Cobb & Co ... Orange, Stony Creek, Ironbarks, Black Rock, Wellington, and Montefiores ; Cobb & Co ... Hartley, Bowenfels, and Mudgee; 33 Cobb and Co ... Bathurst, Peel, and Sofala ; 44 Cobb & Co ... Bathurst, Evans Plains, Blayney, Carcoar, and Cowra ; 49 Cobb & Co ... Orange, Toogong, Murga, and Forbes ; 13 Cobb and Co ... Picton, Yass

1868

6 Jan 1868 Conveyance of Post Office Mails from the 1st January next ... 16 Cobb & Co ... Address Sydney ... Penrith and Orange; 17 Cobb & Co ... Orange, Stony Creek, Ironbarks, Wellington, and Montefiores; ; Orange, Molong, Black Rock, Wellington, and Montefiores; 21 Cobb & Co ... Hartley, Bowenfels, and Mudgee; 36 Cobb and Co ... Bathurst, Peel, and Sofala; 46 Cobb & Co ... Bathurst, Evans Plains, Blayney, Carcoar, and Cowra; 47 Cobb & Co ... Cowra and Grenfell; 52 Cobb & Co ... Orange, Toogong, Murga, and Forbes; 17 Cobb and Co ... Picton and Yass

1869

30 Dec 1868 Conveyance of Post Office Mails from the 1st January next ... 14 Cobb & Co ... Address Sydney ... Penrith and Orange ; 15 Cobb & Co ... Orange, Stony Creek, Ironbarks, Wellington, and Montefiores; Orange, Molong, Black Rock, Wellington, and Montefiores ; 19 Cobb & Co ... Hartley, Bowenfels, and Mudgee ; 37 Cobb and Co ... Bathurst, Peel, and Sofala ; 49 Cobb & Co ... Bathurst, Evans Plains, Blayney, Carcoar, and Cowra ; 50 Cobb & Co ... Cowra and Grenfell ; 2 Cobb and Co ... Picton and Yass ; 73 Cobb and Co ... Hay, Wanganella, and Deniliquin ; 83 Cobb and Co ... Deniliquin, Moama, and Echuca

1870

19 Jan 1870 Goulburn to Albury ; Goulburn to Yass ; 17 Jan 1870 Conveyance of Post Office Mails from the 1st January next ... 1 Cobb & Co ... Address Sydney ... Railway Station, One-tree Hill, and Post Offices, One-tree Hill and Orange ; Hartley, Bowenfells, and Mudgee ; Bathurst, Peel, and Sofala ; Railway Station, Goulburn, and Post Offices, Goulburn and Gundagai ; Gundagai and Albury; 17 Cobb & Co ... Orange, Stony Creek, Ironbarks, Black Rock, Wellington, and Montefiores; Orange, Molong, Black Rock, Wellington, and Montefiores ; 56 Cobb & Co. £2 to be paid for every seat required by Government, other than those for Postal Inspectors and Mail Guards ... Bathurst, Evans Plains, Blayney, Carcoar, and Cowra; 57 Cobb & Co ... Cowra and Grenfell ; 78 Cobb and Co ... Hay, Wanganella, and Deniliquin ; 91 Cobb and Co ... Deniliquin, Moama, and Eucha; 10 May 1870 Telegraph Inn, Gunning

1871

4 Jan 1871 Conveyance of Post Office Mails from the 1st January next ... 1 Cobb & Co ... Address Sydney ... Railway Station, One-tree Hill, and Post Offices, One-tree Hill and Orange ; Hartley, Bowenfells, and Mudgee ; Bathurst, Peel, and Sofala ; Railway Station, Goulburn, and Post Offices, Goulburn and Gundagai ; Gundagai and Albury; 18 Cobb & Co ... Orange, Stony Creek, Ironbarks, Black Rock, Wellington, and Montefiores; Orange, Molong, Black Rock, Wellington, and Montefiores ; 59 Cobb & Co. £2 to be paid for every seat required by Government, other than those for Postal Inspectors and Mail Guards ... Bathurst, Evans' Plains, Blayney, Carcoar, and Cowra; 85 Cobb and Co ... Hay, Wanganella, and Deniliquin; 99 Cobb and Co ... Deniliquin, Moama, and Eucha; 45 Cobb & Co ... Railway Station, Muswellbrook, and Post Office, Armidale; 12 Aug 1871 Cobb & Co's Northern Espress—Scone to Tamworth and Armidale ... Starr's New England Hotel, Armidale ... Green's Caledonion Hotel, Tamworth ; Cobb & Co., Murrurundi and Sydney, and Wright, Barker & Co., Sydney

1872

3 Jan 1872 Conveyance of Post Office Mails ... 1 Cobb & Co ... Address Sydney ... Railway Station, One-tree Hill, and Post Offices, One-tree Hill and Orange ; Hartley, Bowenfells, and Mudgee ; Bathurst, Peel, and Sofala ; Railway Station, Goulburn, and Post Offices, Goulburn and Gundagai ; Gundagai and Albury; 19 Cobb & Co ... Orange, Stony Creek, Ironbarks, Black Rock, Wellington, and Montefiores; Orange, Molong, Black Rock, Wellington, and Montefiores ; 59 Cobb & Co ... Bathurst, Evans' Plains, Blayney, Carcoar ; Carcoar and Cowra; 50 Cobb & Co ... Railway Station, Muswellbrook, and Post Office, Armidale; 29 May 1872 Telegraph Line of Coaches. Cobb & Co.—From Wagga to Tarcutta ... Booking Office : M. Callaghan's, Commercial Hotel, Wagga Wagga; 22 Jun 1872 Telegraph Line of Coaches. Cobb & Co.—From Wagga to Tarcutta, Albury, Sydney and Melbourne ... Booking Office : John Clark's Criterion Hotel, Wagga Wagga; 21 Sep 1872 Telegraph Line of Coaches. Cobb & Co.—From Wagga to Tarcutta, Adelong, Albury, Sydney and Melbourne ... Booking Office : John Clark's Criterion Hotel, Wagga Wagga

1873

16 Jan 1873 Conveyance of Post Office Mails ... 1 Cobb & Co ... Address Sydney ... 1 Railway Station, Macquarie Plains, and Post Offices, Bathurst and Orange ; Railway Station, Wallerawang, and Post Offices, Wallerawang Railway Station and Mudgee ; Dubbo, Warren, Cannonbar, Gongolgon, and Bourke ; Railway Station, Goulburn, and Post Offices, Goulburn and Gundagai ; Gundagai and Albury ; 24 Cobb & Co ... Ilford, Upper Pyramid, Tambaroora, and Hill End, via Tabrabucca Swamp ; 86 Cobb & Co ... Orange, Shepherd's Creek, Ironbarks, Black Rock, Wellington, and Montefiores; Orange, Shepherd's Creek, Molong, Black Rock, Wellington, and Montefiores ; 37 Cobb & Co ... Wellington, Montefiores, and Dubbo ; 42 Cobb & Co ... Bathurst, Peel, Wattle Flat, and Sofala ; 55 Cobb & Co ... Bathurst, Coola, Long Swamp, and Trunkey Creek, via Denis Island ; 61 Cobb & Co Bathurst, Evans' Plains, Blayney, Carcoar ; Carcoar and Cowra ; 75 Cobb & Co ... Murrumburrah, Coramundra, Junee, and Wagga Wagga, via Berthungra and Conjugong ; Wagga Wagga, Urana, Jereelderie, Conargo, and Deniliquin, via Broogong ; 50 Cobb & Co ... Railway Station, Muswellbrook, and Post Office, Murrurundi, Willow-tree, Wallabadah, Goonoo Goonoo, Tamworth, Moonbi, Bendemeer, Uralla, and Armidale; 68 Cobb & Co ... Armidale, Falconer, Glen Innes, via Ben Lomond Station, with branch mail from Armidale to Puddledock ; Glen Innes, Dundee, Deepwater, Tenterfield, Bookookoorara, and Maryland ; Bendemeer, Bundarra, Stanborough, Inverell, via Carlisle Gully; 26 Jul 1873 Reduced Fares.—Cobb and Co.'s Telegraph Line of Coaches.—Raglan to Orange ... Booking Office, 246 Pitt-street [Sydney]; 31 May 1873 Telegraph Line of Coaches. Cobb & Co.—From Wagga to Tarcutta, Adelong, Albury, Sydney and Melbourne ... Booking Office : John Clark's Criterion Hotel, Wagga Wagga

1874

19 Jan 1874 Conveyance of Post Office Mails ... 1 Cobb & Co ... Address Sydney ... Railway Station, Macquarie Plains, and Post Offices, Bathurst and Orange ; Railway Station, Wallerawang, and Post Offices, Wallerawang Railway Station and Mudgee ; Dubbo, Warren, Cannonbar, Gongolgon, and Bourke ; Railway Station, Goulburn, and Post Offices, Goulburn and Gundagai ; Gundagai and Albury; 38 Cobb & Co ... Orange, Shepherd's Creek, Ironbarks, Black Rock, Wellington, and Montefiores; Orange, Shepherd's Creek, Molong, Black Rock, Wellington, and Montefiores; 39 Cobb & Co ... Wellington, Montefiores, and Dubbo; 43 Cobb & Co ... Bathurst, Peel, Wattle Flat, and Sofala; 55 Cobb & Co ... Bathurst, Caloola, Long Swamp, and Trunkey Creek, via Dennis Island; 62 Cobb & Co Bathurst, Evans' Plains, Blayney, Carcoar ; Carcoar and Cowra ; 82 Cobb & Co ... Murrumburrah, Coramundra, Junee, and Wagga Wagga, via Bethungra and Conjugong ; Wagga Wagga, Urana, Jereelderie, Conargo, and Deniliquin, via Broogong ; 92 Cobb & Co ... Tarcutta and Wagga Wagga ; 69 Cobb & Co ... Railway Station, Murrurundi, and Post Offices Murrurundi, Willow-tree, Wallabadah, Goonoo Goonoo, Tamworth, Moonbi, Bendemeer, Uralla, and Armidale; 70 Cobb & Co ... Armidale, Falconer, Glen Innes, via Ben Lomond Station, with branch mail from Armidale to Puddledock ; Glen Innes, Dundee, Deepwater, Tenterfield, Bookookoorara, and Maryland ; Bendemeer, Bundarra, Stanborough, Inverell, via Carlisle Gully; Telegraph Line of Coaches. Cobb & Co.—Wagga to Tarcutta, Adelong, Albury, Sydney and Melbourne ... Booking Office : John Clark's Criterion Hotel, Wagga Wagga

1875

13 Jan 1875 Conveyance of Post Office Mails ... 1 Cobb & Co ... Address Sydney ... Raglan Railway Station, and Post Offices, Raglan, Kelso, Bathurst, Dunkeld, Vittoria, Guyong, Lucknow, and Orange (Week 6x35 miles) ; Wallerawang Railway Station, and Post Offices, Wallerawang, Lidsdale, Cullen Bullen, Ilford, Cudgegong, Apple-tree Flat, and Mudgee (Week 6x56 miles) ; Bathurst, Peel, Wattle Flat, and Sofala (Week 6x29 miles) ; Bathurst, Caloola, Long Swamp, and Trunkey Creek, via Denis Island (Week 3x38 miles) ; Bathurst, Evan's Plains, Blayney, and Carcoar ; and Carcoar, Lyndurst, Sheet of Bark, and Cowra (Week 6or3x59 miles) ; Wellington, Montefiores and Dubbo (Week 6x35 miles) ; Dubbo, Warren, Cannonbar, Gongolgon, and Bourke (Week 2x252miles) ; Railway Station, Goulburn, Mutt Billy, Gunning, Yass, Bookham, Jugiong, and Gundagai ; Gundagai, South Gundagai, Adelong Crossing-place, Hillas Creek, Tarcutta, Garryowen, Ten-mile Creek, Bowna, Thurgoona, and Albury (Week 6x254 miles) ; Murrumburrah, Coramundra, Junee, and Wagga Wagga, via Bethungra and Conjugong (Week 3x100 miles) ; Wagga Wagga, Urana, Jereelderie, Conargo, and Deniliquin, via Broogong (Week 4x180 miles) ; Armidale, Falconer, and Glen Innes, via Ben Lomond, with a branch mail from Armidale to Puddledock (Week 3x60 miles) ; Glen Innes, Dundee, Deepwater, Tenterfield, and Maryland (Week 3x119 miles) ; Bendemeer, Bundarra, Stanborough, Middle Town, Inverell, via Carlisle Gully (Week 3x102 miles) ; 35 Cobb & Co ... Gilgandra and Dubbo, via Terramungamine, Talbrager Bridge, and Coal Boggie Creek (Week 2x46 miles) ; 44 Cobb & Co ... Orange, Shepherd's Creek, Ironbarks, Black Rock, Wellington,

and Montefiores (Week 3x60 miles); Orange, Shepherd's Creek, Molong, Black Rock, Wellington and Montefiores (Week 3x60 miles); 44 Cobb & Co ... Queanbeyan, Rob Roy, Michelago and Cooma (Week 3x? miles); 87 Cobb & Co ... Tarcutta and Wagga Wagga (Week 3x21 miles); 58 Cobb & Co ... Muswellbrook, Denman, Merriwa and Cassilis (Contractor will be required to provide boat at Denman) (Week 3x75 miles) ; 71 Cobb & Co ... Railway Station, Murrurundi, and Post Offices Murrurundi, Willow-tree, Wallabadah, Goonoo Goonoo, Tamworth, Moonbi, Bendemeer, Uralla, and Armidale (Week 6x121 miles) ; 115 Cobb & Co ... Glen Innes, Tent Hill, and Vegetable Creek (Week 3x? miles) ... TOTAL 6956 miles

1876

17 Jan 1876 Conveyance of Post Office Mails ... 1 Cobb & Co ... Address Sydney ... Raglan Railway Station, and Post Offices, Raglan, Kelso, Bathurst, Dunkeld, Vittoria, Guyong, Lucknow, and Orange (Week 6x35 miles) ; Wallerawang Railway Station, and Post Offices, Wallerawang, Lidsdale, Cullen Bullen, Capertee, Ilford, Cudgegong, Apple-tree Flat, and Mudgee (Week 6x56 miles) ; Bathurst, Peel, Wattle Flat, and Sofala (Week 6x29 miles) ; Bathurst, Caloola, Long Swamp, and Trunkey Creek, via Denis Island (Week 3x38 miles) ; Bathurst, Evan's Plains, Blayney, and Carcoar ; and Carcoar, Lyndhurst, Sheet of Bark, and Cowra (Week 6or3x59 miles) ; Wellington, Montefiores, Maryvale, and Dubbo (Week 6x33 miles) ; Dubbo, Minore, Warren, Timbriebungie, Cannonbar, Gongolgon, and Bourke (Week 2x252miles) ; Railway Station, Goulburn, and Post Offices, Goulburn, Breadalbane, Gunning, Yass, Bowning, Bookham, Jugiong, Coolac, and Gundagai ; Gundagai, South Gundagai, Adelong Crossing-place, Hillas Creek, Tarcutta, Little Billabong, Garryowen, Germanton, Woomargama, Bowna, Thurgoona, and Albury (Week 6x254 miles) ; Murrumburrah, Wallendbeen, Coramundra, Cungegong, Bethungra, Junee, Wallaceton, and Wagga Wagga (Week 3x100miles) ; Wagga Wagga, Urana, Jereelderie, Coree, Conargo, and Deniliquin, via Broogong (Week 4x180 miles) ; Armidale, Falconer, and Glen Innes, via Ben Lomond, with a branch mail from Armidale to Puddledock (Week 3x60 miles) ; Glen Innes, Dundee, Deepwater, Tenterfield, Kimberley, and Maryland (Week 3x119 miles) ; Bendemeer, Wilson's Downfall, Bundarra, Stanborough, Kimberley, and Inverell, via Carlisle Gully (Week 3x106 miles) ; 24 Cobb & Co ... Mudgee, Cullenbone, Guntawang, Cobbora, Mundooran, Gilgandra, and Coonamble (to use Government between Mudgee and Cobbora, and to travel in times of floods on the north side of Cudgegong River, via Guntawang.) (Week 2x161 miles) ; 33 Cobb & Co ... Gilgandra and Dubbo, via Terramungamine, Talbragar Bridge, and Coal Boggie Creek (Week 2x46 miles) ; 52 Cobb & Co ... Orange, Shepherd's Creek, Ironbarks, Black Rock, Wellington, and Montefiores (Week 3x60 miles); Orange, Shepherd's Creek, Molong, Black Rock, Wellington and Montefiores (Week 3x60 miles) ; 80 Cobb and Co ... Orange, Heifer Station, Cheeseman's Creek, Cudal, Toogong, Murga, Eugowra, and Forbes (Week 3x80 miles) ; Northern Roads ... 68 Cobb & Co ... Muswellbrook, Denman, Merriwa and Cassillis (Contractor will be required to provide boat at Denman) (Week 3x75 miles) ; 84 Cobb & Co ... Railway Station, Murrurundi, and Post Offices, Haydonton, Murrurundi, Willow-tree, Wallabadah, Goonoo Goonoo, Tamworth, Moonbi, Bendemeer, Carlisle Gully, Uralla, and Armidale (Week 6x121 miles) ; 185 Cobb & Co ... Glen Innes, Tent Hill, and Vegetable Creek (Week 3x31 miles) ... TOTAL 6499 miles

1877

20 Jan 1877 Conveyance of Post Office Mails ... 1 Cobb & Co ... Address Sydney ... Orange, Irvinstone, Shepherd's Creek, Ironbarks, Black Rock, Wellington, and Montefiores (Week 3x60 miles); Orange, Shepherd's Creek, Molong, Black Rock, Wellington and Montefiores (Week 3x60 miles) ; Wellington, Montefiores, Maryvale, and Dubbo (Week 6x33 miles) ; Dubbo, Minore, Timbriebungie, Warren, Cannonbar, Willeroon, Gongolgon, and Bourke (Week 2x252 miles) ; Carcoar, Mandurama, Lyndhurst, Sheet of Bark, and Cowra (Week 6x30 miles) ; Wagga Wagga, Cookardinia, Gerogery, and Albury, via Mangoplah (Week 6x88 miles) ; Tarcutta and Wagga Wagga (Week 6x21 miles) ; Wagga Wagga, Urana, Jereelderie, Coree, Conargo, and Deniliquin, via Broogong (Week 4x180 miles) ; Railway Station, Murrurundi, and Post Offices, Haydonton, Murrurundi, Willowtree, Wallabadah, Goonoo Goonoo, Tamworth, Moonbi, Bendemeer, Carlisle Gully, Uralla, and Armidale (Week 6x121 miles) ; 2 Cobb & Co ... Railway Station and Post Offices Blayney and Carcoar (Week 6x8miles) ; Back Creek Railway Station (Duramana), and Trunkey Creek (Week 3x17 miles) ; Railway Station, Bowning, and Post Offices, Bowning, Bookham, Jugiong, Coolac, and Gundagai, South Gundagai, Adelong Crossing-place, Hillas Creek, Tarcutta, Little Billabong, Garryowen, Germanton, Woomargama, Bowna, Thurgoona, and Albury (Week 6x171 miles) ; 24 Cobb & Co ... Wallerawang Railway Station, and Post Offices, Wallerawang, Lidsdale, Cullen Bullen, Capertee, Ilford, Cudgegong, Apple-tree Flat, and Mudgee (Week 6x56 miles) ; 25 Cobb & Co ... Mudgee, Cullenbone, Guntawang, Cobbora, Mundooran, Gilgandra, and Coonamble (to use Government Road between Mudgee and Cobbora, and to travel in times of floods on the north side of Cudgegong River, via Guntawang.) (Week 2x161 miles) ; 32 Cobb & Co ... Gilgandra and Dubbo, via Terramungamine, Talbragar Bridge, and Coal Boggie Creek (Week 2x46 miles) ; 55 Cobb & Co ... Bathurst Railway Station, and Post Offices, Bathurst, Dunkeld, Vittoria, Guyong, Lucknow, and Orange (Week 6x36 miles); 57 Cobb & Co ... Bathurst, Peel, Wattle Flat, and Sofala (Week 6x29 miles) ; 119 Cobb & Co ... Warren, Mount Harris, and Wammerawa. Via Drungalee (Week 2x120 miles) ; 125 Cobb & Co ... Booligal and Hay (Week 2x51 miles) ; Northern Roads ... 127 Cobb & Co ... Armidale, Falconer, and Glen Innes, via Ben Lomond, with a branch mail from Armidale to Puddledock (Week 3x60 miles) ; 140 Cobb & Co ... Glen Innes, Y water, and Vegetable Creek (Week 3x31 miles) ... TOTAL 6220 miles

1878

23 Jan 1878 Conveyance of Post Office Mails ... 1 Cobb & Co ... Address Sydney ... Orange, March, Shepherd's Creek, Ironbarks, Black Rock, Wellington, and Montefiores (Week 3x60 miles); Orange, March, Shepherd's Creek, Molong, Black Rock, Wellington and Montefiores (Week 3x60 miles) ; Wellington, Montefiores, Maryvale, Murrumbidgerie, Eschol and Dubbo (Week 6x33 miles) ; Dubbo, Minore, Timbriebungie, Warren, Cannonbar, Willeroon, Gongolgon, and Bourke (Week 2x252 miles); Carcoar, Mandurama, Lyndhurst, Sheet of Bark, and Cowra (Week 6x30 miles); Wagga Wagga, Cookardinia, Morven, Gerogery, and Albury, via Mangoplah (Week 6x88 miles) ; Tarcutta and Wagga Wagga (Week 3x21 miles) ; Wagga Wagga, Urana, Jereelderie, Coree, Conargo, and Deniliquin, via Broogong (Week 4x180 miles) ; Railway Station, Murrurundi, and Post Offices, Haydonton, Murrurundi, Willowtree, Wallabadah, Goonoo Goonoo, Tamworth, Moonbi, Bendemeer, Carlisle Gully, Uralla, and Armidale (Week 6x121 miles) ; Bendemeer, Kingston, Bundarra, Stanborough, and Inverell, via Carlisle Gully (Week 3x106 miles) ; 2 Cobb & Co ... Railway Station and Post Offices Blayney and Carcoar (Week 6x8 miles) ; Back Creek Railway Station (Duramana), and Trunkey Creek (Week 3x17 miles) ; Railway Station, Bowning, and Post Offices, Bowning, Bookham, Jugiong, Coolac, and Gundagai, South Gundagai, Adelong Crossing-place,

Hillas Creek, Tarcutta, Kyamba, Little Billabong, Garryowen, Germanton, Woomargama, Mullengandra, Bowna, Thurgoona, and Albury (Week 6x171 miles) ; 23 Cobb & Co ... Wallerawang Railway Station, and Post Offices, Wallerawang, Lidsdale, Cullen Bullen, Capertee Camp, Ilford, Cudgegong, Apple-tree Flat, and Mudgee (Week 6x56 miles) ; 29 Cobb & Co ... Mudgee, Cullenbone, Guntawang, Cobbora, Mundooran, Gilgandra, Gulargambone, and Coonamble (to use Government road between Mudgee and Cobbora, and to travel in times of floods on the north side of Cudgegong River, via Guntawang.) (Week 2or3x161 miles) ; 39 Cobb & Co ... Mundooran, Binnaway, and Coonabarabran, via Luckey's, Caigan, Mobala, and Belar (Week 2x55 miles) ; 48 Cobb & Co ... Gilgandra and Dubbo, via Terramungamine, Talbragar Bridge, and Coal Boggie Creek (Week 2x46 miles) ; 48 Cobb & Co ... Coonamble and Walgett, via Yowee, Bundy, Buggil, Wingadee, and Nugai (Week 1x70 miles) ; 63 Cobb & Co ... Bathurst, Peel, Wattle Flat, and Sofala (Week 6x28 miles) ; and Sofala and Hill End (Week 6x29 miles) ; 80 Cobb & Co ... From Railway Station Blayney and Carcoar (Week 6x8 miles); 122 Cobb & Co ... Warren, Mount Harris, and Wammerawa. Via Drungalee (Week 2x120 miles) ; 125 Cobb & Co ... Gongolgon and Brewarrina (Week 2x28 miles) ; 110 Cobb & Co ... Murrumburrah, Wombat, and Young (Week 3x20 miles) ; 121 Cobb & Co ... Cootamundra, Cungegong, Bethungra, Junee, Wallaceton, and Wagga Wagga (Week 3x57 miles) ; 125 Cobb & Co ... Adelong Crossing-place, Shepard's Town, Adelong, Gilmore, and Tumut (Week 6x26 miles) ; 136 Cobb & Co ... Hay and Booligal (Week 2x51 miles) ; 80 Cobb & Co ... Muswellbrook, Denman, Gungal, Merriwa, and Cassilis (Contractors will be required to provide boat at Denman) ; 144 Cobb & Co ... Armidale, Guyra, Falconer, and Glen Innes, via Ben Lomond, with a branch mail from Armidale to Puddledock (Week 3x60 miles) ; 151 Cobb & Co ... Glen Innes, Dundee, Deepwater, Tenterfield, Willson's Downfall, Amosfield, and Maryland (Week 3x119 miles) ; 153 Cobb & Co ... Glen Innes, Y water, and Vegetable Creek (Week 3x31 miles) ... TOTAL 7660 miles

1879

1 Oct 1879 Dubbo, Warren, Cannonbar, Willeroon, Gongolgan and Bourke is about 250 miles long; ; 13 Jan 1879 Conveyance of Post Office Mails ... 1 Cobb & Co ... Address Sydney ... Orange, March, Shepherd's Creek, Ironbarks, Black Rock, Wellington, and Montefiores (Week 3x60 miles); Orange, March, Shepherd's Creek, Molong, Rexcourt, Black Rock, Wellington and Montefiores (Week 3x60 miles) ; Wellington, Montefiores, Maryvale, Murrumbidgerie, Eschol and Dubbo (Week 6x33 miles) ; Dubbo, Minore, Timbriebungie, Warren, Cannonbar, Willeroon, Gongolgon, and Bourke (Week 2x252 miles) ; Carcoar, Mandurama, Lyndhurst, Sheet of Bark, and Cowra (Week 6x30 miles) ; Wagga Wagga, Cookardinia, Morven, Gerogery, and Albury, via Mangoplah (Week 3x88 miles) ; Tarcutta and Wagga Wagga (Week 3x21 miles) ; Wagga Wagga, Urana, Jereelderie, Coree, Conargo, and Deniliquin, via Broogong (Week 4x180 miles); Railway Station, Murrurundi, and Post Offices, Haydonton, Murrurundi, Willow-tree, Wallabadah, Goonoo Goonoo, Tamworth, Moonbi, Bendemeer, Carlisle Gully, Uralla, and Armidale (Week 6x121 miles) ; Bendemeer, Kingston, Bundarra, Stanborough, and Inverell, via Carlisle Gully (Week 3x106 miles) ; 2 Cobb & Co ... Railway Station and Post Offices Blayney and Carcoar (Week 6x8 miles) ; Railway Station Newbridge, and Post Offices, Newbridge and Trunkey Creek (Week 3x17 miles) ; Railway Station, Bowning, and Post Offices, Bowning, Bookham, Jugiong, Coolac (Week 3x46 miles) ; Railway Station, Cootamundra & Post Offices, Cootamundra, Coolac, Gundagai, South Gundagai, Adelong Crossing-place, Hillas Creek, Tarcutta, Kyamba, Little Billabong, Garryowen, Germanton (Week 6x113 miles) ; Wagga Wagga and Germanton (Week 7x42 miles) ; From Germanton to Woomargama, Mullengandra, Bowna, Thurgoona, and Albury (Week 13x32 miles) From Albury to Thurgoona, Bowna, Mullengandra, Woomargama, and Germanton (Week 14x32 miles) ; 22 Cobb & Co ... Wallerawang Railway Station, and Post Offices, Wallerawang, Lidsdale, Cullen Bullen, Capertee Camp, Ilford, Cudgegong, Apple-tree Flat, and Mudgee (Week 6x72 miles) ; 32 Cobb & Co ... Mudgee, Eurunderee, Home Rule, and Gulgong (Week 6x17 miles) ; and Gulgong, Cobbora (via Goodaman's), Mundooran, Gilgandra, Curban, Gulargambone, and Coonamble. (Week 2x150miles) ; 37 Cobb & Co ... Mundooran, Binnaway, and Coonabarabran, via Luckey's, Caigan, Mobala, and Belar (Week 2x55 miles) ; 41 Cobb & Co ... Gilgandra, Burslem's, and Dubbo, via Terramungamine, Talbragar Bridge, and Coal Boggie Creek (Week 2x46 miles) ; 46 Cobb & Co ... Coonamble, Buggil, and Walgett, via Yowee, Bundy, Wingadee, and Nugal (Week 2x70 miles) ; 63 Cobb & Co ... Bathurst, Peel, Wattle Flat, and Sofala (Week 6x28 miles) ; 82 Cobb & Co ... From Railway Station, Blayney, and Carcoar (Week 6x8 miles) ; 101 Cobb & Co ... Orange, Borenore, Cheeseman's Creek, Cudal, Toogong, Murga, Eugowra, and Forbes (Week 6x80 miles) ; 102 Cobb & Co ... Orange and Molong (Week 3x28 miles) ; 105 Cobb & Co... Forbes, Bedgerebong, Monwonga, Borambil, and Condobolin (Week 2x60 miles) ; 106 Cobb & Co... Forbes, Bedgerebong, Monwonga, Borambil, and Condobolin (Week 1x60 miles) ; 128 Cobb & Co ... Warren, Mount Harris, and Wammerawa, via Drungalee (Week 2x120 miles) ; 131 Cobb & Co ... Gongolgon and Brewarrina (Week 2x28 miles) ; 115 Cobb & Co ... Adelong Crossing-place, Shepard's Town, Adelong, Gilmore, and Tumut (Week 6x26 miles) ; 125Cobb & Co ... Railway Station, Murrumburrah, and Post Office Murrumburrah, Wombat, Young, Musgrave, and Grenfell.(Week 5x59 miles) ; 136 Wagga Railway Station, and Post Offices, Wagga Railway Station and Wagga Wagga (Week 6x4 miles) ; 146 Cobb & Co ... Hay and Booligal (Week 2x51 miles) ; 84 Cobb & Co ... Muswellbrook, Denman, Gungal, Merriwa, and Cassilis (Contractors will be required to provide boat at Denman, and to convey an extra mail from Muswellbrook to Denman on Saturdays) (Week 3x75 miles) ; 152 Cobb & Co ... Armidale, Guyra, Falconer, and Glen Innes, via Ben Lomond, with a branch mail from Armidale to Puddledock three times a week (Week 6x60 miles) ; 159 Cobb & Co ... Glen Innes, Dundee, Deepwater, Tenterfield, Willson's Downfall, Amosfield, and Maryland (Week 3x119 miles); 161 Cobb & Co ... Glen Innes, Y. water, and Vegetable Creek (Week 3x31 miles) ... TOTAL 9252 miles

1880

13 Jan 1880 Conveyance of Post Office Mails ... 1 Cobb & Co ... Address Sydney ... Wallerawang Railway Station, and Post Offices, Wallerawang, Lidsdale, Cullen Bullen, Capertee Camp, Ilford, Cudgegong, Apple-tree Flat, and Mudgee (Week 6x72 miles) ; Gulgong, Dension Town, and Coolah, via Tallewang (Week 2x46 miles) ; Railway Station and Post Offices Blayney and Carcoar (Week 6x8 miles) ; Carcoar, Mandurama, Lyndhurst, Sheet of Bark, and Cowra (Week 6x30 miles) ; Orange, March, Irvinstone, Shepherd's Creek, Farnham, Ironbarks, Black Rock, Wellington, and Montefiores (Week 3x60 miles) ; and Orange, Molong, Rexcourt, Black Rock, Wellington and Montefiores (Week 3x60 miles) ; Wellington, Montefiores, Maryvale, Eschol and Dubbo (Week 6x33 miles) ; Dubbo, Timbriebungie, Warren, Cannonbar, Willeroon, Gongolgon, and Bourke (Week 2x252 miles) ; Railway Station, Cootamundra and Post Offices, Cootamundra, Coolac, Gundagai, South Gundagai, Adelong Crossing-place, Hillas Creek, and Tarcutta (Week 6x73 miles) ; Wagga Wagga, South Wagga Railway Station, Urana, Jereelderie, Coree, Conargo, and Deniliquin, via Broogong (Week 4x180

miles) ; Urana, Colombo Creek, and Narandera, via Urana Station, Coonong, Widgiewa, Yarrabee, Cundle Township, and Gillenbar (Week 2x62 miles) Narrandera, Rankin's Springs, and Lake Cudgellico, via Medium, Mumbledoon, Barellan, North Gogeldra, Binya, Ballandra, and Coonapaira (Week 1x171 miles) ; Tarcutta and Wagga Wagga (Week 3x21 miles) ; Corowa and Wahgunyah (Contractors to provide means for crossing the river Murray when the bridge is flooded) (Week 12x1 miles) ; Tamworth, Moonbi, Bendemeer, Carlisle Gully, Uralla, and Armidale (Week 6x62 miles) ; Bendemeer, Kingston, Bundarra, Stanborough, and Inverell, via Carlisle Gully (Week 3x106 miles) ; Armidale, The Pinch, Guyra, and Glen Innes, via Ben Lomond (Week 6x60 miles) ; Glen Innes, Dundee, Deepwater, Tenterfield (Week 6x52 miles) ; Tenterfield, Willson's Downfall, Sugarloaf, Stanthorpe, and Maryland (Week 6x52 miles) ; Willson's Downfall and Amosfield (Horseback) (Week 3x3 miles) ; 33 Cobb & Co ... Mudgee, Eurunderee, Home Rule, and Gulgong (Week 6x17 miles) ; and Gulgong, Cobbora (via Goodaman's), Mundooran, Gilgandra, Curban, Gulargambone, and Coonamble. (Week 2x150miles); 37 Cobb & Co ... Mundooran, Binnaway, and Coonabarabran, via Luckey's, Caigan, Mobala, and Belar (Week 2x55 miles) ; 41 Cobb & Co ... Gilgandra, Burslem's, and Dubbo, via Terramungamine, Talbragar Bridge, and Coal Boggie Creek (Week 2x46 miles) ; 46 Cobb & Co ... Coonamble, Buggil, and Walgett, via Yowee, Bundy, Wingadee, and Nugal (Week 2x70 miles); 65 Cobb & Co ... Bathurst, Peel, Wattle Flat, and Sofala (Week 6x28 miles) ; 106 Cobb & Co ... Orange, Borenore, Cheeseman's Creek, Cudal, Toogong, Murga, Eugowra, and Forbes (Week 6x80 miles) ; 107 Cobb & Co ... Orange and Molong (Week 3x28 miles) ; 135 Cobb & Co ... Gongolgon and Brewarrina (Week 2x28 miles); 128 Cobb & Co ... Adelong Crossing-place, Shepard's Town, Adelong, Gilmore, and Tumut (Week 6x26 miles) ; 132 Cobb & Co ... Tarcutta, Kyamba, Little Billabong, Garryowen, and Germanton (Week 3x44 miles) ... 139 Cobb & Co ...Railway Platform, Murrumburrah, and Post Office Murrumburrah, Wombat, Young, Musgrave, and Grenfell (Week 7x58 miles) ; 136 Wagga Railway Station, and Post Offices, Wagga Railway Station and Wagga Wagga (Week 6x4 miles) ; 156 Cobb & Co ... Wagga Wagga, South Wagga Railway Station, Jerri Jerri, Germanton, Woomagarma, Mullengandra, Bowns, Thurgoons, and Albury (Week 7x84 miles) ; 157 Cobb & Co ... Jerri Jerri, Cookardinia, Morven, Gerogery, and Albury, via Mangoplah (Week 3x48 miles) ; 182 Cobb & Co ... Little Billabong, Carabost, and Tumberumba (Week 3x48 miles); 87 Cobb & Co ... Muswellbrook, Denman, Gungal, Merriwa (Week 4x46 miles) ; and Merriwa Cassilis (Contractors are required to provide boat at Denman) (Week 3x25 miles) ; 171 Cobb & Co ... Glen Innes, Y. water, and Vegetable Creek (Week 3x31 miles) ... TOTAL 1881 miles

1881

22 Jan 1881 Conveyance of Post Office Mails ... 1 Cobb & Co ... Address Sydney ... Wallerawang Railway Station, and Post Offices, Wallerawang, Lidsdale, Cullen Bullen, Capertee Camp, Ilford, Cudgegong, Apple-tree Flat, and Mudgee (Week 6x72 miles) ; Gulgong, Dension Town, Tallewang, and Coolah (Week 2x46 miles) ; Railway Station and Post Offices Blayney and Carcoar (Week 6x8 miles) ; Carcoar, Mandurama, Lyndhurst, Sheet of Bark, and Cowra (Week 6x30 miles) ; *Orange, March, Irvinstone, Shepherd's Creek, Farnham, Ironbarks, Neurea, Wellington, and Montefiores (Week 3x60 miles) ; and *Orange, Molong, Rexcourt, Black Rock, Neurea, Wellington and Montefiores *THIS PORTION OF CONTRACT CANCELLED IN CONSEQUENCE OF THE EXTENSION OF THE RAILWAY TO WELLINGTON FROM 1ST JUNE 1880 (Week 3x60 miles); Wellington, Montefiores, Maryvale, Eschol and Dubbo (Week 6x33 miles) ; Dubbo, Timbriebungie, Warren, Cannonbar, Willeroon, Gongolgon, and Bourke (Week 2x252 miles) ; Railway Station, Cootamundra and Post Offices, Cootamundra, Coolac, Gundagai, South Gundagai, Adelong Crossing-place, Hillas Creek, and Tarcutta (Week 6x73 miles) ; Wagga Wagga, South Wagga Railway Station, Urana, Jereelderie, Coree, Conargo, and Deniliquin, via Broogong (Week 4x180 miles) ; Urana, Colombo Creek, and Narrandera, via Urana Station, Coonong, Widgiewa, Yarrabee, Cundle Township, and Gillenbar (Week 2x62 miles) Narrandera, Rankin's Springs, and Lake Cudgellico, via Medium, Mumbledoon, Barellan, North Gogeldra, Binya, Ballandra, and Coonapaira (Week 1x171 miles) ; Tarcutta and Wagga Wagga (Week 3x21 miles) ; Corowa and Wahgunyah, (Contractors to provide means for crossing the river Murray when the bridge is flooded.) (Week 12x1miles) ; Tamworth, Moonbi, Bendemeer, Carlisle Gully, Uralla, and Armidale (Week 6x62 miles) ; Bendemeer, Kingstown, Bundarra, Stanborough, and Inverell, via Carlisle Gully (Week 3x106 miles) ; Armidale, The Pinch, Guyra, and Glen Innes, via Ben Lomond (Week 6x60 miles) ; Glen Innes, Dundee, Deepwater, Tenterfield (Week 6x58 miles) ; Tenterfield, Willson's Downfall, Sugarloaf, Stanthorpe, and Maryland (Week 6x52 miles) ; Willson's Downfall and Amosfield (Horseback) (Week 3x3 miles) ; 36 Cobb & Co ... Mudgee, Eurunderee, Home Rule, and Gulgong (Week 6x17 miles) ; and Gulgong, Cobbora (via Goodaman's), Mundooran, Gilgandra, Curban, Gulargambone, and Coonamble. (Week 2x150miles) ; 45 Cobb & Co ... Coonamble, Buggil, and Walgett, via Yowee, Bundy, Wingadee, and Nugal (Week 2x70 miles) ; 64 Cobb & Co ... Bathurst, Peel, Wattle Flat, and Sofala (Week 6x28 miles) ; 102 Cobb & Co ... Orange, Borenore, Cheeseman's Creek, Cudal, Toogong, Murga, Eugowra, and Forbes (Week 6x80 miles) ; 103 Cobb & Co ... Orange and Molong (Week 6x22 miles) ; 114 Cobb & Co ... Condobolin and Cugong, and Eauabalong (Week 1x40 miles) ; 115 Cobb & Co ... Condobolin and Cugong, and Eauabalong, along the north side of the Lachlan River (Week 2x45 miles) ; 135 Cobb & Co ... Wellington, Montefiores, Comobella, Cobbora, Merrygoen, Binnaway, and Coonabarabran, via Luckey's, Caigan, Mobala, and Belar (Week 2x112 miles) ; 136 Cobb & Co ... Dubbo, Brocklehurst, Burslem's, and Gilgandra, via Coal Boggie Creek, Talbragar Bridge, and Terramungamine (Week 2x46 miles) ; 137 Cobb & Co ... Dubbo, Timbriebungie, and Warren (Week 1x86 miles) ; 144 Cobb & Co ... Gongolgon and Brewarrina (Week 2x28 miles) ; 133 Cobb & Co ... Adelong Crossing-place, Shepard's Town, Adelong, Gilmore, and Tumut (Week 6x26 miles) ; 137 Cobb & Co ... Tarcutta, Kyamba, Little Billabong, Garryowen, and Germanton (Week 3x44 miles) ; 139 Cobb & Co ... Little Billabong, Carabost, and Tumberumba (Week 3x38 miles) ; 146 Cobb & Co ... Railway Platform, Murrumburrah, and Post Office Murrumburrah, Wombat, Young, Musgrave, and Grenfell (Week 7x58 miles) ; 155 Cobb & Co ... Cootamundra and Temora, via Cowan's and Combaning (Week 6x32 miles) ; 170 Cobb & Co ... Railway Station, Billabong (Culcairn), Morvan, and Germanton (Contractors to convey mails on either side of the Billabong Creek in times of flood.) (Week 6x18 miles) ; 172 Cobb & Co ... Railway Station, Gerogery, and Post Offices, Gerogery and Albury, including the conveyance of any mails from or to any part of the Australasian Colonies, the United Kingdom, or Foreign Countries, &c., as required. (In order that the mails may reach Wodonga in time for the train leaving for Melbourne ...) (Week 7x20 miles) ; 195 Cobb & Co ... Germanton, Woomargama, Mullengandra, Bowns, Thurgoona, and Albury (Week 3x30 miles) ; 85 Cobb & Co ... Muswellbrook, Denman, Gungal, Merriwa (Week 4x46 miles) ; and Merriwa and Cassilis (Week 3x25 miles) ... TOTAL 7462 miles

1882

24 Jan 1882 Conveyance of Post Office Mails ... 1 Cobb & Co ... Address Sydney ... Wallerawang Railway Station, and Post Offices, Wallerawang, Lidsdale, Cullen Bullen, Capertee Camp, Ilford, Cudgegong, Apple-tree Flat, and Mudgee (Week 6x72 miles) ; Gulgong, Tallewang, Dension Town, and Coolah (Week 2x46 miles) ; Railway Station and Post Offices Blayney and Carcoar (Week 6x8 miles) ; Carcoar, Mandurama, Lyndhurst, Sheet of Bark, and Cowra (Week 6x30 miles) ; Cowra and Grenfell (Week 3x40 miles) ; *Orange, March, Irvinstone, Shepherd's Creek, Farnham, Ironbarks, Neurea, Wellington, and Montefiores (Week 3x60 miles) ; and *Orange, Molong, Rexcourt, Neurea, Wellington and Montefiores *THIS PORTION OF CONTRACT CANCELLED IN CONSEQUENCE OF THE EXTENSION OF THE RAILWAY TO WELLINGTON FROM 1ST JUNE 1880 (Week 3x60 miles); Wellington, Montefiores, Maryvale, Eschol and Dubbo (Week 6x33 miles) ; Dubbo, Timbriebungie, Warren, Cannonbar, Willeroon, Gongolgon, and Bourke (Week 2x252 miles) ; Railway Station, Cootamundra and Post Offices, Cootamundra, Receiving Office, Brawlin, Coolac, Gundagai, South Gundagai, Adelong Crossing-place, Hillas Creek, and Tarcutta (Week 6x73 miles) ; *Wagga Wagga, South Wagga Railway Station, Urana, Jereelderie, Coree, Conargo, and Deniliquin, via Broogong *THIS PORTION OF CONTRACT BETWEEN WAGGA WAGGA AND THE ROCK RAILWAY STATION CANCELLED, IN CONSEQUENCE OF THE EXTENSION OF THE RAILWAY TO GEROGARY FROM 1ST SEPTEMBER, 1880 (Week 4x180 miles); Urana, Colombo Creek, Cundell, Gillenbar, and Narrandera, via Urana Station, Coonong, Widgiewa, Yarrabee, and Cuddle Township (Week 2x62 miles) ; Wagga Wagga and Tarcutta (Week 3x21 miles) ; Corowa and Wahgunyah, (Contractors to provide means for crossing the river Murray when the bridge is flooded.) (Week 12x1miles) ; *Tamworth, Tintin Hull, Moonbi, Bendemeer, Carlisle Gully, Uralla, and Armidale *THIS PORTION OF CONTRACT BETWEEN TAMWORTH AND MOONBI RAILWAY STATION CANCELLED, IN CONSEQUENCE OF THE EXTENSION OF THE RAILWAY TO MOONBI FROM 9th JANUARY, 1882 (Week 6x62 miles) ; Bendemeer, Kingstown, Bundarra, Stanborough, and Inverell, via Carlisle Gully (Week 3x106 miles) ; Armidale, Guyra, 'Ben Lomond Hotel', and Glen Innes, via (Week 6x60 miles) ; Glen Innes, Dundee, Deepwater, Tenterfield (Week 6x58 miles) ; Tenterfield, Willson's Downfall, Sugarloaf, Stanthorpe, and Maryland (Week 6x52 miles) ; Willson's Downfall and Amosfield (Horseback) (Week 3x3 miles) ; 97 Cobb & Co ... Orange, Borenore, Cheeseman's Creek, Cudal, Toogong, Murga, Eugowra, and Forbes (Week 6x80 miles) ; 98 Cobb & Co ... Orange, Kangaroobi, and Molong (Week 6x22 miles) ; 109 Cobb & Co ... Condobolin and Cugong, and Eauabalong, along the south side of the Lachlan River (Week 2x45 miles) ; 118 Cobb & Co ... Molong, Meranburn, Bumberry, and Parkes (Week 6x60 miles) ; 131 Cobb & Co ... Wellington, Montefiores, Comobella, Cobbora, Murrungundy, Cobbora, Merrygoen, Binnaway, and Coonabarabran, via Luckey's, Caigan, Mobala, and Belar (Week 2x112 miles) ; 136 Cobb & Co ... Dubbo, Brocklehurst, Burslem's, and Gilgandra, via Coal Boggie Creek, Talbragar Bridge, and Terramungamine (Week 2x46 miles) ; 137 Cobb & Co ... Dubbo, Brocklehurst, Burslem's, and Gilgandra, via Coal Boggie Creek, Talbragar Bridge, and Terramungamine (Week 1x46 miles) ; 138 Cobb & Co ... Dubbo, Timbriebungie, and Warren (Week 1x86 miles) ; 140 Cobb & Co ... Gilgandra, Curban, Gulargambone, and Coonamble (Week 3x51 miles) ; 144 Cobb & Co ... Coonamble, Buggil, and Walgett, via Yowee, Bundy, Wingadee, and Nugal (Week 2x70 miles) ; 148 Cobb & Co ... Warren, Nyngan, Hermitage Plains, and Cobar, via Pine Ridge (Week 1x141 miles) ; 153 Cobb & Co ... Gongolgon and Brewarrina (Week 2x28 miles) ; 141 Cobb & Co ... Adelong Crossing-place, Grahamstown, Shepard's Town, Adelong, Gilmore, and Tumut (Week 6x26 miles) ; 145 Cobb & Co ... Tarcutta, Kyamba, Little Billabong, Garryowen, and Germanton (Week 3x44 miles) ; 147 Cobb & Co ... Little Billabong, Carabost, and Tumberumba (Week 3x38 miles) ; 155 Cobb & Co ...Railway Platform, Murrumburrah, and Post Office Murrumburrah, Wombat, Young, Musgrave, and Grenfell (Week 7x58 miles) ; 160 Cobb & Co ... Grenfell and Forbes (Week 3x41 miles) ; 168 Cobb & Co ... Cootamundra and Temora, via Cowan's and Combaning (Week 7x32 miles) ; 180 Cobb & Co ... Railway Station, Billabong (Culcairn), Morvan, and Germanton (Contractors to convey mails on either side of the Billabong Creek in times of flood.) (Week 6x18 miles) ; 214 Cobb & Co ... Germanton, Woomargama, Mullengandra, Bowns, Thurgoona, and Albury (Week 3x30 miles) ; 215 Cobb & Co ... Germanton, Woomargama, Mullengandra, Bowns, Thurgoona, and Albury (Week 3x30 miles) ; 91 Cobb & Co ... Muswellbrook, Denman, Gungal, Merriwa (Week 6x46 miles) ; and Merriwa, Bow, and Cassilis (Week 3x25 miles)... TOTAL 6844 miles

1883

24 Jan 1883 Conveyance of Post Office Mails ... 1 Cobb & Co ... Address Sydney ... Ilford and Rylstone (Week 6x11 miles) ; Gulgong, Tallewang, Dension Town, and Coolah (Week 2x46 miles) ; From Railway Station, Blayney, to Post Offices Blayney and Carcoar (Week 6x8 miles) ; Railway Station, Blayney, and Post Offices Blayney and Carcoar Mandurama, Lyndhurst, Sheet of Bark, and Cowra (Week 6x38 miles) ; Cowra and Grenfell (Week 3x40 miles) ; Orange, Kangaroobie, Molong (Week 3x60 miles); Forbes, Carrawobity, Bedgerebong, Monwonga, Borambil, and Condobolin (Week 2x60 miles); Forbes, Waroo, Newlands, and Condobolin, along the south bank of the Lachlan River (Week 2x65 miles); Forbes and Parkes (Week 2x25 miles); Warren, Nyngan, Hermitage Plains, and Cobar, via Pine Ridge (Week 1x141 miles) ; Bourke and Hungerford, via Ford's Bridge, Yantabullabulla, and Brindingabba (Week 1x140 miles) ; Bourke, Louth, Tilpa, Tankerooka, and Wilcannia, travelling on either side of the Darling River (Week 1x250 miles) ; Cobar and Louth (Week 1x90 miles) ; Railway Station, Cootamundra and Post Office, Cootamundra, Receiving Office, Brawlin, Muttama Reef, Coolac, Gundagai, South Gundagai, Adelong Crossing-place, Hillas Creek, and Tarcutta (Week 6x78 miles) ; Tarcutta, Kyamba, Little Billabong, Garryowen, and Germanton (Week 3x44 miles) ; Little Billabong, Carabost, Rosewood, and Tumberumba (Week 3x38 miles); Tumberumba, Burne, Tooma, Welaregang Station, Tintaldra (Victoria), Welaregang Station, Ournie, Maracket, Wagra, Bowna, and Albury, via Camberoona, Dora Dora, Talmalmei, Jingillie, and Ournie Diggings (Week 2x115 miles) ; Railway Station, Culcairn, and Post Offices, Morvan, and Germanton (Contractors to convey mails on either side of the Billabong Creek in times of flood.) (Week 6x18 miles) ; Germanton, Woomargama, Mullengandra, Bowns, Thurgoona, and Albury (Week 6x30 miles) ; Tamworth, Attunga, Manilla, Upper Manilla, Barraba, Cobbadah, Bingera, and Warialda, via Barker's, North Bingera (Week 3x167 miles) ; Armidale, Guyra, 'Ben Lomond Hotel' Glencoe, and Glen Innes (Week 6x60 miles) ; Glen Innes, Dundee, Deepwater, Tenterfield (Week 6x58 miles) ; Tenterfield, Willson's Downfall, Sugarloaf (Queensland), and Stanthorpe (Queensland) (Week 6x44 miles) ; 30 Cobb & Co ... Railway Station, Capertree, and Post Offices, Capertree, Ilford, Cudgegong, Apple-tree Flat, and Mudgee (Week 6x50 miles) ; 61 Cobb & Co ... Bathurst, Peel, Wyagdon, Wattle Flat, and Sofala (Week 6x28 miles) ; 74 Cobb & Co ... Railway Station, Newbridge, and Post Offices, Moorilda, Hobby's Yards, and Trunkey Creek (Week 3x18 miles); 97 Cobb & Co ... Orange, Borenore, Cheeseman's

Creek, Cudal, Toogong, Murga, Eugowra, and Forbes (Week 6x80 miles) ; 106 Cobb & Co ... Condobolin and Eauabalong, along the south side of the Lachlan River (Week 2x45 miles) ; 115 Cobb & Co ... Molong, Meranburn, Bumberry, and Parkes (Week 6x60 miles) ; 127 Cobb & Co ... Wellington, Montefiores, Comobella, Cobbora, Murrungundy, Cobbora, Merrygoen, Binnaway, and Coonabarabran, via Luckey's, Caigan, Mobala, and Belar (Week 2x112 miles) ; 132 Cobb & Co ... Dubbo, Brocklehurst, Burslem's, and Gilgandra, via Coal Boggie Creek, Talbragar Bridge, and Terramungamine (Week 2x46 miles) ; 133 Cobb & Co ... Dubbo, Brocklehurst, Burslem's, and Gilgandra, via Coal Boggie Creek, Talbragar Bridge, and Terramungamine (Week 1x46 miles) ;; 135 Cobb & Co ... Gilgandra, Curban, Gulargambone, and Coonamble (Week 3x51 miles) ; 139 Cobb & Co ... Coonamble, Buggil, and Walgett, via Yowee, Bundy, Wingadee, and Nugal (Week 2x70 miles) ; 144 Cobb & Co ... Railway Station, Nevertire, and Post Office, Warren (Week 6x12 miles) ; Warren, Cannonbar, Willeroon, Gongolgon, and Bourke (Week 2x166 miles) ; 148 Cobb & Co ... Nyngan, Glenariff, Girilambone, and Bourke, via Dulley's Publichouse, 'Bye Rock Hotel,' Bye Rock Station, Kenilworth, and Mulga Creek Station (Cooper's) (Week 1x153 miles); 151 Cobb & Co ... Gongolgon, and Brewarrina (Week 2x28 miles) ; 154 Cobb & Co ... Railway Platform, Murrumburrah, and Post Offices, Murrumburrah, Wombat, Young, and Grenfell (Week 7x58 miles) ; 159 Cobb & Co ... Grenfell and Forbes (Week 3x41 miles); 160 Cobb & Co ... Grenfell and Forbes (Week 3x41 miles) ; 168 Cobb & Co ... Cootamundra, Cowan's, & Temora, via Combaning (Week 7x32 miles) ; 178 Cobb & Co ... Adelong Crossing-place, Grahamstown, Shepard's Town, Adelong, Gilmore, and Tumut (Week 6x26 miles) ; 195 Cobb & Co ... Railway Station, The Rock, Receiving Office, Ferrier's, and Postal Office, Urana, via Broogong (Week 4x57 miles) ; 96 Cobb & Co ... Muswellbrook, Denman, Gungal, Merriwa (Week 6x46 miles) ; and Merriwa, Bow, and Cassilis (Week 3x25 miles); 102 Cobb & Co ... Merriwa, Bow, and Cassilis (Horseback) (Week 3x25 miles); 167 Cobb & Co ... Railway Station, Moonbi, and Post Offices, Moonbi, Bendemeer, Kingstown, Bundarra, Stanborough, and Inverell (Week 3x104 miles) ... TOTAL 9444 miles

1884

24 Jan 1883 Conveyance of Post Office Mails ... 1 Cobb & Co ... Address Sydney ... Ilford and Rylstone (Week 6x11 miles) ; Gulgong, Tallewang, Dension Town, and Coolah (Week 2x46 miles) ; From Railway Station, Blayney, to Post Offices Blayney and Carcoar (Week 6x8 miles) ; Railway Station, Blayney, and Post Offices Blayney and Carcoar Mandurama, Lyndhurst, Sheet of Bark, and Cowra (Week 6x38 miles) ; Cowra and Grenfell (Week 3x40 miles) ; Orange, Kangaroobie, Molong (Week 3x60 miles); Forbes, Carrawobity, Bedgerebong, Monwonga, Borambil, and Condobolin (Week 2x60 miles); Forbes, Waroo, Newlands, and Condobolin, along the south bank of the Lachlan River (Week 2x65 miles); Forbes and Parkes (Week 2x25 miles); Nevertire Railway Station, and Post Offices, Nevertire, Nyngan, Hermitage Plains, and Cobar (Week 1x23 miles) ; Bourke and Hungerford, via Ford's Bridge, Yantabullabulla, and Brindingabba (Week 1x140 miles) ; Bourke, Louth, Tilpa, Tankerooka, and Wilcannia, travelling on either side of the Darling River (Week 2x250 miles) ; Cobar and Louth (Week 1x90 miles) ; Railway Station, Cootamundra and Post Office, Cootamundra, Receiving Office, Brawlin, Muttama Reef, Coolac, Gundagai, South Gundagai, Adelong Crossing-place, Hillas Creek, and Tarcutta (Week 6x73 miles) ; Tarcutta, Kyamba, Little Billabong, Garryowen, and Germanton (Week 3x44 miles) ; Little Billabong, Carabost, Rosewood, and Tumberumba (Week 3x38 miles) ; Tumberumba, Burne, Tooma, Welaregang Station, Tintaldra (Victoria), Welaregang Station, Ournie, Jingellic, Maracket, Wagra, Bowna, and Albury, via Camberoona, Dora Dora, Talmalmei, and Ournie Diggings (Week 2x115 miles) ; Railway Station, Culcairn, and Post Offices, Morvan, and Germanton (Contractors to convey mails on either side of the Billabong Creek in times of flood.) (Week 6x18 miles) ; Germanton, Woomargama, Mullengandra, Bowns, Thurgoona, and Albury (Week 6x30 miles) ; Tamworth, Attunga, Manilla, Upper Manilla, Barraba, Cobbadah, Bingera, and Warialda, via Barker's, North Bingera (Week 6x167 miles) ; ; Armidale, Guyra, 'Ben Lomond Hotel,' Glencoe, and Glen Innes (Week 6x60 miles) ; Glen Innes, Dundee, Deepwater, Bolivia, The Bluff, and Tenterfield (Week 6x58 miles); Tenterfield, Willson's Downfall, Sugarloaf (Queensland), and Stanthorpe (Queensland) (Week 6x44 miles) ; 33 Cobb & Co ... Railway Station, Capertree, and Post Offices, Capertree, Ilford, Cudgegong, Apple-tree Flat, and Mudgee (Week 6x34 miles) ; 44 Cobb & Co ... Mudgee, Eurunderee, Home Rule, and Gulgong (Week 6x17 miles) ; 63 Cobb & Co ... Bathurst, Peel, Wyagdon, Wattle Flat, and Sofala (Week 6x28 miles) ; 70 Cobb & Co ... Railway Station, Newbridge, and Post Offices, Moorilda, Hobby's Yards, and Trunkey Creek (Week 3x18 miles) ; 98 Cobb & Co ... Orange, Borenore, Cheeseman's Creek, Cudal, Toogong, Murga, Eugowra, and Forbes (Week 6x80 miles) ; 106 Cobb & Co ... Condobolin and Eauabalong, along the south side of the Lachlan River (Week 2x45 miles) ; 118 Cobb & Co ... Molong, Meranburn, Bumberry, Bindogandra, and Parkes (Week 6x60 miles) ; 137 Cobb & Co ... Dubbo, Brocklehurst, Burslem's, and Gilgandra, Curban, Gulargambone, and Coonamble, via Coal Boggie Creek, Talbragar Bridge, and Terramungamine (Week 3x97 miles) ; 157 Cobb & Co ... Railway Station, Nyngan, and Post offices, Nyngan, Wicklow, and Nymagee (Week 1x65 miles); 158 Cobb & Co ... Nyngan, Railway Station and Post Offices, Nyngan, Cannonbar, Monkey, Gongolgon, and Bourke (Week 2x192 miles); 159 Cobb & Co ... Nyngan, Hermitage Plains, and Cobar (Week 2x90 miles); 161 Cobb & Co ... Nyngan, Glenariff, Girilambone, and Bourke, via Dulley's Publichouse, 'Bye Rock Hotel,' Bye Rock Station, Kenilworth, and Mulga Creek Station (Cooper's) (Week 1x153 miles); 168 Cobb & Co ... Bourke, Mungunyah, Enngonia, and Barringun, via West Bourke, Gedia Camp Lake, Box-holes, Native Dog Spring, Lila, and Belalie (Week 2x90 miles) ; 156 Cobb & Co ... Railway Platform, Murrumburrah, and Post Offices, Murrumburrah, Wombat, Young, and Grenfell (Week 7x58 miles) ; 157 Cobb & Co ... Murrumburrah and Young, via Ridge Road (Week 3x20 miles) ; 162 Cobb & Co ... Grenfell and Forbes (Week 3x41 miles) ; 163 Cobb & Co ... Grenfell and Forbes (Week 3x41 miles) ; 171 Cobb & Co ... Cootamundra, Cowan's, & Temora, via Combaning (Week 7x32 miles) ; 179 Cobb & Co ... Gundagai and Tumut, via the marked-tree line (Week 3x20 miles) ; and Adelong Crossing-place, Grahamstown, Shepard's Town, Adelong, Gilmore, and Tumut (Week 6x26 miles) ; 198 Cobb & Co ... Railway Station, The Rock, Receiving Office, Ferrier's, and Postal Office, Urana, via Broogong (Week 4x57 miles) ; 100 Cobb & Co ... Muswellbrook, Denman, Giant's Creek, Gungal, Merriwa (Week 6x46 miles) ; 106 Cobb & Co ... Merriwa, Bow, and Cassilis (Week 4x25 miles) ... TOTAL 8667 miles

1885

20 Jan 1885 Conveyance of Mails ... 1 Cobb & Co ... Sydney ... Ilford and Rylstone (Cancelled in consequence of the extension of the Railway to Rylstone, from 9th June 1884.) (Week 6x11 miles) ; Gulgong, Tallewang, Dension Town, and Coolah (Week 2x46 miles) ; From Railway Station, Blayney, to Post Office, Blayney, and Carcoar (Week 6x8 miles) ; Railway Station, Blayney, and Post Office, Blayney, and Carcoar, Mandurama, Lyndhurst, Sheet of Bark, Cowra (Week 6x38 miles) ; Cowra and Grenfell (Week 3x40 miles) ; Orange, Kangaroobie, and

Molong (Week 7x22 miles) ; Forbes, Waroo, Newlands, and Condobolin, along the south bank of the Lachlan river (Week 2x65 miles) ; 127 Cobb & Co ... Molong, Garra, Moranburn, Bumberry, Bindogandra, and Parkes (Week 6x60 miles) ; 165 Cobb & Co ... Warren, Tenandra, Bourbah, and Coonamble, via Donohoe's, on the Merri Merri, and M'Mahon's, on the west bank of the Castlereagh River (Week 1x80 miles) ; Forbes and Parkes (Week 3x25 miles) ; Nevertire Railway Station, and Post Offices, Nevertire, Nyngan, Hermitage Plains, and Cobar (Week 1x123 miles) ; Bourke, North Bourke, and Hungerford, via Ford's Bridge Yantabullabulla, and Brindingabba (Week 1x140 miles) ; Bourke, Louth, Tilpa, Tankerooka, and Wilcannia, travelling on either side of the Darling River (Week 2x250 miles) ; Cobar and Louth (Week 1x90 miles) ; Railway Station, Cootamundra and Post Offices, Cootamundra, Receiving Office, Brawlin, Muttama Reef, Coolac, Gundagai, South Gundagai, Adelong Crossing-place, Hillas Creek, and Tarcutta (Week 6x73 miles) ; Tarcutta, Kyamba, Luntsville, Little Billabong, Garryowen, and Germanton (Week 3x44 miles) ; Little Billabong, Carabost, Rosewood, and Tumbarumba (Week 3x38 miles) ; Tumbarumba, Burns, Tooma, Welaregang Station, Tintaldra (Victoria), Welaregang Station, Ournie, Jingellic, Maracket, Wagra, Bowna, and Albury, via Camberoona, Dora Dora, Talmalmei, and Ournie Diggings (main road to be travelled between Camberoona and Wagra) (Week 2x115 miles); Railway Station, Culcairn, and Post Offices, Morven and Germanton (contractors to convey mails on either; side of the Billabong Creek in times of flood) (Week 6x18 miles) ; Germanton, Woomargama, Mullengandra, Bowna, Thurgoona, and Albury (Week 6x30 miles) ; Tamworth, Attunga, Manilla, Upper Manilla, Barraba, Cobbadah, Bingera, and Warialda, via Barker's, North Bingera (Week 6x167 miles) ; Armidale, Guyra, 'Ben Lomond Hotel,' Glencoe, and Glen Innes, via (Week 6x60 miles) ; Glen Innes, Dundee, Deepwater, Bolivia, The Bluff, and Tenterfield (Week 6x58 miles) ; Tenterfield, Willson's Downfall, Sugarloaf (Queensland), Stanthorpe (Queensland) (Week 6x44 miles) ; 77 Cobb & Co ... Railway Station, Newbridge, and Post Offices, Moorilda, Hobby's Yards, and Trunkey Creek (Week 3x18 miles) ; 99 Cobb & Co ... Orange, Borenore, Cheeseman's Creek, Cudal, Toogong, Murga, Eugowra, and Forbes (Week 6x80 miles) ; 119 Cobb & Co ... Sandy Creek and Nymagee (Week 2x25 miles) ; 121 Cobb & Co ... Molong, Garra, Meranburn, Bumberry, Bindogandra and Parkes (Week 6x60 miles) ; 140 Cobb & Co ... Dubbo, Brocklehurst, Burslem's, and Gilgandra, Curban, Gulargambone, and Coonamble, via Coalboggie Creek, Talbragar Bridge, and Terramungamine (Week 3x97 miles) ; 148 Cobb & Co ... Coonamble, Buggil, and Walgett, via Yowee, Bundy, Wingadee, and Nugal (Week 2x70 miles) ; 168 Cobb & Co ... Nyngan, Wicklow, and Nymagee by surveyed road (Week 3x62 miles) ; 164 Cobb & Co ... Nyngan, Hermitage Plains, and Cobar (Week 2x90 miles) ; 167 Cobb & Co ... Gongolgon and Brewarrina (Week 2x28 miles) ; 172 Cobb & Co ... Byrock and Gongolgon (Week 2x50 miles) ; Byrock and Bourke (Week 4x58 miles) ; 173 Cobb & Co ... Bourke, North Bourke, Mungunyah, Enngonia, and Barringun, via West Bourke, Gedia Camp Lake, Box-holes, Native Dog Spring, Lila, and Belalie (Week 2x90 miles) ; 163 Cobb & Co ... Murrumburrah and Young, via Ridge Road (Week 3x20 miles) ; 165 Cobb & Co ... Young, Weddin, and Grenfell (Week 7x38 miles) ; 186 Cobb & Co ...Gundagai and Tumut, via the marked-tree line (Week 6x20 miles) ; and Adelong Crossing-place, Grahamstown, Shepard's Town, Adelong, Gilmore, and Tumut (Week 6x26 miles) ; 203 Cobb & Co ... Railway Station, The Rock, Receiving Office, Ferrier's, and Post Office, Urana, via Broogong (Week 4x57 miles) ; 101 Cobb & Co ... Muswellbrook, Denman, Giant's Creek, Gungal, and Merriwa (Week 6x46 miles) ; 107 Cobb & Co ... Merriwa, Bow, and Cassilis (Week 4x25 miles) ... TOTAL 8802 miles

1886

21 Jan 1886 Conveyance of Mails ... 48 Cobb & Co ... Sydney ... Gulgong, Tallewang, Dension Town, and Coolah (Week 2x46 miles) ;–105 Cobb & Co ... Orange, Borenore, Cheeseman's Creek, Cudal, Toogong, Murga, Eugowra, and Forbes (Orange and Borenore portion of contract cancelled from 21st January, 1886, in consequence of the extension of the railway to Molong (Week 6x80 miles) ; 115 Cobb & Co ... Forbes and Marsden's, via Wongagong, Bundaburra Creek, Dog and Duck, Green Hills, Boyd, and Battery (Week 1x55 miles) ; 128 Cobb & Co ... Molong, Garra, Meranburn, Bumberry, Bindogandra and Parkes (Week 6x60 miles) ; 140 Cobb & Co ... Dubbo, Brocklehurst, Burslem's, and Gilgandra, Curban, Gulargambone, and Coonamble, via Coalboggie Creek, Talbragar Bridge, and Terramungamine (Week 3x97 miles) ; 154 Cobb & Co ... Coonamble, Buggil, and Walgett, via Yowee, Bundy, Wingadee, and Nugal (Week 2x70 miles) ; 169 Cobb & Co ... Nyngan, Hermitage Plains, and Cobar (Week 3x90 miles) ; 171 Cobb & Co ... Cobar and Louth (Week 1x90 miles); 175 Cobb & Co ... Byrock, Tarcoon, and Brewarina (Week 3x57 miles) ; 180 Cobb & Co ... Bourke, North Bourke, Mungunyah, Enngonia, and Barringun, via West Bourke, Gedia Camp Lake, Box-holes, Native Dog Spring, Lila, and Belalie (Week 2x90 miles) ; 183 Cobb & Co ... Bourke, North Bourke, and Hungerford, via Ford's Bridge, Yantabullabulla, and Brindingabba (Week 1x140 miles) ; 184 Cobb & Co ... Bourke, Louth, Tilpa, Tankerooka, and Wilcannia, travelling on either side of the Darling River (Week 2x250 miles) ; 1 Cobb & Co ... Gundagai, South Gundagai, Adelong Crossing-place (Week 6x10 miles) ; Adelong Crossing-place, Hillas Creek, Lower Tarcutta, and Tarcutta (Week 3x27 miles) ; Tarcutta, Kyamba, Luntsville, Little Billabong, Garryowen, and Germanton (Week 3x44 miles) ; Little Billabong, Carabost, Rosewood, and Tumbarumba (Week 3x38 miles) ; Railway Station, Culcairn, and Post Offices, Morven and Germanton (Contractors to convey mails on either; side of the Billabong Creek in times of flood) (Week 6x18 miles) ; Germanton, Woomargama, Mullengandra, Bowna, Thurgoona, and Albury (Week 6x30 miles) ; Tumberumba, Burns, Tooma, Welaregang Station, Ournie, Jingellic, Maracket, Wagra, Bowna, and Albury, via Camberoona, Dora Dora, Talmalmei, and Ournie Diggings (Week 2x115 miles) ; 174 Cobb & Co ... Young, Weddin, and Grenfell (Week 7x38 miles) ; 178 Cobb & Co ... Grenfell and Forbes (Week 6x41 miles) ; 196 Cobb & Co ...Gundagai, Gocup and Tumut, via the marked-tree line (Week 6x20 miles); and Adelong Crossing-place, Grahamstown, Shepard's Town, Adelong, Gilmore, and Tumut (Week 6x26 miles) ; 238 Cobb & Co ... Junee Junction, The Reefs, Sebastopol, and Temora, via 'Cooney's Inn' (Week 1x38 miles) ; 268 Cobb & Co ... Wilcannia, Victoria Hotel, Tarella, Yandarloo, Cobham, Milperinka, The Albert, and Tibooburra, via Mena Murtie, Kayrunnera, Morden, and Yanderberry (Week 2x207 miles) ; 100 Cobb & Co ... Muswellbrook, Denman, Giant's Creek, Gungal, and Merriwa (Week 6x46 miles) ; 106 Cobb & Co ... Merriwa, Bow, Borambil, and Cassilis (Week 4x25 miles) ; 171 Cobb & Co ... Tamworth, Attunga, Manilla, Upper Manilla, Barraba, Cobbadah, Bingera, and Warialda, via Barker's, North Bingera (Week 6x167 miles) ; 211 Cobb & Co ... Glen Innes, Dundee, Deepwater, Bolivia, The Bluff, and Tenterfield (Week 6x58 miles) ; 224 Cobb & Co ... Tenterfield, Willson's Downfall, Sugarloaf (Queensland),Kyoomba, Stanthorpe (Queensland) (Week 6x44 miles); 77 Cobb & Co ... Railway Station, Newbridge, and Post Offices, Moorilda, Hobby's Yards, and Trunkey Creek (Week 3x18 miles) ; 119 Cobb & Co ... Sandy Creek and Nymagee (Week 2x25 miles) ; 168 Cobb & Co ... Nyngan, Wicklow, and Nymagee by surveyed road (Week 3x62 miles) ; 167 Cobb & Co ... Gongolgon and Brewarrina (Week 2x28 miles) ... TOTAL 7160 miles

1887

25 Jan 1887 Contracts have been entered into as follows for the conveyance of mails ... 47 Cobb & Co ... Address Sydney ... Gulgong, Tallewang, Dension Town, and Coolah (Week 2x46 miles) ; 114 Cobb & Co ... Forbes, Waroo, Newlands, and Condobolin, along the south bank of the Lachlan river (Week 2x65 miles) ; 127 Cobb & Co ... Molong, Garra, Moranburn, Bumberry, Bindogandra, and Parkes (Week 6x60 miles) ; 165 Cobb & Co ... Warren, Tenandra, Bourbah, and Coonamble, via Donohoe's, on the Merri Merri, and M'Mahon's, on the west bank of the Castlereagh River (Week 1x80 miles) ; 168 Cobb & Co ... Nyngan, Wicklow, and Nymagee, by surveyed road (Week 3x62 miles) ; 171 Cobb & Co ... Cobar and Louth (Week 1x90miles); 174 Cobb & Co ... Railway Station and Post Office, Byrock (Week 2x1/7 miles) ; 175 Cobb & Co ... Byrock, Tarcoon, and Brewarrina (Week 3x57 miles) ; 180 Cobb & Co ... Bourke, North Bourke, Mungunyah, Enngonia, and Barringun, via West Bourke, Gedia Camp Lake, Box-holes, Native Dog Springs, Lila, and Belalie (Week 2x90 miles) ; 183 Cobb & Co ... Bourke, North Bourke, Hungerford, via Ford's Bridge Yantabullabulla, and Brindingabba (Week 1x140 miles) ; 184 Cobb & Co ... Bourke, Louth, Tilpa, Tankerooka, and Wilcannia, travelling on either side of the Darling River (Week 2x250 miles) ; 1 Cobb & Co ... Gundagai, South Gundagai, and Adelong Crossing-place (Week 6x10 miles) ; Adelong Crossing-place, Hillas Creek, Lower Tarcutta, and Tarcutta (Week 3x27 miles) ; Tarcutta, Kyamba, Luntsville, Little Billabong, Garryowen, and Germanton (Week 3x44 miles) ; Little Billabong, Carabost, Rosewood, and Tumbarumba (Week 3x38 miles) ; Railway Station, Culcairn, and Post Offices, Morven and Germanton (contractors to convey mails on either; side of the Billabong Creek in times of flood) (Week 6x18 miles) ; Germanton, Woomargama, Mullengandra, Bowna, Thurgoona, and Albury (Week 6x30 miles) ; Tumbarumba, Burns, Tooma, Welaregang Station, Tintaldra (Victoria), Welaregang Station, Ournie, Jingellic, Maracket, Wagra, Bowna, and Albury, via Camberoona, Dora Dora, Talmalmei, and Ournie Diggings (main road to be travelled between Camberoona and Wagra) (Week 2x115 miles) ; 170 Cobb & Co ... Young, Weddin, and Grenfell (Week 7x38 miles) ; 174 Cobb & Co ... Grenfell and Forbes (Week 6x41 miles) ; 193 Cobb & Co ... Gundagai, Gocup, and Tumut, via the marked-tree line (Week 6x20 miles); and Adelong Crossing-place, Grahamstown, Shephard's Town, Adelong, Gilmore, and Tumut (Week 6x26 miles) ; 205 Cobb & Co ... Junee Junction, and The Reefs, Sebastopol, and Temora, via 'Cooney's Inn (Week 1x38miles) ; 264 Cobb & Co ... Wilcannia, Victoria Hotel, Tarella, Yandarloo, Cobham, Milperinka, The Albert, and Tiboolburra, via Mena Murtie, Kayrunnera, Morden, and Yanderberry (Week 2x207 miles) ; 174 Cobb & Co ... Tamworth, Attunga, Manilla, Upper Manilla, Barraba, Cobbadah, Bingera, and Warialda, via Barker's, North Bingera (Week 6x167 miles) ; 229 Cobb & Co ... Tenterfield, Willson's Downfall, Sugarloaf (Queensland), Kyoomba (Queensland), and Stanthorpe (Queensland) (Week 6x44 miles) ... TOTAL 5101 miles. Note: Change of address for Postal Contracts for New South Wales, Cobb & Co ... Sydney until 1887, changed to Bathurst in 1888

1888

3 Feb 1888 Contracts have been entered into as follows for the conveyance of mails ... 49 Cobb & Co ... Address Bathurst ... Gulgong, Tallewang, Dension Town, and Coolah (Week 2x46 miles) ; 98 Cobb & Co ... Cowra, Goolagong, and Forbes (Week 3x58 miles) ; 116 Cobb & Co ... Forbes, Carrawobity, Bedgerebong, Mulguthrie, Borambil, and Condobolin (Week 2x60 miles) ; 117 Cobb & Co ... Forbes, Waroo, Newlands, and Condobolin, along the south bank of the Lachlan river (Week 2x65 miles) ; 129 Cobb & Co ... Molong, Garra, Moranburn, Bumberry, Bindogandra, and Parkes (Week 6x60 miles) ; 170 Cobb & Co ... Nyngan, Wicklow, and Nymagee, by surveyed road (Week 3x62 miles) ; 173 Cobb & Co ... Cobar and Louth (Week 1x90 miles) ; 176 Cobb & Co ... Railway Station and Post Office, Byrock (Week 2x1/7 miles) ; 177 Cobb & Co ... Byrock, Tarcoon, and Brewarrina (Week 3x57 miles) ; 181 Cobb & Co ... Bourke, North Bourke, Mungunyah, Enngonia, and Barringun, via West Bourke, Gedia Camp Lake, Box-holes, Native Dog Springs, Lila, and Belalie (Week 2x90 miles) ; 185 Cobb & Co ... Bourke, North Bourke, Hungerford, via Ford's Bridge Yantabullabulla, and Brindingabba (Week 1x140 miles) ; 186 Cobb & Co ... Bourke, Louth, Tilpa, Tankerooka, and Wilcannia, travelling on either side of the Darling River (Week 2x250 miles) ; 1 Cobb & Co ... Gundagai, South Gundagai, and Adelong Crossing-place (Week 6x10 miles) ; Adelong Crossing-place, Hillas Creek, Lower Tarcutta, and Tarcutta (Week 3x27 miles) ; Tarcutta, Kyamba, Luntsville, Little Billabong, Garryowen, and Germanton (Week 3x44 miles) ; Little Billabong, Carabost, Rosewood, and Tumbarumba (Week 3x38 miles) ; Railway Station, Culcairn, and Post Offices, Morven and Germanton (contractors to convey mails on either; side of the Billabong Creek in times of flood) (Week 6x18 miles) ; Germanton, Woomargama, Mullengandra, Bowna, Thurgoona, and Albury (Week 6x30 miles) ; Tumbarumba, Burns, Tooma, Welaregang Station, Tintaldra (Victoria), Welaregang Station, Ournie, Jingellic, Maracket, Wagra, Bowna, and Albury, via Camberoona, Dora Dora, Talmalmei, and Ournie Diggings (Main road to be travelled between Camberoona and Wagra) (Week 2x115 miles) ; 163 Cobb & Co ... Young, Weddin, and Grenfell (Week 7x38 miles) ; 168 Cobb & Co ... Grenfell and Forbes (Week 6x41 miles) ; 262 Cobb & Co ... Wilcannia, Victoria Hotel, Tarella, Yandarloo, Cobham, Milperinka, The Albert, and Tiboolburra, via Mena Murtie, Kayrunnera, Morden, and Yanderberry (Week 2x207 miles) ; 265 Cobb & Co ... Euriowie and Cobham Lake, via Fowler's Gap, Bancannia Lake, and Packsaddle (Week 1x96 miles) ... TOTAL 3558 miles. Note: Change of address for Postal Contracts for New South Wales, Cobb & Co ... Sydney until 1887, changed to Bathurst in 1888

1889

3 Feb 1888 Contracts have been entered into as follows for the conveyance of mails ... 98 Cobb & Co ... Cowra, Goolagong, and Forbes (Week 3x58 miles) ; 118 Cobb & Co ... Forbes, Carrawobity, Bedgerebong, Mulguthrie, Borambil, and Condobolin (Week 2x60 miles) ; 119 Cobb & Co ... Forbes, Waroo, Newlands, and Condobolin, along the south bank of the Lachlan river (Week 2x65 miles) ; 120 Cobb & Co ... Forbes, Tichborne, and Parkes (Week 3x25 miles) ; 132 Cobb & Co ... Molong, Garra, Meranburn, Bumberry, Bindogandra, and Parkes (Week 6x60 miles) ; 185 Cobb & Co ... Railway Station and Post Office, Byrock (Week 2x1/7 miles) ; 186 Cobb & Co ... Byrock, Tarcoon, and Brewarrina (Week 3x57 miles) ; 190 Cobb & Co ... Bourke, North Bourke, Mungunyah, Enngonia, and Barringun, via West Bourke, Gedia Camp Lake, Box-holes, Native Dog Springs, Lila, and Belalie (Week 2x90 miles) ; 194 Cobb & Co ... Bourke, North Bourke, Hungerford, via Ford's Bridge Yantabullabulla, and Brindingabba (Week 1x140 miles) ; 168 Cobb & Co ... Young, Weddin, and Grenfell (Week 7x38 miles) ; 172 Cobb & Co ... Grenfell and Forbes (Week 6x41 miles) ; 274 Cobb & Co ... Wilcannia, Victoria Hotel, Tarella, Yandarloo, Cobham, Milperinka, The Albert, and Tiboolburra, via Mena Murtie, Kayrunnera, Morden, and Yanderberry (Week 2x207 miles) ; 282 Cobb & Co ... Silverton, Day Dream, Purnamoota, Lady Don, and Euriowie (Week 2x54 miles) ; 283 Cobb & Co ... Euriowie, Poolamacca, Gnalta, and 'Victoria Hotel' (Week 1x122 miles) ; 284 Cobb & Co ... Euriowie and Cobham Lake, via Fowler's Gap, Bancannia Lake, and Packsaddle (Week 1x96 miles) ... TOTAL 2603 miles

1890

15 Feb 1890 Contracts have been entered into as follows for the conveyance of mails ... 97 Cobb & Co ... Cowra, Goolagong, and Forbes (Week 3x58 miles) ; 111 Cobb & Co ... Railway Station, Orange, and Post offices, Borenore, Cheeseman's Creek, Cudal, Toogong, Murga, Nangar, Eugowra, and Forbes (Week 6x97 miles) ; 117 Cobb & Co ... Forbes, Carrawobity, Bedgerebong, Mulguthrie, Borambil, and Condobolin (Week 3x60 miles) ; 118 Cobb & Co ... Forbes, Waroo, Newlands, and Condobolin, along the south bank of the Lachlan river (Week 3x65 miles) ; 120 Cobb & Co ... Forbes, Tichborne, and Parkes (Week 3x25 miles) ; 131 Cobb & Co ... Molong, Garra, Meranburn, Bumberry, Bindogandra, Kamandra, and Parkes (Week 6x60 miles) ; 186 Cobb & Co ... Byrock, Tarcoon, and Brewarrina (Week 3x57 miles) ; 192 Cobb & Co ... Bourke, North Bourke, Mungunyah, Enngonia, and Barringun, via West Bourke, Gedia Camp Lake, Box-holes, Native Dog Springs, Lila, and Belalie (Week 2x90 miles) ; 172 Cobb & Co ... Young, Weddin, and Grenfell (Week 7x38 miles) ; 176 Cobb & Co ... Grenfell and Forbes (Week 6x41 miles) ; 285 Cobb & Co ... Wilcannia, Victoria Hotel, Tarella, Yandarloo, Cobham, Milperinka, The Albert, and Tiboolburra, via Mena Murtie, Kayrunnera, Morden, and Yanderberry (Week 2x207 miles) ; 291 Cobb & Co ... Silverton, Day Dream, Purnamoota, Lady Don, and Euriowie (Week 2x54 miles) ; 293 Cobb & Co ... Euriowie and Cobham Lake, via Fowler's Gap, Bancannia Lake, and Packsaddle (Week 1x96 miles) ... TOTAL 3047 miles

1891

16 Feb 1891 Contracts have been entered into as follows for the conveyance of mails ... 103 Cobb & Co ... Bathurst ... Cowra, Goolagong, Tomanbil, and Forbes (Week 3x58 miles) ; 117 Cobb & Co ... Railway Station, Borenore, and Post offices, Borenore, Cheeseman's Creek, Cudal, Toogong, Murga, Nangar, Eugowra, and Forbes (Week 6x79 miles) ; 125 Cobb & Co ... Forbes, Carrawobity, Bedgerebong, Mulguthrie, Borambil, and Condobolin (Week 3x60 miles) ; 126 Cobb & Co ... Forbes, Waroo, Newlands, and Condobolin, along the south bank of the Lachlan river (Week 3x65 miles) ; 127 Cobb & Co ... Forbes, Tichborne, and Parkes (Week 3x25 miles) ; 128 Cobb & Co ... Forbes, Tichborne, and Parkes (Week 3x25 miles) ; 142 Cobb & Co ... Molong, Garra, Meranburn, Bumberry, Bindogandra, Kamandra, and Parkes (Week 6x60 miles) ; 204 Cobb & Co ... Railway Station and Post Office, Bourke (Week 1x3/8 miles) ; 205 Cobb & Co ... Bourke, North Bourke, Mungunyah, Enngonia, and Barringun, via West Bourke, Gedia Camp Lake, Box-holes, Native Dog Springs, Lila, and Belalie (Week 2x90 miles) ; 209 Cobb & Co ... Bourke, North Bourke, Ford's Bridge, Yantabulla, and Hungerford, via Bringabba (Week 1x140 miles) ; 210 Cobb & Co ... Bourke, North Bourke, Ford's Bridge, Yantabulla, and Hungerford, via Bringabba (Week 1x140 miles) ; 211 Cobb & Co ... Bourke, Louth, Tilpa, Tankerooka, and Wilcannia, travelling on either side of the Darling River (Week 2x250 miles) ; 179 Cobb & Co ... Young, Weddin, and Grenfell (Week 7x38 miles) ; 183 Cobb & Co ... Grenfell and Forbes (Week 6x41 miles) ; 297 Cobb & Co ... Wilcannia, Victoria Hotel, Tarella, Yandarloo, Cobham, Milperinka, The Albert, and Tiboolburra, via Mena Murtie, Kayrunnera, Morden, and Yanderberry (Week 2x207 miles) ; 304 Cobb & Co ... Silverton, Day Dream, Purnamoota, Gainer's Hotel, and Euriowie (Week 2x54 miles) ; 305 Cobb & Co ... Euriowie, Poolamacca, Pampira, Gnalta, and 'Victoria Hotel' (Week 1x122 miles) ; 306 Cobb & Co ... Euriowie and Cobham Lake, via Fowler's Gap, Bancannia Lake, and Packsaddle (Week 1x96 miles) ... TOTAL 3854 miles

1892

24 Feb 1892 Contracts have been entered into as follows for the conveyance of mails ... 119 Cobb & Co ... Railway Station, Borenore, & Post offices, Borenore, Cheeseman's Creek, Cudal, Toogong, Murga, Nangar, Eugowra, and Forbes (Week 6x79 miles) ; 126 Cobb & Co ... Forbes, Carrawobity, Bedgerebong, Mulguthrie, Borambil, and Condobolin (Week 3x60 miles) ; 127 Cobb & Co ... Forbes, Waroo, Newlands, and Condobolin, along the south bank of the Lachlan river (Week 3x65 miles) ; 128 Cobb & Co ... Forbes, Tichborne, and Parkes (Week 6x25 miles) ;; 142 Cobb & Co ... Molong, Garra, Manildra, Meranburn, Porcupine Gap, Bumberry, Bindogandra, Kamandra, and Parkes (Week 6x60 miles) ; ; 204 Cobb & Co ... Railway Station and Post Office, Bourke (Week 1x3/8 miles) ; 205 Cobb & Co ... Bourke, North Bourke, Mungunyah, Enngonia, and Barringun, via West Bourke, Gedia Camp Lake, Box-holes, Native Dog Springs, Lila, and Belalie (Week 2x90 miles) ; 182 Cobb & Co ... Young, Weddin, and Grenfell (Week 7x38 miles) ; 186 Cobb & Co ... Grenfell and Forbes (Week 6x41 miles) ; 316 Cobb & Co ... Wilcannia, 'Victoria Hotel,' Tarella, Yandarloo, Cobham, Milperinka, The Albert, and Tiboolburra, via Mena Murtie, Kayrunnera, Morden, and Yanderberry (Week 2x207 miles) ; 317 Cobb & Co ... Wilcannia, Mount Gipps, Round Hill, and Broken Hill (Week 2x113 miles) ; 321 Cobb & Co ... Broken Hill, Torrowangee, and Euriowie, via Mount Gipps Station, 'Maybell Hotel,' Albion Town, and 'Gainor's Hotel' (Week 2x53 miles) ; 324 Cobb & Co ... Euriowie, Poolamacca, Pampira, Gnalta, and 'Victoria Hotel' (Week 1x123 miles) ; 325 Cobb & Co ... Euriowie and Cobham Lake, via Fowler's Gap, Bancannia Lake, and Packsaddle (Week 2x96 miles) ... TOTAL 3113 miles

1893

18 Feb 1893 Contracts have been entered into as follows for the conveyance of mails ... 123 Cobb & Co ... Railway Station, Borenore, & Post offices, Borenore, Cheeseman's Creek, Cudal, Toogong, Murga, Nangar, Eugowra, and Forbes (Week 6x79 miles) ; 127 Cobb & Co ... Forbes, Bogan Gate, Trundle, Barnett, and Dandaloo, via Nelungaloo, Gunning Bland, Todd and West's, Christie's, Troffs', A. T. Medcalf's, Gobondry, Jumble Plains, Block H, Woodlands, & Albert Waterholes (Week 2x136 miles) ; 129 Cobb & Co ... Forbes, Carrawobity, Bedgerebong, Mulguthrie, Borambil, and Condobolin (Week 3x60 miles) ; 127 Cobb & Co ... Forbes, Waroo, Newlands, and Condobolin, along the south bank of the Lachlan river (Week 3x65 miles) ; 131 Cobb & Co ... Forbes, Tichborne, and Parkes (Week 6x25 miles) ;; 147 Cobb & Co ... Molong, Garra, Manildra, Meranburn, Athey's, Porcupine Gap, Bumberry, Bindogandra, Kamandra, and Parkes (Week 6x60 miles) ; 155 Cobb & Co ... Parkes, Alectown, Kadina, Mingelo, and Peak Hill, via Bachelor's Reef (Week 3x36 miles) ; 206 Cobb & Co ... Cobar and Wilcannia (Week 2x160 miles) ; 210 Cobb & Co ...Tarcoon and Beemery (Week 1x28 miles); 216 Cobb & Co ... Railway Station and Post Office, Bourke (Week 1x3/8 miles) ; 217 Cobb & Co ... Bourke and North Bourke (Week 6x3½ miles) ; 218 Cobb & Co ... Bourke, Louth, Tilpa, Tankerooka, and Wilcannia, traveling on either side of the Darling River (Week 2x90 miles) ; 223 Cobb & Co ... Bourke, North Bourke, Mungunyah, Enngonia, and Barringun, via West Bourke, Gedia Camp Lake, Box-holes, Native Dog Springs, Lila, and Belalie (Week 2x250 miles) ; 189 Cobb & Co ... Grenfell and Forbes (Week 6x41 miles) ; 824 Cobb & Co ... Wilcannia, 'Victoria Hotel,' Tarella, Yandarloo, Cobham Lake, Milperinka, The Albert, and Tiboolburra, via Mena Murtie, Kayrunnera, Morden, and Yanderberry (Week 2x207 miles) ; 325 Cobb & Co ... Wilcannia, Mount Gipps, Round Hill, and Broken Hill (Week 2x110 miles) ; 329 Cobb & Co ... Broken Hill, Torrowangee, and Euriowie, via Mount Gipps Station, 'Maybell Hotel,' Albion

Town, and 'Gainor's Hotel' (Week 2x53 miles) ; 323 Cobb & Co ... Euriowie and Cobham Lake, via Fowler's Gap, Bancannia Lake, and Packsaddle (Week 2x96) ... TOTAL 4167 miles

1894

15 Feb 1894 Contracts have been entered into as follows for the conveyance of mails ... 123 Cobb & Co ... Railway Station, Borenore, & Post offices, Borenore, Cheeseman's Creek, Cudal, Toogong, Murga, Nangar, Eugowra, and Forbes (Week 6x79 miles) ; 127 Cobb & Co ... Forbes, Bogan Gate, Trundle, Barnett, and Dandaloo, via Nelungaloo, Gunning Bland, Todd and West's, Christie's, Troffs', A. T. Medcalf's, Gobondry, Jumble Plains, Block H, Woodlands, & Albert Waterholes (Week 2x136 miles) ; 129 Cobb & Co ... Forbes, Carrawobity, Bedgerebong, Mulguthrie, Borambil, and Condobolin (Week 3x60 miles) ; 127 Cobb & Co ... Forbes, Waroo, Newlands, and Condobolin, along the south bank of the Lachlan river (Week 3x65 miles) ; 131 Cobb & Co ... Forbes, Tichborne, and Parkes (Week 6x25 miles) ; 147 Cobb & Co ... Molong, Garra, Manildra, Meranburn, Athey's, Porcupine Gap, Bumberry, Bindogandra, Kamandra, and Parkes (Week 6x60 miles) ; 155 Cobb & Co ... Parkes, Alectown, Kadina, Mingelo, and Peak Hill, via Bachelor's Reef (Week 3x36 miles) ; 206 Cobb & Co ... Cobar and Wilcannia (Week 2x160 miles) ; 210 Cobb & Co ... Tarcoon and Beemery (Week 1x28 miles); 216 Cobb & Co ... Railway Station and Post Office, Bourke (Week 1x3/8 miles) ; 217 Cobb & Co ... Bourke and North Bourke (Week 6x3½ miles) ; 218 Cobb & Co ... Bourke, Louth, Tilpa, Tankerooka, and Wilcannia, traveling on either side of the Darling River (Week 2x90 miles) ; 223 Cobb & Co ... Bourke, North Bourke, Mungunyah, Enngonia, and Barringun, via West Bourke, Gedia Camp Lake, Box-holes, Native Dog Springs, Lila, and Belalie (Week 2x250 miles) ; 189 Cobb & Co ... Grenfell and Forbes (Week 6x41 miles) ; 824 Cobb & Co ... Wilcannia, 'Victoria Hotel,' Tarella, Yandarloo, Cobham Lake, Milperinka, The Albert, and Tiboolburra, via Mena Murtie, Kayrunnera, Morden, and Yanderberry (Week 2x207 miles) ; 325 Cobb & Co ... Wilcannia, Mount Gipps, Round Hill, and Broken Hill (Week 2x110 miles) ; 329 Cobb & Co ... Broken Hill, Torrowangee, and Euriowie, via Mount Gipps Station, 'Maybell Hotel,' Albion Town, and 'Gainor's Hotel' (Week 2x53 miles) ; 323 Cobb & Co ... Euriowie and Cobham Lake, via Fowler's Gap, Bancannia Lake, and Packsaddle (Week 2x96 miles) ... TOTAL 4167 miles

1895

16 Feb 1895 Contracts have been entered into as follows for the conveyance of mails ... 129 Cobb & Co ... Railway Station, Borenore, & Post offices, Borenore, Cheeseman's Creek, Cudal, Toogong, Murga, Nangar, Eugowra, and Forbes (Week 3x79 miles) ; 154 James Rutherford ... Forbes, Carrawobity, Bedgerebong, Mulguthrie, Borambil, and Condobolin (Week 3x60 miles) ; 182 James Rutherford ... Dubbo, Brocklehurst, Coalbaggie, Burslem's, and Gilgandra, via Talbragar Bridge and Terramungamine (Week 3x41 miles) ; 230 James Rutherford (Cobb & Co) Railway Station and Post office Bourke (Week 1x3/8 mile) ; 231 Cobb & Co ... Bourke and North Bourke (Week 6x3½ mile) ; 232 Cobb & Co ... Bourke, North Bourke, Mungunyah, Enngonia, and Barringun, via West Bourke, Gedia Camp Lake, Box-holes, Native Dog Springs, Lila, and Belalie (Week 2x90 miles) ; 193 Cobb & Co ... Young, Weddin, and Grenfell (Week 6x38 miles) ; 197 Cobb & Co ... Grenfell and Forbes (Week 6x41 miles) ; 338 James Rutherford (Cobb & Co) ... Broken Hill, Round Hill, Mount Gipps, and Wilcannia (Week 2x110 miles) ; 152 James Rutherford (Cobb & Co) ... Narrabri, Wee Waa, Cuttabri, Pilliga, Come-by-chance, and Walgett (Week 3x125 miles) ; 153 Cobb & Co ... Narrabri, Millie, Bumble, & Moree (Week 6x70 miles) ; 166 Cobb & Co ... Walgett and Goodooga (Week 1x97 miles) ; 171 James Rutherford (Cobb & Co) ... Weetalibalh and New Angledool (Week 2x14 miles) ... TOTAL 2266 miles Note: James Rutherford and/or Cobb and Co listed on mail contracts

1896

17 Oct 1896 Cobb & Co.'s Coaches—Mansfield, Jamieson; Cobb & Co.'s Telegraph Line of Coaches runs daily between Moe and Walhalla ... A. Grant, proprietor.; 13 Jan 1899 Cobb & Co's. Coaches—Jerilderie to Deniliquin ... Booking Office Royal Mail, Hotel, Jerilderie; 19 Feb 1896 Conveyance of Post Office Mails ... 156 James Rutherford ... Forbes, Carrawobity, Bedgerebong, Mulguthrie, Borambil, and Condobolin (Week; x60 miles) ; 240 James Rutherford (Cobb & Co) Railway Station and Post office Bourke (Week 1x3/8 mile) ; 196 Cobb & Co ... Young, Weddin, and Grenfell (Week 6x38 miles) ; 212 Cobb & Co ... Temora, Gidginbung, Barmedman (Week 6x30 miles) ; 158 James Rutherford (Cobb & Co) ... Narrabri, Wee Waa, Cuttabri, Pilliga, Come-by-chance, and Walgett (Week; x125 miles) ; 159 Cobb & Co ... Narrabri, Bumble, & Moree (Week 7x70 miles) ... TOTAL 1204 miles Note: James Rutherford and/or Cobb and Co listed on mail contracts

1897

16 Feb 1897 Conveyance of Post Office Mails ... 155 James Rutherford ... Forbes, Carrawobity, Bedgerebong, Mulguthrie, Borambil, and Condobolin (Week 3x60 miles) ; 157 James Rutherford ... Bogan Gate and Condobolin (Week 6x87 miles) ; 241 James Rutherford (Cobb & Co) Railway Station and Post office Bourke (Week 1x3/8 mile) ; 220 James Rutherford ... Temora, Gidginbung, Barmedman, Wyalong, and West Wyalong (Week 6x45 miles) ; 160 James Rutherford (Cobb & Co) Narrabri, Wee Waa, Cuttabri, Pilliga, Come-by-chance, and Walgett (Week 1x125 miles) ; 163 Cobb & Co ... Bathurst ... Narrabri, and Collarenebri, via 'Myall Vale Hotel,' Boolcarroll Station, 'Rosehill Hotel', Harden Brothers'. Lower Boolcarroll, 'Yarranbar Hotel,' Nowley Station, Maloney's 'Bulyeroi Hotel,' Barrett's, Lord's, G. Shearer's, Merrywinebone, and Pockataroo (Week 2x110 miles) ... With a branch mail to and from 'Myall Vale Hotel,; Wall's, Power's, Wyatt's, Cohen's, Maxwell's, and Lehane's (Horseback) (Week 2x13 miles) ... TOTAL 1344 miles Note: James Rutherford and/or Cobb and Co listed on mail contracts

1898

Note: James Rutherford not Cobb and Co now listed on mail contracts

Appendix 3: £4,000 Reward for the apprehension of John Gilbert, John O'Meally, Benjamin Hall, and John Vane

V. R.

£4,000 REWARD,
FOR THE APPREHENSION OF JOHN GILBERT, JOHN O'MEALLEY, BENJAMIN HALL, AND JOHN VANE,
AND £100 REWARD FOR ACCOMPLICES.

WHEREAS the abovenamed persons are charged with the commission of numerous and serious offences, and have hitherto eluded the efforts to apprehend them: It is hereby notified that the Government will pay a Reward of One Thousand Pounds for such information as will lead to the apprehension of each of the offenders named.

The Government will also pay a reward of One Hundred Pounds for such information as will lead to the conviction of any person or persons for harbouring, assisting, or maintaining any of the abovenamed offenders.

All such information communicated by any person charged with the commission of an offence, will entitle his case to favorable consideration by the Crown, and will in all cases be regarded by the Police Authorities as strictly confidential; and in the event of payment of any of the Rewards above offered, the name of the recipient will not be disclosed.

The above Rewards are offered in lieu of all others previously payable by Government for the apprehension or conviction of the offenders abovenamed.

WILLIAM FORSTER.
Colonial Secretary's Office,
Sydney, 27th October, 1863.

(Courtesy State Library New South Wales)

Reference List

ADVERTISING': 1852 Bathurst Free Press and Mining Journal (NSW : 1851 - 1862; 1872; 1882; 1885 - 1897; 1899 - 1904), 10 April, p. 3. ; 1853 Bathurst Free Press and Mining Journal (NSW : 1851 - 1862; 1872; 1882; 1885 - 1897; 1899 - 1904), 18 June, p. 3. ; 1853 Geelong Advertiser and Intelligencer (Vic. : 1851 - 1856), 9 June, p. 1. (DAILY.) ; 1853 The Argus (Melbourne, Vic. : 1848 - 1957), 10 September, p. 8. ; 1853 The Argus (Melbourne, Vic. : 1848 - 1957), 13 May, p. 11. ; 1853 The Argus (Melbourne, Vic. : 1848 - 1957), 13 June, p. 2. ; 1853 The Argus (Melbourne, Vic. : 1848 - 1957), 14 May, p. 5. ; 1853 The Argus (Melbourne, Vic. : 1848 - 1957), 16 July, p. 8. ; 1853 The Argus (Melbourne, Vic. : 1848 - 1957), 2 June, p. 7. ; 1853 The Argus (Melbourne, Vic. : 1848 - 1957), 21 June, p. 6. ; 1853, 22 June, p. 4 ; 1853, 26 April, p. 8. ; 1853, 27 September, p. 2. ; 1853, 8 October, p. 3. ; 1854 Mount Alexander Mail (Vic. : 1854 - 1917), 27 May, p. 1. ; 1854 The Age (Melbourne, Vic. : 1854 - 1954), 10 November, p. 1. ; 1854, 17 November, p. 3. ; 1854, 2 November, p. 1. ; 1854, 20 October, p. 1. ; 1854, 23 November, p. 3. ; 1854, 25 November, p. 8. ; 1854 The Argus (Melbourne, Vic. : 1848 - 1957), 12 October, p. 8. ; 1854, 12 April, p. 1. ; 1854, 12 October, p. 8. ; 1854, 2 December, p. 6.; 1854, 20 October, p. 3. ; 1854, 24 November, p. 6. ; 1854, 25 November, p. 6. ; 1854, 3 May, p. 2. ; 1854, 30 November, p. 8. ; 1854, 31 January, p. 3. ; 1854 The Banner (Melbourne, Vic. : 1853 - 1854), 27 June, p. 13. ; 1855 Bendigo Advertiser (Vic. : 1855 - 1918), 25 October, p. 1. ; 1855, 6 October, p. 1. ; 1855 Geelong Advertiser and Intelligence (Vic. : 1851 - 1856), 5 Jun, p. 1. ; 1855 Mount Alexander Mail (Vic. : 1854 - 1917), 13 July, p. 4. ; 1855, 28 September, p. 4. ; 1855 The Age (Melbourne, Vic. : 1854 - 1954), 16 February, p. 2. ; 1855, 17 February, p. 2. ; 1855, 18 January, p. 8. ; 1855, 19 June, p. 2. ; 1855, 21 November, p. 8. ; 1855, 24 January, p. 2. ; 1855, 24 January, p. 1. ; 1855, 30 January, p. 1. ; 1855, 5 September, p. 2. ; 1855, 8 February, p. 2. ; 1855, 9 November, p. 1. ; 1855 The Argus (Melbourne, Vic. : 1848 - 1957), 1 February, p. 8. ; 1855, 15 January, p. 7. ; 1855, 17 January, p. 8. ; 1855, 2 June, p.1. ; 1855, 2 November, p. 7. ; 1855, 20 October, p. 7. ; 1855, 21 September, p. 1. ; 1855, 23 May, p. 3. ; 1855, 25 January, p. 3. ; 1855, 26 November, p. 8. ; 1855, 26 March, p. 8 ; 1855, 27 October, p. 7. ; 1855, 4 December, p. 3. ; 1855, 6 October, p. 1. ; 1855, 6 November, p. 7. ; 1855, 8 June, p. 7. ; 1856 Bendigo Advertiser (Vic. : 1855 - 1918), 12 December, p. 3 ; 1856 Bendigo Advertiser (Vic. : 1855 - 1918), 16 May, p. 1. ; 1856 Bendigo Advertiser (Vic. : 1855 - 1918), 18 October, p. 1. ; 1856, 23 May, p. 3. ; 1856 Mount Alexander Mail (Vic. : 1854 - 1917), 27 May, p. 4. ; 1856, 29 April, p. 3. ; 1856, 3 June, p. 4. ; 1856 The Age (Melbourne, Vic. : 1854 - 1954), 2 December, p. 8. ; 1856 The Age (Melbourne, Vic. : 1854 - 1954), 20 February, p. 1. ; 1856 'Advertising', The Age (Melbourne, Vic. : 1854 - 1954), 23 June, p. 1. ; 1856, 25 June, p. 1. ; 1856, 28 June, p. 1. ; 1856, 3 December, p. 8. ; 1856, 31 May, p. 1. ; 1856, 8 December, p. 7. ; 1856 The Argus (Melbourne, Vic. : 1848 - 1957), 1 January, p. 2. ; 1856, 1 May, p. 1. ; 1856, 13 March, p. 3. ; 1856, 5 July, p. 8. ; 1856 19 May, p. 7. ; 1856, 22 April, p. 10. ; 1856, 24 April, p. 1. ; 1856, 27 February, p. 8. ; 1856 28 April, p. 8. ; 1856, 29 May, p. 8. ; 1856, 29 May, p. 8. ; 1856, 29 August, p. 8. ; 1856, 3 April, p. 2. ; 1856, 30 April, p. 8. ; 1856 31 May, p.3. ; 1856, 9 April, p. 3. ; 1856 Williamstown Chronicle (Vic. : 1856 - 1954), 29 November, p. 1. ; 1856 Williamstown Chronicle (Vic. : 1856 - 1954), 8 November, p. 1. ; 1857 Bell's Life in Victoria and Sporting Chronicle (Melbourne, Vic. : 1857 - 1868), 6 June, p. 1. ; 1857 Bell's Life in Victoria and Sporting Chronicle (Melbourne, Vic. : 1857 - 1868), 25 July, p. 1. ; 1857 Mount Alexander Mail (Vic. : 1854 - 1917), 10 July, p. 2. ; 1857, 12 January, p. 4. ; 1857, 21 December, p. 4. ; 1857, 22 June, p. 3. ; 1857, 28 October, p. 4. ; 1857, 4 November, p. 3. ; 1857 The Age (Melbourne, Vic. : 1854 - 1954), 14 January, p.1. ; 1857, 18 July, p. 3. ; 1857, 26 October, p. 1. ; 1857, 27 April, p. 1. ; 1857, 3 January, p. 1. ; 1857 The Argus (Melbourne, Vic. : 1848 - 1957), 1 July, p. 8. ; 1857, 10 November, p. 3. ; 1857, 10 October, p. 8. ; 1857, 11 August, p. 8. , ; 1857, 13 October, p. 8. ; 1857, 13 October, p. 8. ; 1857, 19 August, p. 8. ; 1857, 2 September, p. 8. ; 1857, 23 September, p.8. ; 1857, 26 September, p. 8. ; 1857, 27 April, p. 8. ; 1857, 29 October, p. 8. ; 1857, 3 February, p. 6. ; 1857, 30 June, p. 8. ; 1857, 30 December, p. 3. ; 1857, 4 May, p. 3. ; 1857, 6 November, p. 8. ; 1857, 7 September, p. 8. ; 1857 The Star (Ballarat, Vic. : 1855 - 1864), 1 September, p. 4. ; 1857, 2 November, p. 1. ; 1857, 3 December, p. 1. ; 1857, 4 November, p. 1. 1858 Bendigo Advertiser (Vic. : 1855 - 1918), 17 November, p. 1. ; 1858, 19 July, p. 1. ; 1858, 24 February, p. 1. ; 1858 Launceston Examiner (Tas. : 1842 - 1899), 9 October, p. 1. ; 1858 Mount Alexander Mail (Vic. : 1854 - 1917), 1 January, p. 2. ; 1858, 14 May, p. 2. ; 1858, 21 May, p. 8. ; 1858, 23 April, p. 2. ; 1858, 3 August, p. 4. ; 1858, 27 August, p. 2.; 1858, 28 July, p. 4. 1858 The Age (Melbourne, Vic. : 1854 - 1954), 1 October, p. 3. ; 1858, 19 January, p. 8. ; 1858, 4 February, p. 8. ; 1858, 6 January, p. 2. ; 1858 The Argus (Melbourne, Vic. : 1848 - 1957), 17 June, p. 8. ; 1858, 23 February, p. 6. ; 1858, 29 October, p. 8. ; 1858, 30 September, p. 8. ; 1858, October, p. 8. ; 1858, 8 November, p. 8. ; 1858 The Star (Ballarat, Vic. : 1855 - 1864), 1 February, p.1. ; 1858, 10 February, p. 1. ; 1858, 10 February, p. 1. ; 1858, 25 November, p. 1. ; 1858, 4 February, p. 1. ; 1859 Bell's Life in Victoria and Sporting Chronicle (Melbourne, Vic. : 1857 - 1868), 5 February, p.4. ; 1859, 12 February, p.4. ; 1859, 9 July, p.1. ; 1859, 1 November, p.1. ; 1859, 16 August, p.1. ; 1859, 6 January, p. 1. ; 1859 Geelong Advertiser (Vic. : 1859 - 1929), 16 March, p.1. ; 1859, 18 February, p.1. ; 1859, 29 October, p.1. ; 1859 Maryborough and Dunolly Advertiser (Vic. : 1857 - 1867 ; 1914 - 1918), 4 July, p.1. ; 1859, 1 March, p. 4. ; 1859 Mount Alexander Mail (Vic. : 1854 - 1917), 14 January, p. 8. ; 1859, , 17 October, p. 4. ; 1859, 2 March, p.4. ; 1859, 21 October, p.2. ; 1859, 7 November, p.4. ; 1859 The Age (Melbourne, Vic. : 1854 - 1954), 10 September, p.3. ; 1859, 17 June, p. 7. ; 1859, 2 June, p.7. ; 1859, 31 December, p.2. ; 1859 The Argus (Melbourne, Vic. : 1848 - 1957), 1 January, p. 8. ; 1859, 10 February, p.8. ; 1859, 10 May, p.8. ; 1859, 15 March, p. 8. ; 1859, 19 January, p.8. ; 1859, 22 February, p.1. ; 1859, 25 November, p. 3. ; 1859 The Star (Ballarat, Vic. : 1855 - 1864), 20 April, p. 1. ; 1859, 25 April, p.3. ; 1860 Bendigo Advertiser (Vic. : 1855 - 1918) 3 August 1860: 1. ; 1860 Bell's Life in Victoria and Sporting Chronicle (Melbourne, Vic. : 1857 - 1868), 3 November, p.1. ; 1860 Bendigo Advertiser (Vic. : 1855 - 1918), 9 April, p.1. ; 1860 Geelong Advertiser (Vic. : 1859 - 1929), 12 December, p.1. ; 1860, 21 January, p.1. ; 1860, 24 December, .1. ; 1860, 24 January, p.1. ; 1860, 4 December, p.1. ; 1860 Maryborough and Dunolly Advertiser (Vic. : 1857 - 1867 ; 1914 - 1918), 9 November, p.3. ; 1860 Mount Alexander Mail (Vic. : 1854 - 1917), 10 August, p.2. ; 1860, 11 June, p. 1. ; 1860, 27 February, p.1. ; 1860, 7 November, p.4. ; 1860, 13 December, p.1. ; 1860 The Age (Melbourne, Vic. : 1854 - 1954), 14 August, p. 8. ; 1860, 14 September, p. 3. ; 1860, 22 March, p.3. ; 1860, 4 July, p.3. ; 1860 The Argus (Melbourne, Vic. : 1848 - 1957), 11 June, p. 8. ; 1860, 12 November, p.8. ; 1860, 12 June, p. 3. ; 1860, 13 June, p. 8. ; 1860, 15 August, p.8. ; 1860, 16 April, p. 8. ; 1860, 21 June, p.8. ; 1860, 25 October, p.8. ; 1860, 27 January, p.8. ; 1860, 27 July, p. 3. ; 1860, 28 May, p. 8. ; 1860, October, p.8. ; 1860, 7 May, p. 8. ; 1860, 7 August, p.8. ; 1860 The Kyneton Observer (Vic. : 1856 - 1900), 10 November, p.1. ; 1860, 18 October, p.1. ; 1860 The Star (Ballarat, Vic. : 1855 - 1864), 13 December, p. 1. ; 1860, 21 July, p. 3. ; 1860, 7 March, p 4. ; 1860, 8 November, p.1. ; 1860 The Tarrangower Times and Maldon District Advertiser (Vic. : 1858 - 1862), 13 July, p. 1. ; 1861 Portland Guardian and Normanby General Advertiser (Vic. : 1842 - 1843; 1854 - 1876), 14 January, p.1. ; 1861 The Age (Melbourne, Vic. : 1854 - 1954) 1 July 1861, p.8. ; 1861 29 June 1861, p.8. ; 1861 Bendigo Advertiser (Vic. : 1855 - 1918), 3 October, p.3. ; 1861 Empire (Sydney, NSW : 1850 - 1875), 1 January, p. 8. ; 1861 Maryborough and Dunolly Advertiser (Vic. : 1857 - 1867 ; 1914 - 1918), 2 January, p.1. ; 1861, 2 January, p.1. ; 1861, 14 January, p.1. ; 1861, 5 June, p.1. ; 1861, 5 July, p.1. ; 1861 Mount Alexander Mail (Vic. : 1854 - 1917), 1 November, p.2. ; 1861, 1 November, p.8. ; 1861, 14 June, p.2. ; 1861, 24 June, .3. ; 1861, 8 March, p.2. ; 1861 The Age (Melbourne, Vic. : 1854 - 1954), 1 January, p. 7. ; 1861, 16 August, p.1. ; 1861 22 March, p.8. ; 1861, 23 March, p.8. ; 1861, 6 April, p 8. ; 1861 The Argus (Melbourne, Vic. : 1848 - 1957), 1 July, p.8. ; 1861,1 February, p. 8. , viewed 17 Aug 2023, http://nla.gov.au/nla.newsarticle5697196; 1861 The Argus (Melbourne, Vic. : 1848 - 1957), 11 February, p.8. ; 1861, 13 June, p.8. ; 1861, 16 January, p.8. ; 1861, 18 March, p.8. ; 1861, 18 June, p.8. ; 1861, 2 April, p.8. ; 1861, 22 June, p. 8. ; 1861, 28 March, p. 3.; 1861, 5 June, p.8. ; 1861 The Herald (Melbourne, Vic. : 1861 - 1954), 22 April, p.1. ; 1861 The Herald (Melbourne, Vic. : 1861 - 1954), 4 June, p.1. ; 1861 The Kyneton Observer (Vic. : 1856 - 1900), 17 January, p.4. ; 1861, 8 January, p. 1. ; 1861 The Star (Ballarat, Vic. : 1855 - 1864), 14 January, p.1. ; 1861, 14 June, p. 1. ; 1861, 14 March, p.3. ; 1861, 15 January, p.1. ; 1861, 16 January, p.1. ; 1861, 22 May, p.1. ; 1861, 28 January, p. 1. ; 1861, 30 January, p.1. ; 1861, 4 March, p.3. ; 1861, 5 October, p.1. ; 1862 Maryborough and Dunolly Advertiser (Vic. :

1857 - 1867 ; 1914 - 1918) 11 June 1862, p.1. ; 1862 Bathurst Free Press and Mining Journal (NSW : 1851 - 1904), 28 June, p. 3. 3 Sep, p. 3. ; 1862, 15 October, p. 1. ; 1862 Empire (Sydney, NSW : 1850 - 1875), 21 July, p. 5. ; 1862 Geelong Advertiser (Vic. : 1859 - 1929), 8 November, p.1. ; 1862 Maryborough and Dunolly Advertiser (Vic. : 1857 - 1867 ; 1914 - 1918), 10 February, p.1. ; 1862, 9 May, p. 1. ; 1862, 14 May, p.1. ; 1862 Mount Alexander Mail (Vic. : 1854 - 1917), 27 January, p.3. ; 1862, 5 May, p. 3. ; 1862, 7 April, p.3. ; 1862 The Age (Melbourne, Vic. : 1854 - 1954), 13 May, p.1. ; 1862, 22 February, p. 3. ; 1862, 5 May, p. 1. ; 1862 The Argus (Melbourne, Vic. : 1848 - 1957), 16 January, p.8. ; 1862 The Herald (Melbourne, Vic. : 1861 - 1954), 15 January, p.1. ; 1862, 15 March, p.1. ; 1862, 3 May, p.1. ; 1862 The Star (Ballarat, Vic. : 1855 - 1864), 13 September, p.1. ; 1862, 24 May, p. 1. ; 1862, 29 December, p. 1. ; 1862 The Sydney Morning Herald (NSW : 1842 - 1954), 21 March, p. 2. ; 21 June, p.10. ; 22 July, p. 6. ; 1862, 15 December, p. 1. ; 1862 The Tarrangower Times and Maldon and Newstead Advertiser (Vic. : 1862 - 1873), 1 August, p.4. ; 1862 The Tarrangower Times and Maldon District Advertiser (Vic. : 1858 - 1862), 21 March, p 5. ; 1863 Bell's Life in Victoria and Sporting Chronicle (Melbourne, Vic. : 1857 - 1868), 17 January, p. 1. ; 1863 Hamilton Spectator and Grange District Advertiser (Vic. : 1860 - 1870), 20 March, p.1. ; 1863, 3 April, p. 1. ; 1863, 10 April, p.1. ; 1863 Portland Guardian and Normanby General Advertiser (Vic. : 1842 - 1843; 1854 - 1876), 16 April, p.1.; 1863 The Argus (Melbourne, Vic. : 1848 - 1957), 30 May, p. 8. ; 1863 The Herald (Melbourne, Vic. : 1861 - 1954), 14 April, p. 1. ; 1863 The Star (Ballarat, Vic. : 1855 - 1864), 11 April, p. 1. ; 1863, 11 July, p. 1. ; 1863, 16 June, p. 1. ; 1863, 20 January, p. 1. ; 1863, 27 February, p. 1. ; 1863 The Sydney Morning Herald (NSW : 1842 - 1954), 11 May, p. 8. ; 1863, 16 June, p. 6. ; 1863, 27 November, p. 6. ; 1863 The Tarrangower Times and Maldon and Newstead Advertiser (Vic. : 1862 - 1873), 31 March, p. 1. ; 1863, 23 June, p. 1. ; 1863, 20 November, p. 1. ; 1863 The Yass Courier (NSW : 1857 - 1929), 25 March, p. 1. ; 1864 Empire (Sydney, NSW : 1850 - 1875), 14 June, p. 1. ; 1864 Geelong Advertiser (Vic. : 1859 - 1929), 23 July, p. 1. ; 1864, 4 January, p. 1. ; 1864 Mount Alexander Mail (Vic. : 1854 - 1917), 1 February, p. 1. ; 1864, 6 October, p. 3. ; 1864 The Star (Ballarat, Vic. : 1855 - 1864), 2 August, p. 1. ; 1864, 23 July, p. 1. ; 1864, 28 November, p. 1. ; 1864, 5 January, p. 1. ; 1864 The Sydney Morning Herald (NSW : 1842 - 1954), 5 December, p. 1. ; 1864 The Tarrangower Times and Maldon and Newstead Advertiser (Vic. : 1862 - 1873), 12 February, p. 1. ; 1865 Pastoral Times and Echuca and Moama Chronicle (Deniliquin, NSW : 1863 - 1866), 1 July, p. 4. ; 1865, 26 August, p. 1. ; 1865 The Argus (Melbourne, Vic. : 1848 - 1957), 11 January, p. 8. ,; 1865 The Ballarat Star (Vic. : 1865 - 1924), 10 January, p. 1. ; 1865, 3 May, p. 1. ; 1865, 4 December, p. 1. ; 1866 Geelong Advertiser (Vic. : 1859 - 1929), 27 December, p. 1. ; 1866 The Ballarat Star (Vic. : 1865 - 1924), 12 March, p. 1. ; 1866, 5 March, p. 1. ; 1866 The Pastoral Times (South Deniliquin, NSW : 1866 - 1895), 26 May, p. 4. ; 1866 The Telegraph, St Kilda, Prahran and South Yarra Guardian (Vic. : 1864 - 1888), 3 March, p. 6. ; 1867 Geelong Advertiser (Vic. : 1859 - 1929), 5 January, p. 1. ; 1867 Maryborough and Dunolly Advertiser (Vic. : 1857 - 1867 ; 1914 - 1918), 9 January, p. 1. ; 1867 Queensland Times, Ipswich Herald and General Advertiser (Qld. : 1861 - 1908), 9 April, p. 1. ; 1867 The Ballarat Star (Vic. : 1865 - 1924), 1 April, p. 1. ; 1868 Dalby Herald and Western Queensland Advertiser (Qld. : 1866 - 1879), 22 February, p. 1. ; 1868 Geelong Advertiser (Vic. : 1859 - 1929), 1 February, p. 1. ; 1868, 22 April, p. 1. ; 1868 Gippsland Times (Vic. : 1861 - 1954), 15 September, p. 1. (Morning.) ; 1868 Hamilton Spectator and Grange District Advertiser (Vic. : 1860 - 1870), 4 March, p. 1. ; 1868 The Ballarat Star (Vic. : 1865 - 1924), 2 January, p. 1. ; 1868, 7 September, p. 1. ; 1868 The Pastoral Times (South Deniliquin, NSW : 1866 - 1895), 23 May, p. 1. ; 1869 Geelong Advertiser (Vic. : 1859 - 1929), 1 January, p. 1. ; 1869, 26 January, p. 1. ; 1869 The Ballarat Star (Vic. : 1865 - 1924), 26 August, p. 1. ; 1869 The Riverine Herald (Echuca, Vic. : Moama, NSW : 1869 - 1954; 1998 - 2002), 26 March, p. 4. ; 1869 The Sydney Morning Herald (NSW : 1842 - 1954), 18 May, p. 1. ; 1869, 29 November, p. 10.; 1870 Geelong Advertiser (Vic. : 1859 - 1929), 2 July, p. 1. ; 1870 The Ballarat Courier (Vic. : 1869 - 1886; 1914 - 1918), 14 April, p. 1. ; 1870 The Ballarat Star (Vic. : 1865 - 1924), 27 May, p. 1. ; 1870 Western Press and Camperdown, Colac, Mortlake and Terang Representative (Vic. : 1866-1867 ; 1870), 7 May, p. 1. ; 1871 Geelong Advertiser (Vic. : 1859 - 1929), 7 September, p. 1. ; 1871 The Argus (Melbourne, Vic. : 1848 - 1957), 23 December, p. 3. ; 1871 The Ballarat Star (Vic. : 1865 - 1924), 1 March, p. 1. ; 1871 The Ballarat Star (Vic. : 1865 - 1924), 10 October, p. 1. ; 1871, 16 September, p. 1. ; 1871, 4 November, p. 1. ; 1871 The Maitland Mercury and Hunter River General Advertiser (NSW : 1843 - 1893), 12 August, p. 1.; 1871 The Sydney Morning Herald (NSW : 1842 - 1954), 20 January, p. 8. ; 1871, 30 December, p. 8. ; 1872 The Argus (Melbourne, Vic. : 1848 - 1957) 9 October 1872: 1. ; 1872 Empire (Sydney, NSW : 1850 - 1875), 1 January, p. 1. ; 1872 Geelong Advertiser (Vic. : 1859 - 1929), 12 March, p. 1.; 1872 Hamilton Spectator (Vic. : 1870 - 1918), 13 March, p. 1. ; 1872 The Ballarat Star (Vic. : 1865 - 1924), 21 September, p. 1. ; 1872, 4 January, p. 1. ; 1872 Wagga Wagga Express and Murrumbidgee District Advertiser (NSW : 1858 - 1859; 1866; 1872 - 1875), 29 May, p. 1. ; 1872, 22 June, p. 1. ; 1872, 21 September, p. 1. ; 1873 Geelong Advertiser (Vic. : 1859 - 1929), 18 March, p. 1. ; 1873, 3 January, p. 1. ; 1873 Hamilton Spectator (Vic. : 1870 - 1918), 22 March, p. 1. ; 1873, 25 January, p. 1. ; 1873 Portland Guardian and Normanby General Advertiser (Vic. : 1842 - 1843; 1854 - 1876), 27 March, p. 1. ; 1873 The Argus (Melbourne, Vic. : 1848 - 1957), 19 March, p. 8. ; 1873 The Ballarat Star (Vic. : 1865 - 1924), 12 May, p. 1. ; 1873, 14 June, p. 1. ; 1873, 30 June, p. 1. ; 1873 The Sydney Morning Herald (NSW : 1842 - 1954), 26 July, p. 6. ; 1873 Wagga Wagga Express and Murrumbidgee District Advertiser (NSW : 1858 - 1859; 1866; 1872 - 1875), 31 May, p. 1. ; 1874 Bendigo Advertiser (Vic. : 1855 - 1918), 3 October, p. 4. ; 1874 Geelong Advertiser (Vic. : 1859 - 1929), 7 January, p. 1. ; 1874 The Ballarat Star (Vic. : 1865 - 1924), 1 January, p. 1. ; 1874, 16 January, p. 1. ; 1874, 7 March, p. 1. ; 1874 Wagga Wagga Express and Murrumbidgee District Advertiser (NSW : 1858 - 1859; 1866; 1872 - 1875), 3 October, p. 1. ; 1875 The Ballarat Courier (Vic. : 1869 - 1886; 1914 - 1918), 30 January, p. 1. ; 1875, 4 February, p. 1. ; 1875 The Ballarat Star (Vic. : 1865 - 1924), 11 March, p. 1. ; 1876 Camperdown Chronicle (Vic. : 1875 - 1954), 13 April, p. 1. ; 1876 The Ballarat Courier (Vic. : 1869 - 1886; 1914 - 1918), 15 February, p. 1. ; 1876 The Ballarat Star (Vic. : 1865 - 1924), 6 March, p. 1. ; 1876 The Sydney Morning Herald (NSW : 1842 - 1954), 10 May, p. 6. ; 1877 The Ballarat Star (Vic. : 1865 - 1924), 10 May, p. 1. ; 1877, 31 January, p. 1. ; 1878 The Argus (Melbourne, Vic. : 1848 - 1957), 19 November, p. 8. ; 1878 The Ballarat Star (Vic. : 1865 - 1924), 11 January, p. 1. ; 1879 Camperdown Chronicle (Vic. : 1875 - 1954), 18 November, p. 1. ; 1879 Evening News (Sydney, NSW : 1869 - 1931), 27 October, p. 1. ; 1879 The Argus (Melbourne, Vic. : 1848 - 1957), 13 January, p. 3. ; 1879 The Ballarat Star (Vic. : 1865 - 1924), 28 January, p. 1. ; 1880, 18 September, p. 4. ; 1881 Bendigo Advertiser (Vic. : 1855 - 1918), 7 June, p. 1. ; 1881 The Ballarat Star (Vic. : 1865 - 1924), 19 March, p. 4. ; 1882 The Avoca Mail (Vic. : 1863 - 1900; 1915 - 1918), 25 August, p. 3. ; 1882 The Ballarat Star (Vic. : 1865 - 1924), 17 March, p. 4. ; 1883 Border Watch (Mount Gambier, SA : 1861 - 1954), 5 September, p. 1. ; 1883 The Avoca Mail (Vic. : 1863 - 1900; 1915 - 1918), 1 May, p. 1. ; 1883, 13 July, p. 4. ; 1883 The Ballarat Star (Vic. : 1865 - 1924), 22 March, p. 4. ; 1884 Geelong Advertiser (Vic. : 1859 - 1929), 5 January, p. 1. ; 1884 Gippsland Mercury (Sale, Vic. : 1871 - 1894; 1914 - 1918), 23 September, p. 1. ; 1884 Gippsland Times (Vic. : 1861 - 1954), 15 December, p. 1.; 1884, 24 November, p. 1. ; 1884, 31 December, p. 1. ; 1884 The Age (Melbourne, Vic. : 1854 - 1954), 15 March, p. 7. ; 1884 The Argus (Melbourne, Vic. : 1848 - 1957), 29 November, p. 7. ,; 1884 The Ballarat Courier (Vic. : 1869 - 1886; 1914 - 1918), 5 February, p. 1. ,; 1884 The Ballarat Star (Vic. : 1865 - 1924), 24 September, p. 1. ; 1884 Toowoomba Chronicle and Darling Downs General Advertiser (Qld. : 1875 - 1902), 16 February, p. 5. ; 1885 Bendigo Advertiser (Vic. : 1855 - 1918), 9 June, p. 1. ; 1885 Gippsland Mercury (Sale, Vic. : 1871 - 1894; 1914 - 1918), 20 January, p. 1. ; 1885, 28 March, p. 1. ; 1885 Gippsland Times (Vic. : 1861 - 1954), 26 January, p. 1. (Morning.) ; 1885 The Ballarat Star (Vic. : 1865 - 1924), 13 October, p. 1. ; 1885, 24 March, p. 1. ; 1885 The McIvor Times and Rodney Advertiser (Heathcote, Vic. : 1863 - 1918), 27 February, p. 4. ; 1886 Bendigo Advertiser (Vic. : 1855 - 1918), 10 February, p. 1. ; 1886 Gippsland Mercury (Sale, Vic. : 1871 - 1894; 1914 - 1918), 23 January, p. 1.; 1886 The Age (Melbourne, Vic. : 1854 - 1954), 27 August, p. 1. ; 1886 The Ballarat Star (Vic. : 1865 - 1924), 10 March, p. 1. ; 1886 The Sydney Morning Herald (NSW : 1842 - 1954), 21 July, p. 2. ; 1887 Bairnsdale Advertiser and Tambo and Omeo Chronicle (Vic. : 1882 - 1946), 29 January, p. 1. ; 1887 The Ballarat Star (Vic. : 1865 - 1924), 26

October, p. 1. ; 1887 The McIvor Times and Rodney Advertiser (Heathcote, Vic. : 1863 - 1918), 8 July, p. 4. ; 1887 The Riverine Herald (Echuca, Vic. : Moama, NSW : 1869 - 1954; 1998 - 2002), 8 January, p. 3; 1887 The Riverine Herald (Echuca, Vic. : Moama, NSW : 1869 - 1954; 1998 - 2002), 28 March, p. 3. ; 1888 Geelong Advertiser (Vic. : 1859 - 1929), 3 April, p. 1. ; 1888 The Ballarat Star (Vic. : 1865 - 1924), 16 August, p. 1. ; 1888, 24 July, p. 1. ; 1888 The McIvor Times and Rodney Advertiser (Heathcote, Vic. : 1863 - 1918), 21 December, p. 4.; 1888 The Sydney Morning Herald (NSW : 1842 - 1954), 10 September, p. 14. ; 1889 The Argus (Melbourne, Vic. : 1848 - 1957), 29 October, p. 2. ; 1889 The Ballarat Star (Vic. : 1865 - 1924), 31 August, p. 3. ; 1889 The McIvor Times and Rodney Advertiser (Heathcote, Vic. : 1863 - 1918), 22 August, p. 4.; 1890 National Advocate (Bathurst, NSW : 1889 - 1954), 7 May, p. 4. ; 1890 The Ballarat Star (Vic. : 1865 - 1924), 19 February, p. 1.; 1890, 26 September, p. 1. ; 1890 The Riverine Grazier (Hay, NSW : 1873 - 1954), 29 April, p. 1. ; 1891 Geelong Advertiser (Vic. : 1859 - 1929), 13 May, p. 1. ; 1891, 14 December, p. 4. ; 1891 The Ballarat Star (Vic. : 1865 - 1924), 25 March, p. 1. ; 1892 Geelong Advertiser (Vic. : 1859 - 1929), 20 December, p. 1. ; 1892 The Ballarat Star (Vic. : 1865 - 1924), 20 May, p. 1. ; 1892, 20 May, p. 1. ; 1892 The Riverine Grazier (Hay, NSW : 1873 - 1954), 30 August, p. 3. ; 1893, 18 April, p. 3. ; 1894 Geelong Advertiser (Vic. : 1859 - 1929), 1 May, p. 1. ; 1895 The Age (Melbourne, Vic. : 1854 - 1954), 20 April, p. 5. ; 1895 The Riverine Grazier (Hay, NSW : 1873 - 1954), 17 September, p. 1. ; 1896 Bairnsdale Advertiser and Tambo and Omeo Chronicle (Vic. : 1882 - 1946), 7 January, p. 1. (morning.); 1896 Geelong Advertiser (Vic. : 1859 - 1929), 14 January, p. 1.; 1896, 14 January, p. 1.; 1896, 22 May, p. 1.; 1896 Riverina Recorder (Balranald, Moulamein, NSW : 1887 - 1944), 25 March, p. 4. ; 1896 Riverina Recorder (Balranald, Moulamein, NSW : 1887 - 1944), 5 August, p. 4. ; 1896 Riverina Recorder (Balranald, Moulamein, NSW : 1887 - 1944), 16 September, p. 4. ; 1896 The Age (Melbourne, Vic. : 1854 - 1954), 17 October, p. 10. ; 1896, 25 November, p. 1. ; 1896 The Ballarat Star (Vic. : 1865 - 1924), 6 October, p. 1. ; 1896 The Daily Telegraph (Sydney, NSW : 1883 - 1930), 3 September, p. 2. ; 1896 The Hay Standard and Advertiser for Balranald, Wentworth, Maude...(Hay, NSW : 1871 - 1873; 1880 - 1881; 1890 - 1900), 8 January, p. 4. ; 1896 The Riverine Grazier (Hay, NSW : 1873 - 1954), 21 January, p. 1. ; 1896, 7 February, p. 3. ; 1897 Riverina Recorder (Balranald, Moulamein, NSW : 1887 - 1944), 24 February, p. 4. ; 1897 The Age (Melbourne, Vic. : 1854 - 1954), 8 July, p. 2. ; 1897 The Ballarat Star (Vic. : 1865 - 1924), 19 May, p. 1. ; 1898 Hamilton Spectator (Vic. : 1870 - 1918), 8 October, p. 2. (Supplement To The Hamilton Spectator); 1898 The Ballarat Star (Vic. : 1865 - 1924), 7 June, p. 1. ; 1899 Jerilderie Herald and Urana Advertiser (NSW : 1898 - 1958), 13 January, p. 1. ; 1899 The Ballarat Star (Vic. : 1865 - 1924), 12 January, p. 1. ; 1899 The Riverine Grazier (Hay, NSW : 1873 - 1954), 12 May, p. 4. ; 1900 Geelong Advertiser (Vic. : 1859 - 1929), 10 January, p. 1. ; 1900 The Age (Melbourne, Vic. : 1854 - 1954), 27 June, p. 2. ; 1900 The Argus (Melbourne, Vic. : 1848 - 1957), 28 July, p. 3. ; 1902 Geelong Advertiser (Vic. : 1859 - 1929), 14 February, p. 1. ; 1903, 13 February, p. 1. ; 1904, 20 January, p. 1. ; 1907, 8 June, p. 1. ; 1908 The Riverine Grazier (Hay, NSW : 1873 - 1954), 3 April, p. 3. ; 1910 East Murchison News (WA : 1901 - 1911), 9 April, p. 1. ; 1910 Geelong Advertiser (Vic. : 1859 - 1929), 22 March, p. 1.; 1911, 18 January, p. 1.; 1913, 4 January, p. 1. ; 1914, 8 June, p. 1. ; 1915, 5 January, p. 1. ; 1917, 16 May, p. 1. ; 1918, 20 February, p. 1. ; 1919, 6 February, p. 1. ; 1920, 11 March, p. 1. ; 1920, 5 August, p. 1. ; 1927 The Sydney Morning Herald (NSW : 1842 - 1954), 5 November, p. 4. ; 1929 The Brisbane Courier (Qld. : 1864 - 1933), 31 August, p. 3. ; 1929 The Telegraph (Brisbane, Qld. : 1872 - 1947), 14 January, p. 40.

'CLASSIFIED ADVERTISING': 1867 The Brisbane Courier (Qld. : 1864 - 1933), 8 January, p. 1. ; 1867, 7 June, p. 1. ; 1869, 8 January, p. 1. ; 1869, 11 September, p. 1. ; 1869, 6 December, p. 1. ; 1870, 9 February, p. 1. ; 1871, 28 January, p. 2. ; 1871, 27 October, p. 1. ; 1872, 21 October, p. 1.; 1873, 11 January, p. 8. ; 1874, 2 March, p. 1. ; 1874, 23 November, p. 4. ; 1875, 4 February, p. 4. ; 1875, 21 June, p. 1. ; 1877, 13 January, p. 2. ; 1878, 29 January, p. 4. ; 1879, 22 January, p. 6. ; 1880, 14 September, p. 6. ; 1881, 3 August, p. 4. ; 1882, , 4 April, p. 4. ; 1883, 29 November, p. 7. ; 1885, 4 June, p. 2. ; 1886, 7 May, p. 8. ; 1887 , 18 February, p. 7. ; 1890, 27 September, p. 619. ; 1891, 31 October, p. 855. ; 1892, 16 January, p. 141.; 1893 'Classified Advertising', The Queenslander (Brisbane, Qld. : 1866 - 1939), 21 October, p. 770.; 1894 The Queenslander (Brisbane, Qld. : 1866 - 1939), 26 May, p. 963. ; 1895 The Queenslander (Brisbane, Qld. : 1866 - 1939), 10 August, p. 242. ; 1896 The Queenslander (Brisbane, Qld. : 1866 - 1939), 16 May, p. 914. ; 1897 The Queenslander (Brisbane, Qld. : 1866 - 1939), 22 May, p. 1149. ; 1900 The Queenslander (Brisbane, Qld. : 1866 - 1939), 7 April, p. 626 ; 1901 The Queenslander (Brisbane, Qld. : 1866 - 1939), 2 March, p. 390. ; 1904 The Queenslander (Brisbane, Qld. : 1866 - 1939), 5 March, p. 2. ; 1918 'Cobb & Co.', The Corowa Free Press (NSW : 1875 - 1954), 18 June, p. 4.

'GOVERNMENT GAZETTE NOTICES': 1865 'Government Gazette Notices', New South Wales Government Gazette (Sydney, NSW : 1832 - 1900), 22 December, p. 2883. ; 1870 New South Wales Government Gazette (Sydney, NSW : 1832 - 1900), 17 January, p. 116. ; 1882 New South Wales Government Gazette (Sydney, NSW : 1832 - 1900), 24 January, p. 468.; 1883 New South Wales Government Gazette (Sydney, NSW : 1832 - 1900), 24 January, p. 483. ; 1885 New South Wales Government Gazette (Sydney, NSW : 1832 - 1900), 20 Janu-ary, p. 623.; 1886 New South Wales Government Gazette (Sydney, NSW : 1832 - 1900), 21 January, p. 459. ; 1887 New South Wales Government Gazette (Sydney, NSW : 1832 - 1900), 25 January; 1894 New South Wales Government Gazette (Sydney, NSW : 1832 - 1900), 15 February, p. 995. ; 1898 New South Wales Government Gazette (Sydney, NSW : 1832 - 1900), 26 February, p. 1755.

'GOVERNMENT GAZETTE TENDERS AND CONTRACTS': 1862 New South Wales Government Gazette (Sydney, NSW : 1832 - 1900), 24 December, p. 2654. ; 1863, 22 December, p. 2813. ; 1866, 18 December, p. 3130. ; 1868, 6 January, p. 24. ; 1868, 30 December, p. 4641. ; 1871, 4 January, p. 24. ; 1872, 3 January, p. 17. ; 1873, 16 January, p. 141. ; 1874, 19 January, p. 176. ; 1875, 13 January, p. 85.; 1876, 17 January, p. 217.; 1877, 20 January, p. 301. ; 1878; 1879, 13 January, p. 183.; 1880; 1881, 22 January, p. 453. ; 1884; 1888, 3 February, p. 903. ; 1889, 29 January, p. 799. ; 1890, 15 February, p. 1405. ; 1891, 16 February, p. 1315.; 1892), 24 February, p. 1547.; 1893, 18 February, p. 1415.; 1895, 16 February, p. 1041. ; 1896, 19 February, p.1242. ; 1897, 16 February, p. 1165.

1842 'FAMILY NOTICES', The Sydney Herald (NSW : 1831 - 1842), 19 July, p. 3. , viewed 16 Sep 2023, http://nla.gov.au/nla.news-article12876232

1850 'THE GOLDEN DREAM.', South Australian (Adelaide, SA : 1844 - 1851), 16 September, p. 4. , viewed 11 Sep 2023, http://nla.gov.au/nla.news-article71627169

1851 'NEWS FROM THE DIGGINGS.', Geelong Advertiser (Vic. : 1847 - 1851), 29 September, p. 2. (DAILY and MORNING), viewed 11 Sep 2023, http://nla.gov.au/nla.news-article91919965

1851 'THE ABERCROMBIE.', Bell's Life in Sydney and Sporting Reviewer (NSW : 1845 - 1860), 18 October, p. 1. , viewed 06 Jun 2023, http://nla.gov.au/nla.newsarticle59773348

1853 'CIRCULAR.', Empire (Sydney, NSW : 1850 - 1875), 12 February, p. 5. , viewed 09 Sep 2023, http://nla.gov.au/nla.news-article60138257

1853 'GEELONG.', The Argus (Melbourne, Vic. : 1848 - 1957), 6 July, p. 3. , viewed 06 Sep 2023, http://nla.gov.au/nla.news-article4794181

1853 'SHIPPING INTELLIGENCE.', The Argus (Melbourne, Vic. : 1848 - 1957), 3 June, p. 4. , viewed 01 Jun 2023, http://nla.gov.au/nla.news-article4793155

1853 'SHIPPING INTELLIGENCE', The Moreton Bay Courier (Brisbane, Qld. : 1846 - 1861), 7 May, p. 2. , viewed 20 Jun 2023, http://nla.gov.au/nla.news-article3710114

1853 'THE FOURTH OF JULY.', The Argus (Melbourne, Vic. : 1848 - 1957), 21 June, p. 7. , viewed 26 May 2023, http://nla.gov.au/nla.news-article4793692

1854 'MEMOIR OF THE LATE MAJOR-GENERAL STEWART.' (1854, April 15). Bathurst Free Press and Mining Journal (NSW : 1851 - 1862; 1872; 1882; 1885 - 1897; 1899 - 1904), p. 2. Retrieved September 27, 2023, from http://nla.gov.au/nla.news-article62048048

1854 'SHIPPING INTELLIGENCE.', The Maitland Mercury and Hunter River General Advertiser (NSW : 1843 - 1893), 13 May, p. 2. , viewed 27 May 2023, http://nla.gov.au/nla.news-article689200

1854 'SHIPPING INTELLIGENCE.', The People's Advocate and New South Wales Vindicator (Sydney, NSW : 1848-1856), 13 May, p. 2. , viewed 26 May 2023, http://nla.gov.au/nla.news-article251544420

1854 'THE LATE MR. CHARLES CLAPP.', The Argus (Melbourne, Vic. : 1848 - 1957), 28 November, p. 5. , viewed 01 Jun 2023, http://nla.gov.au/nla.news-article4800913

1855 'GLANCES AT THE GOLD-FIELDS OF VICTORIA NO. 1.', Empire (Sydney, NSW : 1850 - 1875), 26 June, p. 3. , viewed 29 May 2023, http://nla.gov.au/nla.news-article60176762

1855 'MELBOURNE.', Geelong Advertiser and Intelligencer (Vic. : 1851 - 1856), 31 January, p. 2. (DAILY), viewed 09 Sep 2023, http://nla.gov.au/nla.news-article91860154

1855 'NOTES OF A JOURNEY THROUGH THE WESTERN DISTRICT.', The Age (Melbourne, Vic. : 1854 - 1954), 2 February, p. 3. , viewed 16 Sep 2023, http://nla.gov.au/nla.news-article154853026

1855 'THE FAILURE OF MESSRS ADAMS AND CO., OF SAN FRANCISCO.', The Age (Melbourne, Vic. : 1854 - 1954), 25 June, p. 3. , viewed 02 Aug 2023, http://nla.gov.au/nla.news-article154896289 (The Failure of Messrs. Adams and Co., of San Francisco, 25 Jun 1855, p.3)

1856 'SHIPPING INTELLIGENCE.', The Argus (Melbourne, Vic. : 1848 - 1957), 29 October, p. 4. , viewed 26 May 2023, http://nla.gov.au/nla.news-article7139145

1857 'G. F. TRAIN AT HOME.', The Age (Melbourne, Vic. : 1854 - 1954), 7 February, p. 3. , viewed 26 May 2023, http://nla.gov.au/nla.newsarticle154822033

1859 'KYNETON.', Bendigo Advertiser (Vic. : 1855 - 1918), 16 September, p. 3. , viewed 21 Sep 2023, http://nla.gov.au/nla.news-article87992186

1859 'NO TITLE', Mount Alexander Mail (Vic. : 1854 - 1917), 14 September, p. 3. , viewed 13 Oct 2023, http://nla.gov.au/nla.news-article199052910

1859 'PORTLAND.', Geelong Advertiser (Vic. : 1859 - 1929), 4 January, p. 3. , viewed 16 Aug 2023, http://nla.gov.au/nla.news-article150074880

1859 'TITLE DEEDS.', Mount Alexander Mail (Vic. : 1854 - 1917), 16 September, p. 3. , viewed 26 Jul 2023, http://nla.gov.au/nla.news-article199046906

1861 '[COPY.]', The Age (Melbourne, Vic. : 1854 - 1954), 20 November, p. 6. , viewed 14 Oct 2023, http://nla.gov.au/nla.news-article154900827

1861 'GALLANT CAPTURE OF BUSHRANGERS ON THE LACHLAN.', The Star (Ballarat, Vic. : 1855 - 1864), 24 June, p. 3. , viewed 20 Sep 2023, http://nla.gov.au/nla.news-article66340141

1861 'LACHLAN GOLD FIELDS.', Illawarra Mercury (Wollongong, NSW : 1856 - 1950), 6 December, p. 2. , viewed 20 Sep 2023, http://nla.gov.au/nla.news-article136376642

1861 'LOCAL & GENERAL INTELLIGENCE.', The Yass Courier (NSW : 1857 - 1929), 19 June, p. 2. , viewed 01 Oct 2023, http://nla.gov.au/nla.newsarticle263875696

1862 'COUNTRY NEWS.', Sydney Mail (NSW : 1860 - 1871), 16 August, p. 3. , viewed 19 Mar 2024, http://nla.gov.au/nla.news-article166695204

1862 'DENILIQUIN POLICE COURT.', The Pastoral Times and Southern Courier (Deniliquin, N.S.W : 1861 - 1862), 13 June, p. 3. , viewed 20 Aug 2023, http://nla.gov.au/nla.news-article270951190

1862 'LOCAL AND DOMESTIC.', Bathurst Free Press and Mining Journal (NSW : 1851 - 1862; 1872; 1882; 1885 - 1897; 1899 - 1904), 2 July, p. 2. , viewed 20 Aug 2023, http://nla.gov.au/nla.news-article62720331

1862 'LOCAL AND GENERAL INTELLIGENCE.', The Yass Courier (NSW : 1857 - 1929), 5 July, p. 2. , viewed 13 Sep 2023, http://nla.gov.au/nla.newsarticle263977461

1862 'LOCAL AND GENERAL INTELLIGENCE.', The Yass Courier (NSW : 1857 - 1929), 2 July, p. 2. , viewed 19 Mar 2024, http://nla.gov.au/nla.news-article263976139

1862 'LOCAL AND GENERAL INTELLIGENCE', The Yass Courier (NSW : 1857 - 1929), 18 June, p. 2. , viewed 20 Aug 2023, http://nla.gov.au/nla.newsarticle263974000

1862 'LOCAL AND GENERAL INTELLIGENCE.', The Yass Courier (NSW : 1857 - 1929), 18 June, p. 2. , viewed 20 Aug 2023, http://nla.gov.au/nla.newsarticle263974000

1862 'LOCAL AND PROVINCIAL.', Goulburn Herald (NSW : 1860 - 1864), 14 June, p. 2. , viewed 19 Mar 2024, http://nla.gov.au/nla.news-article102586828

1862 'LOCAL AND PROVINCIAL.', Goulburn Herald (NSW : 1860 - 1864), 2 July, p. 2. , viewed 25 Jul 2023, http://nla.gov.au/nla.news-article102587355

1862 'MODERN COLONIAL COACHING.', Mount Alexander Mail (Vic. : 1854 - 1917), 6 June, p. 5. , viewed 19 Aug 2023, http://nla.gov.au/nla.news-article197094196

1862 'MUDGEE.', Bathurst Free Press and Mining Journal (NSW : 1851 - 1904), 5 November, p. 2. , viewed 06 Jun 2023, http://nla.gov.au/nla.news-article62719470

1862 'NEW SOUTH WALES MEMS.', The Albury Banner and Wodonga Express (NSW : 1860 - 1927; 1929 - 1931; 1933 - 1938), 20 September, p. 3. , viewed 19 Mar 2024, http://nla.gov.au/nla.news-article264151586

1862 'NEW SOUTH WALES.', Adelaide Observer (SA : 1843 - 1904), 30 August, p. 5. , viewed 19 Mar 2024, http://nla.gov.au/nla.news-article158188462

1862 'SOCIAL.', The Star (Ballarat, Vic. : 1855 - 1864), 24 September, p. 1. (Supplement to the star), viewed 09 Aug 2023, http://nla.gov.au/nla.newsarticle66327398

1862 'SUMMARY.', Sydney Mail (NSW : 1860 - 1871), 3 May, p. 4. , viewed 09 Sep 2023, http://nla.gov.au/nla.news-article166691028

1862 'SYDNEY NEWS.', The Maitland Mercury and Hunter River General Advertiser (NSW : 1843 - 1893), 3 July, p. 3. , viewed 06 Jun 2023, http://nla.gov.au/nla.news-article18689254

1862 'THE CIVIL WAR IN AMERICA.', The Argus (Melbourne, Vic. : 1848 - 1957), 3 October, p. 7. , viewed 06 Jun 2023, http://nla.gov.au/nla.news-article6479978

1862 'THE LACHLAN GOLDFIELDS.', Mount Alexander Mail (Vic. : 1854 - 1917), 16 July, p. 2. , viewed 19 Mar 2024, http://nla.gov.au/nla.news-article197095571

1862 'THE SYDNEY MONTHLY OVERLAND MAIL.', The Sydney Morning Herald (NSW : 1842 - 1954), 21 May, p. 5. , viewed 23 Mar 2024, http://nla.gov.au/nla.news-article13228972

1862 'THE SYDNEY MONTHLY OVERLAND MAIL.', The Sydney Morning Herald (NSW : 1842 - 1954), 21 May, p. 5. , viewed 25 Jul 2023, http://nla.gov.au/nla.newsarticle13228972i

1862 'WEEKLY REGISTER.', Empire (Sydney, NSW : 1850 - 1875), 3 May, p. 3. , viewed 31 Dec 2024, http://nla.gov.au/nla.news-article60474885

1863 'MISCELLANEOUS.', Empire (Sydney, NSW : 1850 - 1875), 21 September, p. 3. , viewed 09 Sep 2023, http://nla.gov.au/nla.news-article60548616

1863 'MORUYA REGATTA.', Empire (Sydney, NSW : 1850 - 1875), 3 February, p. 2. , viewed 06 Jun 2023, http://nla.gov.au/nla.news-article60522296

1863 'NEW ZEALAND.', Mount Alexander Mail (Vic. : 1854 - 1917), 12 February, p. 3. , viewed 17 Aug 2023, http://nla.gov.au/nla.news-article200382795

1863 'SPECIAL CRIMINAL COMMISSION.', Sydney Mail (NSW : 1860 - 1871), 28 February, p. 12. , viewed 01 Oct 2023, http://nla.gov.au/nla.news-article166651470

1864 'BEN HALL NEAR BATHURST.', The Age (Melbourne, Vic. : 1854 - 1954), 16 July, p. 5. , viewed 06 Jun 2023, http://nla.gov.au/nla.newsarticle155017974

1864 'COUNTRY NEWS.', The Argus (Melbourne, Vic. : 1848 - 1957), 31 March, p. 6. , viewed 31 May 2023, http://nla.gov.au/nla.news-article5746563

1864 'GEOFFREY EAGAR.', New South Wales Government Gazette (Sydney, NSW : 1832 - 1900), 23 December, p. 2928. , viewed 31 Aug 2023, http://nla.gov.au/nla.news-article225362274

1864 'GOVERNMENT GAZETTE.', Freeman's Journal (Sydney, NSW : 1850 - 1932), 26 October, p. 6. , viewed 15 Sep 2023, http://nla.gov.au/nla.news-article128800600

1865 'GENERAL NEWS.', The Maitland Mercury and Hunter River General Advertiser (NSW : 1843 - 1893), 7 December, p. 4. , viewed 14 Sep 2023, http://nla.gov.au/nla.news-article18699996

1865 'NO TITLE', Empire (Sydney, NSW : 1850 - 1875), 7 March, p. 4. , viewed 16 Jun 2023, http://nla.gov.au/nla.news-article60567176 (No Title, 7 Mar 1865, p.4)

1865 'TELEGRAPHIC.', The Brisbane Courier (Qld. : 1864 - 1933), 24 November, p. 2. , viewed 12 Jun 2023, http://nla.gov.au/nla.news-article1282769

1866 'MONDAY, MARCH 12, 1866.', The Argus (Melbourne, Vic. : 1848 - 1957), 12 March, p. 5. , viewed 07 Aug 2023, http://nla.gov.au/nla.news-article5776954

1866 'MONDAY, OCTOBER 22, 1866.', The Argus (Melbourne, Vic. : 1848 - 1957), 22 October, p. 4. , viewed 19 Aug 2023, http://nla.gov.au/nla.news-article5776555

1866 'PENOLA.', Border Watch (Mount Gambier, SA : 1861 - 1954), 20 January, p. 2. , viewed 14 Sep 2023, http://nla.gov.au/nla.news-article77131518

1866 'SUMMARY OF LATE NEWS.', Border Watch (Mount Gambier, SA : 1861 - 1954), 24 October, p. 2. , viewed 19 Aug 2023, http://nla.gov.au/nla.news-article77132931

1866 'THE SKETCHER.', The Queenslander (Brisbane, Qld. : 1866 - 1939), 19 May, p. 12. , viewed 02 May 2023, http://nla.gov.au/nla.news-article20307621

1867 'BATHURST.', Sydney Mail (NSW : 1860 - 1871), 6 July, p. 4. , viewed 22 Mar 2024, http://nla.gov.au/nla.news-article166798754

1867 'SUMMARY FOR EUROPE.', The Argus (Melbourne, Vic. : 1848 - 1957), 26 January, p. 1. (The Argus Supplement), viewed 19 Aug 2023, http://nla.gov.au/nla.news-article5784510

1867 'THE NEWS OF THE DAY.', The Age (Melbourne, Vic. : 1854 - 1954), 6 August, p. 5. , viewed 13 Sep 2023, http://nla.gov.au/nla.news-article185504663

1867 'TUESDAY, JANUARY, 1867.', The Argus (Melbourne, Vic. : 1848 - 1957), 8 January, p. 5. , viewed 19 Aug 2023, http://nla.gov.au/nla.news-article5783069

1868 'BATHURST.', The Maitland Mercury and Hunter River General Advertiser (NSW : 1843 - 1893), 22 February, p. 2. , viewed 17 Jun 2023, http://nla.gov.au/nla.news-article18714950

1868 'THE GIPPSLAND TIMES.', Gippsland Times (Vic. : 1861 - 1954), 7 July, p. 2. (Morning), viewed 10 Sep 2023, http://nla.gov.au/nla.news-article61341267

1868 'TOWN AND COUNTRY.', Sydney Mail (NSW : 1860 - 1871), 23 May, p. 11. , viewed 22 Mar 2024, http://nla.gov.au/nla.news-article166805034

1868 'TUESDAY, JANUARY 14, 1868.', The Argus (Melbourne, Vic. : 1848 - 1957), 14 January, p. 5. , viewed 18 Aug 2023, http://nla.gov.au/nla.news-article5788479

1869 'UNDER THE VERANDAH.', Leader (Melbourne, Vic. : 1862 - 1918, 1935), 27 March, p. 17. , viewed 13 Oct 2022, http://nla.gov.au/nla.news-article196482306

1870 'JOTTINGS BY THE WAY.', Evening News (Sydney, NSW : 1869 - 1931), 15 July, p. 4. , viewed 06 Jun 2023, http://nla.gov.au/nla.newsarticle107135720

1870 'MISCELANEOUS ITEMS.', Evening News (Sydney, NSW : 1869 - 1931), 9 July, p. 4. , viewed 08 Oct 2023, http://nla.gov.au/nla.news-article107130776

1870 'SOUTH AUSTRALIA.', Ovens and Murray Advertiser (Beechworth, Vic. : 1855 - 1955), 22 October, p. 2. , viewed 31 May 2023, http://nla.gov.au/nla.newsarticle196416188

1870 'THE AUSTRALIAN TOWN & COUNTRY JOURNAL', Australian Town and Country Journal (Sydney, NSW : 1870 - 1919), 18 June, p. 8. , viewed 21 Sep 2023, http://nla.gov.au/nla.news-article70460222

1871 'KING COBB.', Upper Hunter Courier (Murrurundi, NSW : 1871), 15 August, p. 2. , viewed 11 Sep 2023, http://nla.gov.au/nla.newsarticle111066321

1871 'TALK ON 'CHANGE.', The Australasian (Melbourne, Vic. : 1864 - 1946), 11 November, p. 17. , viewed 26 May 2023, http://nla.gov.au/nla.news-article138086703

1872 'BATHURST.', The Newcastle Chronicle (NSW : 1866 - 1876), 21 May, p. 2. , viewed 22 Mar 2024, http://nla.gov.au/nla.news-article111149515

1872 'ERECTION OF POST AND TELEGRAPH OFFICE, AT HILL END.', New South Wales Government Gazette (Sydney, NSW : 1832 - 1900), 25 June, p. 1639. , viewed 24 Mar 2024, http://nla.gov.au/nla.news-article225842556

1872 'SANDHURST STOCK MARKET.', The Pastoral Times (South Deniliquin, NSW : 1866 - 1895), 19 October, p. 2. , viewed 31 May 2023, http://nla.gov.au/nla.newsarticle268007210

1872 'THE AUSTRALIAN HANDBOOK AND ALMANAC AND SHIPPERS' AND IMPORTERS' DIRECTORY' Gordon and Gotch, London, p.86 viewed 30 July 2023 http://nla.gov.au/nla.obj-2900579722

1873 'AUSTRALIAN NEWS IN ENGLISH NEWSPAPERS.', The Sydney Morning Herald (NSW : 1842 - 1954), 13 March, p. 3. , viewed 21 Sep 2023, http://nla.gov.au/nla.news-article13308941

1874 'NOTICE IS HEREBY GIVEN, THAT MR. WILLIAM BROWN BRADLEY HAS RETIRED THIS DAY FROM THE PARTNERSHIP KNOWN AS COBB & CO.', New South Wales Government Gazette (Sydney, NSW : 1832 - 1900), 13 January, p. 76. , viewed 14 Oct 2023, http://nla.gov.au/nla.news-article223691360

1875 'COBB AND CO.', Wagga Wagga Express and Murrumbidgee District Advertiser (NSW : 1858 - 1859; 1866; 1872 - 1875), 24 July, p. 5. , viewed 21 Mar 2024, http://nla.gov.au/nla.news-article271087564
1918 'Cobb & Co.', The Corowa Free Press (NSW : 1875 - 1954), 18 June, p. 4. , viewed 02 May 2023, http://nla.gov.au/nla.news-article235525858

1875 'COBB'S BOX.', Wagga Wagga Advertiser and Riverine Reporter (NSW : 1868 - 1875), 6 February, p. 4. , viewed 11 Sep 2023, http://nla.gov.au/nla.news-article104117694

1875 'DESTRUCTIVE FIRE. FEARFUL LOSS OF PROPERTY.', The Yass Courier (NSW : 1857 - 1929), 9 April, p. 2. , viewed 29 Jun 2023, http://nla.gov.au/nla.news-article263897786

1875 'SOFALA POST AND TELEGRAPH OFFICE BURNT DOWN.', Evening News (Sydney, NSW : 1869 - 1931), 22 June, p. 2. , viewed 06 Jun 2023, http://nla.gov.au/nla.news-article130494770

1876 'NEWS AND NOTES.', The Ballarat Star (Vic. : 1865 - 1924), 15 July, p. 2. , viewed 17 Sep 2023, http://nla.gov.au/nla.news-article200231738

1877 'GEORGE F. TRAIN ON HIMSELF.', The Daily Northern Argus (Rockhampton, Qld. : 1875 - 1896), 8 September, p. 3. , viewed 06 Sep 2023, http://nla.gov.au/nla.news-article213474332

1878 'COBB AND CO.'S COACH FACTORY.', Glen Innes Examiner and General Advertiser (NSW : 1874 - 1908), 23 October, p. 3. , viewed 16 Aug 2023, http://nla.gov.au/nla.news-article217826151nd

1878 'DEATH OF THE FOUNDER OF COBB AND CO.', The Goulburn Herald and Chronicle (NSW : 1864 - 1881), 28 September, p. 3. , viewed 21 Sep 2023, http://nla.gov.au/nla.news-article100879416

1878 'FATAL COACH ACCIDENT NEAR GULGONG.', Geelong Advertiser (Vic. : 1859 - 1929), 18 June, p. 4. , viewed 06 Jun 2023, http://nla.gov.au/nla.news-article149825812

1879 'TELEGRAPHIC BREVITIES.', Evening News (Sydney, NSW : 1869 - 1931), 29 October, p. 2. , viewed 18 Sep 2023, http://nla.gov.au/nla.news-article107158938

1881 'GILGANDRA.', Australian Town and Country Journal (Sydney, NSW : 1870 - 1919), 26 February, p. 38. , viewed 24 Mar 2024, http://nla.gov.au/nla.news-article70953203

1881 'LAW INTELLIGENCE.', The Sydney Daily Telegraph (NSW : 1879 -1883), 28 July, p. 4. , viewed 22 Mar 2024, http://nla.gov.au/nla.news-article238311961

1881 'NARROW ESCAPE AT BATHURST.', Evening News (Sydney, NSW : 1869 - 1931), 21 October, p. 2. , viewed 22 Mar 2024, http://nla.gov.au/nla.news-article107222650

1881 'NEWS AND NOTES.', Southern Argus (Goulburn, NSW : 1881 - 1885), 14 September, p. 3. , viewed 15 Sep 2023, http://nla.gov.au/nla.news-article102059932

1885 'NOTES AND QUERIES.', Australian Town and Country Journal (Sydney, NSW : 1870 - 1919), 12 September, p. 19. , viewed 13 Oct 2023, http://nla.gov.au/nla.news-article70983698

1886 'NEW SOUTH WALES GOVERNMENT GAZETTE' (Sydney, NSW : 1832 - 1900), 29 January, p. 748. , viewed 02 May 2023, http://nla.gov.au/nla.news-page13128780

1886 'ORIGINAL POETRY.', The Australasian (Melbourne, Vic. : 1864 - 1946), 26 June, p. 45. , viewed 14 Sep 2023, http://nla.gov.au/nla.news-article138027973

1887 'GOVERNMENT GAZETTE: JANUARY [?]', The Riverine Grazier (Hay, NSW : 1873 - 1954), 28 January, p. 3. , viewed 30 Aug 2023, http://nla.gov.au/nla.news-article140461060

1887 'NEW SOUTH WALES MAIL CONTRACTS.', The Albury Banner and Wodonga Express (NSW : 1860 - 1938), 28 January, p. 14. , viewed 30 Aug 2023, http://nla.gov.au/nla.news-article254559239

1887 'PENRITH NEWS.', Evening News (Sydney, NSW : 1869 - 1931), 8 August, p. 5. , viewed 21 Sep 2023, http://nla.gov.au/nla.news-article108004002

1888 'DUNKELD.', Hamilton Spectator (Vic. : 1870 - 1918), 2 August, p. 4. , viewed 14 Sep 2023, http://nla.gov.au/nla.news-article225803422

1889 'MESSRS. COBB AND CO'S FACTORY.', Western Herald (Bourke, NSW : 1887 - 1970), 9 November, p. 4. , viewed 18 Sep 2023, http://nla.gov.au/nla.news-article143222729

1890 'BUSY BATHURST.', National Advocate (Bathurst, NSW : 1889 - 1954), 27 August, p. 2. , viewed 02 May 2023, http://nla.gov.au/nla.newsarticle156383878

1890 'PICTURES FROM THE PLAINS.', National Advocate (Bathurst, NSW : 1889 - 1954), 11 October, p. 2. , viewed 26 Mar 2024, http://nla.gov.au/nla.news-article156385561

1891 'A SNAKE YARN.', Windsor and Richmond Gazette (NSW : 1888 - 1965), 12 September, p. 10. , viewed 21 Sep 2023, http://nla.gov.au/nla.news-article72540894

1891 'LOCAL AND GENERAL.', National Advocate (Bathurst, NSW : 1889 - 1954), 20 July, p. 2. , viewed 08 Jun 2023, http://nla.gov.au/nla.newsarticle157161670

1892 'LATER LACHLAN NEWS.', The Albury Banner and Wodonga Express (NSW : 1860 - 1927; 1929 - 1931; 1933 - 1938), 9 December, p. 17. , viewed 21 Sep 2023, http://nla.gov.au/nla.news-article254576915

1892 'MESSRS. COBB & CO.', National Advocate (Bathurst, NSW : 1889 - 1954), 24 December, p. 3. (SUPPLEMENT TO THE NATIONAL ADVOCATE), viewed 23 Mar 2024, http://nla.gov.au/nla.news-article156653951

1893 'COBB AND COMPANY.', The Australian Star (Sydney, NSW : 1887 - 1909), 22 March, p. 6. , viewed 15 Aug 2023, http://nla.gov.au/nla.newsarticle227167669

1893 'FIRE AT COBB AND CO'S FACTORY', The Hay Standard and Advertiser for Balranald, Wentworth, Maude...(Hay, NSW : 1871 - 1873; 1880 - 1881; 1890 - 1900), 13 December, p. 2. , viewed 14 Sep 2023, http://nla.gov.au/nla.news-article144688720

1893 'TOWN TALK.', Geelong Advertiser (Vic. : 1859 - 1929), 11 April, p. 2. , viewed 08 Sep 2023, http://nla.gov.au/nla.news-article1502854691868 1868

1894 'COBB AND CO.', The Burrangong Argus (NSW : 1865 - 1913), 14 November, p. 2. , viewed 11 Sep 2023, http://nla.gov.au/nla.newsarticle247682211

1894 'COBB AND CO.', The Sydney Mail and New South Wales Advertiser (NSW : 1871 - 1912), 17 November, p. 1016. , viewed 02 May 2023, http://nla.gov.au/nla.news-article162836401

1894 'MEMORIAL TO MR. WHITNEY', The Australian Star (Sydney, NSW : 1887 - 1909), 25 December, p. 5. , viewed 02 May 2023, http://nla.gov.au/nla.news-article227487818

1894 'THE LATE MR. F. WHITNEY.', Dubbo Dispatch and Wellington Independent (NSW : 1887 - 1932), 6 November, p. 2. , viewed 15 Sep 2023, http://nla.gov.au/nla.news-article228223042

1894 'THE WYALONG GOLDFIELD.', The Riverine Grazier (Hay, NSW : 1873 - 1954), 3 April, p. 2. , viewed 08 Sep 2023, http://nla.gov.au/nla.news-article139997479

1895 'COBB & CO'S. ON FIRE.', Riverina Recorder (Balranald, Moulamein, NSW : 1887 - 1944), 27 November, p. 2. , viewed 17 Sep 2023, http://nla.gov.au/nla.news-article137608067

1895 'LADIES' COLUMN.' (1895, April 27). The Bendigo Independent (Vic. : 1891 - 1918), p. 3 (Bendigo Independent (Vic. : 1891 - 1901)). Retrieved October 9, 2023, from http://nla.gov.au/nla.news-article194367419

1895 'LATEST INTELLIGENCE.', Goulburn Evening Penny Post (NSW : 1881 - 1940), 11 July, p. 3. , viewed 21 Sep 2023, http://nla.gov.au/nla.newsarticle98553286

1896 'INTERVIEW WITH MR. JAMES RUTHERFORD.', National Advocate (Bathurst, NSW : 1889 - 1954), 6 November, p. 2. , viewed 07 Jun 2023, http://nla.gov.au/nla.news-article156717021

1896 'OBITUARY.', The Australasian (Melbourne, Vic. : 1864 - 1946), 18 July, p. 34. , viewed 13 Sep 2023, http://nla.gov.au/nla.news-article139728162

1897 'COBB & CO.'S CATALOGUE OF HIGH CLASS VEHICLES.', One Search (State Library of Queensland), pp.1-28 bishop.slq.qld.gov.au, viewed 17March 2021, Record number 997321704702061, 21111147640002061

1897 'DISASTROUS FIRE AT CHARLEVILLE.', Toowoomba Chronicle and Darling Downs General Advertiser (Qld. : 1875 - 1902), 18 November, p. 2., viewed 14 Sep 2023, http://nla.gov.au/nla.news-article217726450

1897 'ORIGINAL POETRY.', The Australasian (Melbourne, Vic. : 1864 - 1946), 2 January, p. 42. , viewed 09 Sep 2023, http://nla.gov.au/nla.news-article139735739

1898 '[?] POLICE COURT', National Advocate (Bathurst, NSW : 1889 - 1954), 16 August, p. 2. , viewed 08 Jun 2023, http://nla.gov.au/nla.news-article156749479

1898 'REMINISCENCES OF COBB AND CO.', The Riverine Grazier (Hay, NSW : 1873 - 1954), 14 January, p. 2. , viewed 21 Sep 2023, http://nla.gov.au/nla.newsarticle140688564

1898 'REMINISCENCES OF COBB AND CO.', Western Grazier (Wilcannia, NSW : 1896 - 1951), 26 January, p. 4. , viewed 11 Sep 2023, http://nla.gov.au/nla.newsarticle133815378

1898 'THE OLD COACHING DAYS.', Australian Town and Country Journal (Sydney, NSW : 1870 - 1919), 2 April, p. 47. , viewed 03 Oct 2023 http://nla.gov.au/nla.news-article71284871

1899 'CURRENT NEWS.', Newcastle Morning Herald and Miners' Advocate (NSW : 1876 - 1954), 27 April, p. 4. , viewed 17 Sep 2023, http://nla.gov.au/nla.news-article132787035

1899 'MR. JAMES RUTHERFORD.', National Advocate (Bathurst, NSW : 1889 - 1954), 30 September, p. 2. , viewed 07 Jun 2023, http://nla.gov.au/nla.news-article156811526

1899 'THE CITY COACH AND BUGGY WORKS.', Western Herald (Bourke, NSW : 1887 - 1970), 26 April, p. 2. , viewed 18 Sep 2023, http://nla.gov.au/nla.newsarticle104092448

1899 'WEDDING AT MOUNT PLEASANT.', National Advocate (Bathurst, NSW : 1889 - 1954), 22 February, p. 3. , viewed 21 Sep 2023, http://nla.gov.au/nla.newsarticle156801382

1900 'LATE TELEGRAMS.', The Sun (Kalgoorlie, WA : 1898 - 1929), 8 July, p. 1. , viewed 07 Oct 2023, http://nla.gov.au/nla.news-article211733496

1900 'PARTNERSHIP CASE.', Bathurst Free Press and Mining Journal (NSW : 1851 - 1862; 1872; 1882; 1885 - 1897; 1899 - 1904), 1 March, p. 3. , viewed 22 Mar 2024, http://nla.gov.au/nla.news-article63866590

1900 'SNOW IN MUDGEE.', Mudgee Guardian and North-Western Representative (NSW : 1890 - 1954), 6 July, p. 15. , viewed 07 Oct 2023, http://nla.gov.au/nla.news-article156268794

1901 'DEATH OF MR JOHN WAGNER.', Geelong Advertiser (Vic. : 1859 - 1929), 29 January, p. 2. , viewed 01 Jun 2023, http://nla.gov.au/nla.newsarticle147712112

1902 'MY LIFE IN MANY STATES AND IN FOREIGN LANDS.', Train, George Francis. Pp. Xxi. 340. D. Appleton: New York. SR 910.4 T768 Available from: The National Library of Australia

1903 'DEATH OF MR J. M. PECK', Geelong Advertiser (Vic. : 1859 - 1929), 21 November, p. 1. , viewed 11 Sep 2023, http://nla.gov.au/nla.newsarticle149004624

1903 'LOCAL BREVITIES.', Mudgee Guardian and North-Western Representative (NSW : 1890 - 1954), 8 January, p. 13. , viewed 25 Mar 2024, http://nla.gov.au/nla.news-article157570326

1905 'MAIL SERVICE.', Geelong Advertiser (Vic. : 1859 - 1929), 22 May, p. 1. , viewed 11 Sep 2023, http://nla.gov.au/nla.news-article150089098

1905 'WEDDINGS.', National Advocate (Bathurst, NSW : 1889 - 1954), 1 May, p. 3. , viewed 26 Mar 2024, http://nla.gov.au/nla.news-article157311885

1906 'CONVEYANCE OF MAILS IN QUEENSLAND.', Commonwealth of Australia Gazette (National : 1901 - 1973), 8 December, p. 1505. , viewed 05 Sep 2023, http://nla.gov.au/nla.news-article232352630

1906 'MOUNT PLEASANT", National Advocate (Bathurst, NSW : 1889 - 1954), 12 October, p. 2. , viewed 16 Sep 2023, http://nla.gov.au/nla.news-article157295366

1906 'THE RATTLE OF THE COACH.' (1906, December 26). The Sydney Mail and New South Wales Advertiser (NSW : 1871 - 1912), p. 1650. Retrieved October 1, 2023, from http://nla.gov.au/nla.news-article163683489

1907 'HENRY LAWSON', The Southern Cross Times (WA : 1900 - 1920), 14 December, p. 2. , viewed 01 Oct 2023, http://nla.gov.au/nla.newsarticle209363941

1907 'SHEARERS FINED.', The Sydney Stock and Station Journal (NSW : 1896 - 1924), 5 November, p. 4. , viewed 08 Jun 2023, http://nla.gov.au/nla.newsarticle121608352

1908 'AMONG THE BUSHRANGERS.', The Advertiser (Adelaide, SA : 1889 - 1931),

10 October, p. 13. , viewed 08 Jun 2023, http://nla.gov.au/nla.news-article5192127

1908 'COBB AND CO'S FACTORY.', The Dubbo Liberal and Macquarie Advocate (NSW : 1894 - 1954), 18 November, p. 2. , viewed 14 Sep 2023, http://nla.gov.au/nla.news-article76952561

1908 'FIRE AT BOURKE.', The Daily Telegraph (Sydney, NSW : 1883 - 1930), 9 April, p. 5. , viewed 17 Sep 2023, http://nla.gov.au/nla.newsarticle238142924

1908 'ITEMS OF INTEREST.', Shepparton Advertiser (Vic. : 1887 - 1953), 11 August, p. 4. , viewed 17 Sep 2023, http://nla.gov.au/nla.newsarticle269969569

1908 'OLD FACTORY BURNT', National Advocate (Bathurst, NSW : 1889 - 1954), 9 April, p. 2. , viewed 17 Sep 2023, http://nla.gov.au/nla.news-article157194670

1908 'THE CONTRIBUTOR', The Sydney Mail and New South Wales Advertiser (NSW : 1871 - 1912), 25 November, p. 1405. , viewed 10 Sep 2023, http://nla.gov.au/nla.news-article163229756

1908 'TRUNKEY.', Lithgow Mercury (NSW : 1898 - 1954), 27 May, p. 4. , viewed 07 Oct 2023, http://nla.gov.au/nla.news-article219292875

1910 'CONTRACTS FOR THE CONVEYANCE OF MAILS IN THE STATE OF QUEENSLAND.', Commonwealth of Australia Gazette (National : 1901 - 1973), 8 January, p. 10. , viewed 05 Sep 2023, http://nla.gov.au/nla.news-article232460259

1911 'A PIONEER OF THE COACHING DAYS: THE LATE JAMES RUTHERFORD.', The Sydney Mail and New South Wales Advertiser (NSW : 1871 - 1912), 20 September, p. 26. , viewed 14 Sep 2023, http://nla.gov.au/nla.news-article164334352

1911 'EX-BUSHRANGER IN BATHURST.', National Advocate (Bathurst, NSW : 1889 - 1954), 4 February, p. 4. , viewed 22 Mar 2024, http://nla.gov.au/nla.news-article157784437

1912 'MOUNT PLEASANT SHOW.', The Advertiser (Adelaide, SA : 1889 - 1931), 22 March, p. 11. , viewed 16 Sep 2023, http://nla.gov.au/nla.news-article5329224

1912 'MOUNT PLEASANT.', Daily Advertiser (Wagga Wagga, NSW : 1911 - 1954), 9 March, p. 5. , viewed 26 Mar 2024, http://nla.gov.au/nla.news-article142558431

1912 'POINTED PARS.', Wellington Times (NSW : 1899 - 1954), 28 March, p. 3. , viewed 01 Jun 2023, http://nla.gov.au/nla.news-article137881575

1912 'THE MT. PLEASANT ESTATE.', Leader (Orange, NSW : 1899 - 1945), 3 July, p. 2. , viewed 06 Jun 2023, http://nla.gov.au/nla.news-article117798897

1913 'AFTER 90 YEARS', National Advocate (Bathurst, NSW : 1889 - 1954), 8 November, p. 3. , viewed 06 Jun 2023, http://nla.gov.au/nla.newsarticle157810401

1913 'CONTRACTS FOR THE CONVEYANCE OF MAILS IN THE STATE OF QUEENSLAND.', Commonwealth of Australia Gazette (National : 1901 - 1973), 15 February, p. 399. , viewed 05 Sep 2023

1913 'THE HOUSEHOLD.', The Sydney Wool and Stock Journal (NSW : 1899 - 1917), 29 August, p. 13. , viewed 09 Oct 2023, http://nla.gov.au/nla.news-article106891321

1914 'CONTRACTS FOR THE CONVEYANCE OF MAILS IN THE STATE OF QUEENSLAND.', Commonwealth of Australia Gazette (National : 1901 - 1973), 7 February, p. 206. , viewed 05 Sep 2023, http://nla.gov.au/nla.news-article232365754

1914 'LOCAL BREVITIES', Mudgee Guardian and North-Western Representative (NSW : 1890 - 1954), 23 July, p. 29. , viewed 16 Sep 2023, http://nla.gov.au/nla.news-article156832450

1914 'WEDDING', National Advocate (Bathurst, NSW : 1889 - 1954), 8 January, p. 2. , viewed 06 Jun 2023, http://nla.gov.au/nla.news-article158039294

1915 '[?] AT MOUNT PLEASANT.', Willaura Farmer (Vic. : 1914 - 1916), 4 November, p. 2. , viewed 16 Sep 2023, http://nla.gov.au/nla.newsarticle154603947

1915 'CONTRACTS FOR THE CONVEYANCE OF MAILS IN THE STATE OF QUEENSLAND.', Commonwealth of Australia Gazette (National : 1901 - 1973), 20 February, p. 278. , viewed 05 Sep 2023, http://nla.gov.au/nla.news-article232450920

1915 'VEHICLE ACCIDENT AT BATHURST', Leader (Orange, NSW : 1899 - 1945), 23 August, p. 4. , viewed 13 Oct 2023, http://nla.gov.au/nla.news-article117839754

1916 'CONTRACTS FOR THE CONVEYANCE OF MAILS IN THE STATE OF QUEENSLAND.', Commonwealth of Australia Gazette (National : 1901 - 1973), 15 February, p. 266. , viewed 05 Sep 2023, http://nla.gov.au/nla.news

1917 'AFTER 40 YEARS', The Bathurst Times (NSW : 1909 - 1925), 13 November, p. 1. , viewed 02 May 2023, http://nla.gov.au/nla.newsarticle111554630

1917 'AFTER 40 YEARS', The Bathurst Times (NSW : 1909 - 1925), 6 November, p. 1. , viewed 01 May 2023, http://nla.gov.au/nla.newsarticle111554830

1917 'AFTER 40 YEARS', The Bathurst Times (NSW : 1909 - 1925), 9 November, p. 1. , viewed 01 May 2023, http://nla.gov.au/nla.newsarticle1115739321917

1917 'COBB AND CO.'S FACTORY.', The Bathurst Times (NSW : 1909 - 1925), 9 November, p. 2. , viewed 13 Oct 2023, http://nla.gov.au/nla.newsarticle111573901

1917 'HISTORY OF COBB AND CO.', Toowoomba Chronicle (Qld. : 1917 - 1922), 23 August, p. 4. , viewed 18 Oct 2023, http://nla.gov.au/nla.newsarticle252909055

1917 'THE GENESIS OF COBB & CO', The Western Champion and General Advertiser for the Central-Western Districts (Barcaldine, Qld. : 1892 - 1922), 15 September, p. 11. , viewed 09 Jul 2023, http://nla.gov.au/nla.news-article77790761

1918 'FATHER FOUGHT NAPOLEON', The Inverell Times (NSW : 1899 - 1907, 1909 - 1954), 17 September, p. 7. , viewed 06 Jun 2023, http://nla.gov.au/nla.news-article183601800

1918 'NOTES & ANSWERS.', The Australasian (Melbourne, Vic. : 1864 - 1946), 4 May, p. 25. , viewed 18 Aug 2023, http://nla.gov.au/nla.news-article140205489

1919 'ANZAC DAY', National Advocate (Bathurst, NSW : 1889 - 1954), 27 May, p. 2. , viewed 09 Sep 2023, http://nla.gov.au/nla.news-article158574067

1919 'NO TITLE', The Riverine Grazier (Hay, NSW : 1873 - 1954), 2 September, p. 2. , viewed 18 Sep 2023, http://nla.gov.au/nla.news-article141024928

1920 'COBB AND CO'S FACTORY.', Darling Downs Gazette (Qld. : 1881 - 1922), 20 December, p. 2. , viewed 14 Sep 2023, http://nla.gov.au/nla.news-article174105965

1920 'LATE MR. J. H. STEWART.', The Sydney Morning Herald (NSW : 1842 - 1954), 25 August, p. 9. , viewed 16 Sep 2023, http://nla.gov.au/nla.news-article15903804

1920 'LATE MR. J. H. STEWART', Mudgee Guardian and North-Western Representative (NSW : 1890 - 1954), 26 August, p. 10. , viewed 26 Mar 2024, http://nla.gov.au/nla.news-article157034411

1920 'STORIES OF THE COBB & CO. COACHING DAYS.', Sunday Times (Sydney, NSW : 1895 - 1930), 19 December, p. 18., viewed 14 Oct 2022, http://nla.gov.au/nla.news-article120522761

1920 'THE STEWART ESTATE.', National Advocate (Bathurst, NSW : 1889 - 1954), 14 January, p. 2. , viewed 27 Sep 2023, http://nla.gov.au/nla.news-article158638710

1921 'COMPANY NEWS.', Daily Commercial News and Shipping List (Sydney, NSW : 1891 - 1954), 2 November, p. 5. (Weekly Summary), viewed 23 Mar 2024, http://nla.gov.au/nla.news-article159597500

1921 'HENRY LAWSON', The Grenfell Record and Lachlan District Advertiser (NSW : 1876 - 1951), 28 February, p. 2. , viewed 13 Oct 2023, http://nla.gov.au/nla.news-article112991475

1921 'REMINISCENCES OF BATHURST', Sydney Mail (NSW : 1912 - 1938), 27 July, p. 16. , viewed 13 Oct 2023, http://nla.gov.au/nla.news-article162033717

1921 'SYDNEY MAIL.', The Sydney Morning Herald (NSW : 1842 - 1954), 20 April, p. 10. , viewed 20 Mar 2024, http://nla.gov.au/nla.news-article15955127

1922 'INTERSTATE.', The Queenslander (Brisbane, Qld. : 1866 - 1939), 7 January, p. 29. , viewed 11 Sep 2023, http://nla.gov.au/nla.newsarticle27426816

1922 'MOTOR TRANSPORT', The Daily Telegraph (Sydney, NSW : 1883 - 1930), 2 December, p. 20. , viewed 27 Sep 2023, http://nla.gov.au/nla.news-article245777570

1922 'OLD COACHING DAYS.', The Argus (Melbourne, Vic. : 1848 - 1957), 10 June, p. 7. , viewed 06 Aug 2021, http://nla.gov.au/nla.news-article4629678

1922 'STORY OF COBB AND CO.', The Argus (Melbourne, Vic. : 1848 - 1957), 20 May,

p. 5. , viewed 21 Sep 2023, http://nla.gov.au/nla.news-article4643657

1922 'STORY OF COBB AND CO.', The Argus (Melbourne, Vic. : 1848 - 1957), 20 May, p. 5. , viewed 21 Sep 2023, http://nla.gov.au/nla.news-article4643657

1922 'STORY OF THE BATHURST PIONEERS', The Daily Telegraph (Sydney, NSW : 1883 - 1930), 18 November, p. 13. , viewed 16 Sep 2023, http://nla.gov.au/nla.newsarticle245792869

1922 'STORY OF THE BATHURST PIONEERS', The Daily Telegraph (Sydney, NSW : 1883 - 1930), 25 November, p. 13. , viewed 27 Sep 2023, http://nla.gov.au/nla.newsarticle245787064

1924 'EXIT COBB'S.', The Southern Mail (Bowral, NSW : 1889 - 1954), 5 September, p. 3. , viewed 06 Jun 2023, http://nla.gov.au/nla.newsarticle114063569

1924 'GOOD-BYE TO COBB & CO.', The Cessnock Eagle and South Maitland Recorder (NSW : 1913 - 1954), 5 September, p. 4. , viewed 11 Sep 2023, http://nla.gov.au/nla.news-article99376376

1924 'PASSING OF COBB AND CO.', Cairns Post (Qld. : 1909 - 1954), 24 September, p. 6. , viewed 11 Sep 2023, http://nla.gov.au/nla.news-article40480102

1924 'PERSONAL', The Bathurst Times (NSW : 1909 - 1925), 10 July, p. 2. , viewed 26 Mar 2024, http://nla.gov.au/nla.news-article112109271

1924 'THE FOUNDER OF COBB & CO.', The Scone Advocate (NSW : 1887 - 1954), 12 December, p. 4. , viewed 08 Jun 2023, http://nla.gov.au/nla.news-article157136209

1925 'COACHING IN THE COMMONWEALTH', Sunday Times (Perth, WA : 1902 - 1954), 17 May, p. 9. , viewed 14 Oct 2023, http://nla.gov.au/nla.newsarticle58258535

1925 'MOTOR SHOW.', The Age (Melbourne, Vic. : 1854 - 1954), 6 May, p. 14. , viewed 16 Sep 2023, http://nla.gov.au/nla.news-article155751115

1925 'MOUNT PLEASANT', The Dubbo Liberal and Macquarie Advocate (NSW : 1894 - 1954), 20 February, p. 7. , viewed 26 Mar 2024, http://nla.gov.au/nla.news-article76098247

1925 'PERSONAGRAPHS', Truth (Sydney, NSW : 1894 - 1954), 4 January, p. 8. , viewed 09 Jun 2023, http://nla.gov.au/nla.news-article168708005

1926 '115 YEARS!', The Capricornian (Rockhampton, Qld. : 1875 - 1929), 29 May, p. 61. , viewed 17 Sep 2023, http://nla.gov.au/nla.news-article72017296

1926 'EVENTS TO COME.', Mudgee Guardian and North-Western Representative (NSW : 1890 - 1954), 23 December, p. 17. , viewed 08 Oct 2023, http://nla.gov.au/nla.news-article155943488

1926 'HISTORIC FAMILY', The Daily Mail (Brisbane, Qld. : 1903; 1916 - 1926), 22 May, p. 6. , viewed 14 Sep 2023, http://nla.gov.au/nla.newsarticle219034546

1927 'A FEW NOTES ON HENRY LAWSON.', Freeman's Journal (Sydney, NSW : 1850 - 1932), 15 September, p. 25. , viewed 13 Sep 2023, http://nla.gov.au/nla.news-article116753248

1927 'CHARITY WORKER'S DEATH', The Sun (Sydney, NSW : 1910 - 1954), 18 October, p. 16. (FINAL EXTRA), viewed 26 Mar 2024, http://nla.gov.au/nla.news-article222435916

1927 'LATE MRS. ATHOL STEWART.', The Sydney Morning Herald (NSW : 1842 - 1954), 19 October, p. 16. , viewed 26 Mar 2024, http://nla.gov.au/nla.news-article16412655

1927 'MOUNT PLEASANT SALE', National Advocate (Bathurst, NSW : 1889 - 1954), 30 November, p. 2. , viewed 16 Sep 2023, http://nla.gov.au/nla.news-article159156193

1927 'THE MOUNT.', The Sydney Morning Herald (NSW : 1842 - 1954), 10 December, p. 13. , viewed 26 Mar 2024, http://nla.gov.au/nla.news-article16425460

1927 'THE SALE AT STEWART'S MOUNT', National Advocate (Bathurst, NSW : 1889 - 1954), 1 December, p. 2. , viewed 26 Mar 2024, http://nla.gov.au/nla.news-article159164902

1931 'A RELIC OF THE PAST.', The World's News (Sydney, NSW : 1901 - 1955), 14 January, p. 9. , viewed 04 Oct 2023, http://nla.gov.au/nla.newsarticle136309068

1931 'EARLY DAYS.', Narromine News and Trangie Advocate (NSW : 1898 - 1955), 24 July, p. 7. , viewed 06 Jun 2023, http://nla.gov.au/nla.newsarticle98921371

1932 'COBB AND CO. COACHMAN', The Gundagai Independent (NSW : 1928 - 1954), 21 November, p. 4. , viewed 19 Sep 2023, http://nla.gov.au/nla.news-article224984605

1932 'EARLY SETTLEMENT AND SETTLERS OF COWRA, 1815-1836', The Carcoar Chronicle (NSW : 1878 - 1943), 22 April, p. 3. , viewed 16 Sep 2023, http://nla.gov.au/nla.news-article103554474

1932 'IN THE DAYS OF COBB & CO.', The Port Macquarie News and Hastings River Advocate (NSW : 1882 - 1950), 8 October, p. 6. , viewed 01 Jun 2023, http://nla.gov.au/nla.news-article105959477

1932 'IN THE DAYS OF COBB & CO.', The Port Macquarie News and Hastings River Advocate (NSW : 1882 - 1950), 15 October, p. 6. , viewed 01 Jun 2023, http://nla.gov.au/nla.news-article105962626

1932 'THE COACHING DAYS.', Western Mail (Perth, WA : 1885 - 1954), 10 March, p. 7. (Edition 2), viewed 16 Sep 2023, http://nla.gov.au/nla.news-article37833141

1933 'COBB'S COACHES', Balonne Beacon (St. George, Qld. : 1909 - 1954), 26 January, p. 9. , viewed 28 May 2023, http://nla.gov.au/nla.newsarticle215393584

1933 'COBB'S COACHES', Balonne Beacon (St. George, Qld. : 1909 - 1954), 26 January, p. 9. , viewed 28 May 2023, http://nla.gov.au/nla.newsarticle215393584

1934 'MR. JAMES RUTHERFORD.', Wellington Times (NSW : 1899 - 1954), 24 September, p. 2. , viewed 07 Jun 2023, http://nla.gov.au/nla.news-article143426623

1935 'SOFALA', National Advocate (Bathurst, NSW : 1889 - 1954), 1 March, p. 8. , viewed 25 Mar 2024, http://nla.gov.au/nla.news-article159816344

1936 'COBB AND CO.', The Central Queensland Herald (Rockhampton, Qld. : 1930 - 1956), 1 October, p. 67. , viewed 31 May 2023, http://nla.gov.au/nla.news-article70574919

1936 'WITH COBB AND CO.', The Central Queensland Herald (Rockhampton, Qld. : 1930 - 1956), 22 October, p. 61. , viewed 29 May 2023, http://nla.gov.au/nla.news-article70569253

1937 'A [?] DRIVE', The Australasian' (Melbourne, Vic. : 1864 - 1946), 31 July, p. 7. , viewed 12 Oct 2022, http://nla.gov.au/nla.newsarticle141807670

1941 'BEN HALL', The North-Western Watchman (Coonabarabran, NSW : 1936 - 1949), 2 October, p. 10. , viewed 01 Oct 2023, http://nla.gov.au/nla.news-article263822919

1941 'DEATH OF MRS. WHITNEY.', Leader (Orange, NSW : 1899 - 1945), 29 August, p. 1. , viewed 02 May 2023, http://nla.gov.au/nla.newsarticle254459672

1942 'STEWART MANSION AS WOMEN'S HOSTEL', National Advocate (Bathurst, NSW : 1889 - 1954), 5 October, p. 2. , viewed 26 Mar 2024, http://nla.gov.au/nla.news-article160898114

1946 'LEGENDS OF MT. PLEASANT', Newcastle Morning Herald and Miners' Advocate (NSW : 1876 - 1954), 27 July, p. 5. , viewed 26 Mar 2024, http://nla.gov.au/nla.news-article133174333

1948 'BATHAMPTON MAN'S FOSSIL WAS 125 MILLION YEARS OLD', Lithgow Mercury (NSW : 1898 - 1954), 8 December, p. 8. (CITY EDITION), viewed 07 Jun 2023, http://nla.gov.au/nla.news-article219749603

1948 'READERS' LETTERS', Mountain District Free Press (Tecoma, Vic. : 1947 - 1954), 6 August, p. 6. , viewed 20 Sep 2023, http://nla.gov.au/nla.news-article254771041

1949 'JAS. RUTHERFORD OF COBB & CO.', The Longreach Leader (Qld. : 1923 - 1954), 14 December, p. 19. , viewed 18 Oct 2023, http://nla.gov.au/nla.news-article125790767

1952 'BLACK THURSDAY 1851', Balonne Beacon (St. George, Qld. : 1909 - 1954), 31 December, p. 2. , viewed 09 Sep 2023, http://nla.gov.au/nla.news-article213721495

1953 'WHEN COBB AND CO. CAME TO CUNNAMULLA', Queensland Country Life (Qld. : 1900 - 1954), 10 September, p. 15. , viewed 01 Jun 2023, http://nla.gov.au/nla.news-article100664189

1955 'COBB & CO. IN QUEENSLAND', Balonne Beacon (St. George, Qld. : 1909 - 1954), 7 July, p. 4. , viewed 23 Mar 2024, http://nla.gov.au/nla.news-article215346078

Index

1848 Bathurst Map 51

A

Abercrombie House 5, 110, 111, 112, 121, 122, 123, 124
Abercrombie House Stables 123, 124
Accidents 43, 78, 125
Adam and Co. 10
Adams' Express Office 10
Adelong 105
Anakie Hills 16
Anderson & M'Phee 30, 31, 32
Anderson's Creek 16
Anzac Day Poem 55
Australian Stage Company 29, 30, 128
Avoca 16, 44, 60, 80, 129

B

Bail up! 77
Ballaarat 12, 17, 77, 126, 127, 129
Ballarat 10, 15, 16, 17, 30, 33, 58, 116, 126, 128, 129, 131
Ballarat Stage Company 30
Batesford 16
Bathampton 42
Bathurst 4, 5, 6, 16, 17, 18, 19, 20, 32, 36, 40, 41, 42, 43, 44, 45, 46, 47, 50, 51, 52, 53, 54, 55, 56, 57, 58, 59, 60, 61, 64, 65, 66, 67, 68, 69, 70, 72, 77, 78, 84, 85, 86, 87, 96, 97, 104, 106, 110, 111, 112, 113, 114, 115, 116, 117, 118, 119, 120, 121, 122, 125, 129, 131, 133, 134, 135, 136, 137, 139, 141, 142, 144
Bendigo 10, 13, 17, 29, 34, 43, 71, 128
Ben Lomond Hotel 138, 139, 140
Bill and Deakin 34
Black Bull Hotel 53, 68
Blake, Arthur Lincoln 29, 33, 126, 127, 128, 129
Bourke-street 10, 126, 127, 128

Bowenfels 91, 113, 133
Bradley, William Brown 29, 30, 31, 33, 41, 44, 45, 70, 128, 130, 131, 132
Braidwood Penny Bank 18
Brayton, W. H. 29
Brisbane 4, 40, 42, 43, 65, 70, 71, 112, 113, 115, 117, 129, 131, 132
Buckinguy 42, 44
Buninyong 16
Bushranger - Alexander Fordyce 19
Bushranger - Ben Hall 18, 19, 20, 23, 24, 53, 54, 86, 87
Bushranger - Burke 18
Bushranger - Frank Gardiner 18, 20, 23, 25
Bushranger - Henry Munns 19
Bushranger - John Bow 19, 20
Bushranger - John Gilbert 19, 20, 25, 144
Bushranger - John Maguire 19
Bushranger - John O'Meally 144
Bushranger - John Vane 18, 144
Bushranger - Ned Kelly 24
Bushrangers 6, 16, 18, 20, 43, 54, 55, 65, 77, 78, 117
Bye Rock Hotel 139

C

Caledonion Hotel 134
Cambridge Hotel 69
Cameron and Jones 29
Campbell's River 54
Captain Battye 55
Captain Browne 16
Carcoar 18, 20, 44, 46, 84, 87, 105, 131, 133, 134, 135, 136, 137, 138, 139, 140
Carcoar Hotel 84
Castlemaine 17, 64, 68, 69, 71, 126, 127, 128, 129
Castlemaine Hotel 127
Cawker, J. 30
Cawker, T. 32
Chambers, W. 34
Clubhouse Hotel 53, 85
Clunes 16
Coaching Lines 77, 133
Cobb and Co. Coach Factory 33, 64, 68, 69, 70, 71, 72, 73
Cobb and Co. Ltd. 33
Cobb, E. Winslow 10
Cobb, Freeman 10, 29, 31, 33, 126, 127
Colclough, Chas. 29
Collins-street 10
Combing Park 44, 131
Commercial Hotel 93, 94, 104, 106, 107, 134
Coolgardie 34
Copper Mines 54
Cordillera 16
Cowra 18, 112, 115, 133, 134, 135, 136, 137, 138, 139, 140, 141, 142
Cox, Mrs. 34
Crane and Roberts 34, 116, 132
Criterion Hotel 11, 134

D

Davies, Thomas 29, 126
Deniliquin 9, 17, 30, 133, 134, 135, 136, 137, 138, 143
Droughts 6, 53, 70, 125
Duke of Cornwall Hotel 102
Durack's Inn 52

E

Emerald Hill 10
E. Moore and Co. 30
England 10, 40, 43, 53, 64, 77, 86, 96, 97, 105, 113, 117, 134
Eugowra Escort Robbery 19, 53

F

Fagan, John 53
F. B. Clapp and Co. 29, 127
Fiery Creek 16
Fires 19, 20, 40, 55, 64, 68, 69, 70, 71, 78, 86, 87, 96, 129
First Nugget Hotel 55
Floods 45, 88, 104, 105, 137, 138
Forbes 18, 19, 20, 44, 65, 86, 105, 133, 135, 136, 137, 138, 139, 140, 141, 142, 143
Forest Creek 10, 11
Fossil 42

Foster and Vinge 10, 34

G

Geelong 12, 17, 40, 116, 126, 127, 128, 129
Gill Bros. 34
Glanmire 54, 113
Goldfields 16, 17, 40, 45
Goulburn 16, 40, 45, 52, 71, 104, 105, 107, 133, 134, 135
Grand Hotel 54
Grenfell 15, 133, 134, 136, 137, 138, 139, 140, 141, 142, 143
Gulgong 72, 88, 89, 92, 96, 97, 98, 99, 100, 101, 136, 137, 138, 139, 140, 141
Gundagai 18, 20, 104, 133, 134, 135, 136, 137, 138, 139, 140, 141
Gundaroo 16

H

Hall, Walter Russell 29, 30, 31, 130
Hartley 52, 133, 134
Hereford 41
Hill End 54, 65, 85, 88, 90, 96, 97, 98, 102, 134, 136
Horr, J. C. 29
Hoyt, Henry 29

J

Jackson, Peleg Whitford 29, 37, 127
James Bevan and Co. 34
Jehus (drivers) 18, 53, 129
Jones, Charles Henry 34

K

Kelso 4, 20, 40, 53, 54, 84, 113, 114, 134, 135
Kerosene Lamps 54
Kidman, Sydney 34
King, Emanuel 10

L

Lachlan River 18, 105, 137, 138, 139
Ladies' Column 87
Lamber, John B. 29, 33, 126
Lambing Flat 16, 18, 65, 133
Lawson, Henry 15
Lithgow 41

Lithgow Ironworks 44, 49
Lord Bathurst 54
Lucknow 93, 134, 135

M

Mail Contracts 32, 140, 141, 142, 143
Major-General William Stewart 112, 113
Matthew Veal and Co. 30, 31
Maybell Hotel 142, 143
Meigs & Anderson 29, 30
Melbourne 10, 11, 12, 13, 18, 24, 29, 33, 34, 40, 45, 53, 77, 96, 104, 126, 127, 128, 129, 130, 134, 138
Melbourne Cricket Club 45
Memorial to Frank Whitney 44
Michel and Hughes 29
M'Ivor Hotel 127
Moorabool 16
Mount Alexander 10, 16, 33
Mount Emu Creek 16
Mount Lambie 52, 96
Mount Morgan Gold-mining Company, 43
Mowton, George 10
M'Phee & Co. 29, 30, 31, 32
Mudgee 18, 20, 24, 52, 65, 78, 86, 96, 97, 99, 101, 103, 133, 134, 135, 136, 137, 138, 139
Myall Vale Hotel 144
Mylecharane and Elliott 34

N

New England Hotel 134
Newmarket Hotel 18, 155
News along the tracks 5, 74, 77, 86, 96, 104
Nicholas, James 34
Nowland Bros. 34

O

Orange 16, 18, 40, 42, 44, 45, 53, 65, 78, 86, 94, 95, 133, 134, 135, 136, 137, 138, 139, 140, 142
Oriental Bank 17

P

Paramatta 18, 133
Pascoevale 33
Peck, John Murray 29, 33, 35, 126, 127, 129
Penrith 18, 77, 133
Post Offices 59, 81, 88, 95, 104, 117, 133, 134, 135, 136, 137, 138, 139, 140, 141, 142, 143
Proprietors of Cobb and Co. 5, 6, 17, 20, 26, 27, 33, 34, 67, 69, 126, 128, 129, 130, 131

Q

Queanbeyan 16, 105, 135

R

Randwick Coach and Horses Hotel 80
Roads of New South Wales 40
Robertson, A. W. 29
Robertson, Britton and Co. 17, 29, 131
Robertson, Colin 30, 45, 104, 130
Robertson, Wagner and Co. 29, 30, 31, 32, 33, 68
Rosehill Hotel 144
Rounsevell, J. 34
Royal Hotel 53, 58, 68, 78, 103, 133
Royal Mail Hotel 127
Rutherford, James 6, 29, 30, 31, 32, 33, 36, 39, 40, 41, 42, 43, 44, 63, 65, 125, 129, 130, 131, 132, 133, 143, 144
Rutherford, Norman 42

S

Sandhurst 10, 17, 126, 127, 128, 129
Saville's Hotel 54
Scott & Nugent 30
Shamrock Hotel 17, 128
Sharp, Seth 31, 32
Snake Anecdotes 41
Snow Storm 53, 54
Sofala 54, 96, 133, 134, 135, 136, 137, 139
South Melbourne 10
Stables 17, 20, 53, 65, 70, 78, 112, 129
Steam Engine Hotel 94
Stewarts - Mt. Pleasant 111, 112, 113
Stoneman, Thomas 29, 30, 31
Strath Ghost Anecdote 117
Strath - Mt. Pleasant 112, 117
Surat 33, 45, 125
Swan Hill 34
Swanton, Blake, and Co. 29, 126, 127
Swanton, James 29, 33, 126, 127
Sydney 10, 16, 17, 18, 32, 34, 40, 41, 42, 43, 44, 45, 48, 52, 53, 54, 55, 61, 64, 65, 66, 67, 69, 76, 77, 78, 79, 86, 96, 103, 104, 105, 113, 114, 115, 116, 117, 119, 120, 121, 125, 129, 130, 131, 133, 134, 135, 136, 137, 138, 139, 140, 141

T

Tasmania 34, 126
Tattersall's Hotel 69
Telegraph Hotel 45
Test Team of 1881 105
The Abercrombie 52
The Bushrangers' Cave Poem 21
The Lachlan 15, 16, 17, 18, 19, 53, 77, 86, 98, 105, 129, 133, 137, 138, 139, 140, 141, 142, 143
The Mount 112, 115, 121
The Rattle of the Coach Poem 76
To Detect the Adulteration of Flour 87
To Freshen Salt Butter 87
To prevent Mould on Ink 87
To Protect Gilt Frames from Flies 87
To relieve Hiccoughs 87
To Restore Black Leather 87
To Toughen Glass 87
Train, George Francis 10
Trunkey 105

U

Uhl, Alfred 33

V

Victoria 10, 30, 33, 43, 44, 54, 64, 67, 68, 69, 97, 113, 130
Victoria Hotel 140, 141, 142, 143
Victoria Stage Company 29, 127
Vines, A. N. 33
Vines and M'Phee 31, 32, 33
Vines, Joshua 30

W

Wagner, John 6, 17, 29, 30, 31, 33, 34, 37, 44, 69, 129, 130, 131
Walker, Alexander 36
Wardiyallock Ranges 16
Watson and Hewitt 29, 33, 126, 127, 128, 129
Wattle Flat 54, 134, 135, 136, 137, 139
Weddings 105, 114, 116
Weddin Mountains 20
Wellington 42, 44, 95, 96, 133, 134, 135, 136, 137, 138, 139
Western Stage Company 30, 31, 32, 33
Whips (drivers) 10, 18, 53
Whitney, William Franklin 6, 29, 30, 31, 32, 33, 37, 41, 44, 45, 47, 128, 130, 131, 132
William-street 18, 54, 55, 65, 67
Wingello Park 16
Womersley 33

Y

Yarra 16, 44
Yarranbar Hotel 144
Yass 16

www.ingramcontent.com/pod-product-compliance
Lightning Source LLC
Chambersburg PA
CBHW041711290426
44109CB00028B/2839